PERU
TIME OF FEAR

Deborah Poole & Gerardo Rénique

LATIN AMERICA
BUREAU

First published in the UK in November 1992 by the Latin America Bureau
(Research and Action) Ltd, 1 Amwell Street, London EC1R 1UL

A CIP catalogue record for this book is available from the British Library

ISBN 0 906156 70 X (pbk)
ISBN 0 906156 71 8 (hbk)

Consultant Editor: Colin Harding

Cover photograph: Joseph Castro
Cover design: Andy Dark
Maps vi and vii: Michael Green

Typeset, printed and bound by Russell Press, Nottingham NG7 3HN
Trade distribution in UK by Central Books, 99 Wallis Road, London E9 5LN
Distribution in North America by Monthly Review Press, 122 West 27th Street,
New York, NY 10001

Contents

Peru in Brief

The People

Population	21.6 million (1990)
Annual Growth Rate	2.0% (1990-2000)
Urban	70% (1990)

Principal Cities	Lima 5,600
(thousands, mid 1989 estimates)	Arequipa 613 Callao 574 Trujillo 512
Official languages:	Spanish and Quechua

Economically active population
employed in (1986-89):

Agriculture	35.1%
Industry	12.3%
Services	52.6%

Social Indicators

Infant mortality	82 per thousand live births (1990)
Life expectancy	63.0 years
Adult male literacy rate	92.0% (1990)
Adult female literacy rate	75.0% (1990)

Rural population with access to safe water	22% (1987-90)
Urban population with access to safe water	78% (1987-90)

The Economy

Total Gross Domestic Product (GDP, 1988 dollars)	$28.3bn (1990)
Per capita GDP (1988 dollars)	$1,312
Trade	Exports (1990) $4.046bn
	Imports (1990) $3.903bn

Principal exports (1988)	Non-traditional products $734m
	Copper $607m Fishmeal $379m
	Zinc $263m Lead $205m

Trading Partners (1987):

Exports	USA 27.5% Japan 10.4% UK 5.6%
	Belgium and Luxembourg 4.9%
Imports	USA 26.5% West Germany 8.0%
	Japan 7.4% Brazil 5.9%

Annual inflation	7,482% (1990)
Total disbursed foreign debt (1990)	$20.1bn

Sources: Human Development Report 1992, UNDP; *Economic and Social Progress in Latin America 1991*, IDB; *Peru Country Profile 1989/90*, Economist Intelligence Unit

PERU
POLITICAL

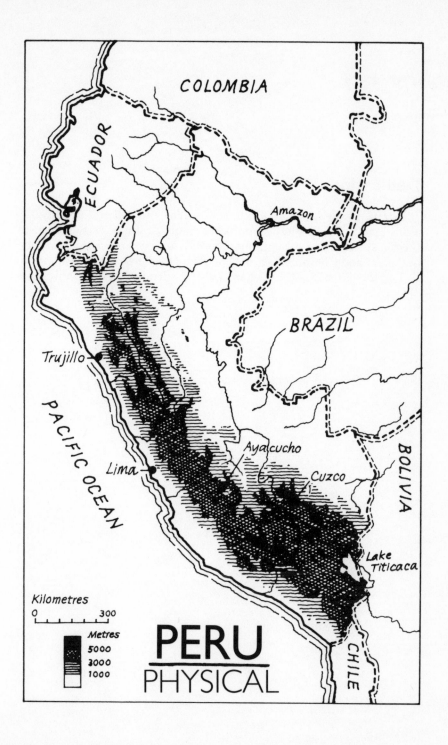

COLOMBIA

ECUADOR

Amazon

BRAZIL

PACIFIC OCEAN

Trujillo

Ayacucho

Lima

Cuzco

BOLIVIA

Lake
Titicaca

CHILE

Kilometres
0   300

Metres
5000
3000
1000

PERU
PHYSICAL

Dedication

To Maria Elena Moyano, Enrique Castilla, and Alberto Pumayala, assassinated by Sendero Luminoso; Saúl Cantoral and Consuelo García, killed by the paramilitary *Comando Rodrigo Franco*; the peasants of Cayara and Chumbivilcas, massacred by the Peruvian armed forces; and all the other 27,000 Peruvians killed by Sendero and the military.

Foreword

When, on the night of his capture, Abimael Guzmán, leader of Sendero Luminoso, came face to face with General Antonio Vidal, head of Peru's elite anti-terrorist police (DIRCOTE), he apparently told him: 'sometimes you win, sometimes you lose. This time it was my turn to lose.'

This equanimity, appropriate to a former philosophy professor, has been echoed in statements by his followers abroad. According to Adolfo Olaechea, spokesman for Sendero Luminoso in London: 'it's more of a problem for Fujimori's regime than for us, really. They have relieved the party of the responsibility of looking after the Chairman.' He added, almost as an afterthought: 'it is a big blow, of course, losing the Chairman. It will delay a few things, but in the end it will change nothing.'

Such apparent nonchalance suggests a bullet-proof confidence in the eventual outcome of the 'people's war' launched by Sendero Luminoso more than twelve years ago. Olaechea said that the 'strategic equilibrium' which Sendero claims to have reached with the forces of the Peruvian state would not be affected by Guzmán's detention; nor would the 'rottenness' of the regime and the Peruvian people's determination to be rid of it.

Nevertheless, the arrest of 'Chairman Gonzalo' and seven members of the central committee raises all manner of questions about what might happen next. Predictions of an early defeat for Sendero Luminoso from 'Senderologists' such as the US academic David Scott Palmer, are almost certainly premature. But quite how the organisation will react to the loss of its founder, leader, ideological mentor and foremost military strategist remains to be seen.

It is quite possible that Sendero Luminoso has well-prepared contingency plans to replace the detained leader and to carry on, with unwavering discipline and commitment, as if nothing has happened. The experience of clandestine organisation accumulated in the years since Abimael Guzmán, Hildebrando Pérez, Antonio Díaz Martínez and the rest slipped away from the old University of San Cristóbal de Huamanga in Ayacucho and began their preparations for the long march to Lima and the overthrow of the state, is unlikely to be wasted.

It is equally possible that the party will go through a period of confusion and internal dissension while competing factions struggle for ascendancy. Deep divisions over strategy may emerge, and rumoured splits over Guzmán's murderous policy of car bombings and assassinations of left-wing rivals could come to the fore. Dissension within Sendero Luminoso could even mean that the violence on the streets gets worse in the short term, as the factions fight it out. The military structure embodied in the People's Guerrilla Army (EGP) which, as this book shows, is parallel and subordinate to the political organisation, could acquire a life of its own. Only time will tell.

Sendero Luminoso is both a charismatic and a bureaucratic organisation — the personality and dominant role of its leader have apparently been vital to its internal cohesion and morale, but it is also a tightly-run revolutionary party with a cell-based structure that should theoretically be able to absorb the loss of its top leader, as it has withstood apparently crippling losses, such as the jail massacres of 1986 and 1992, in the past.

This book provides a lucid account of Sendero Luminoso's rise from obscure beginnings in a small provincial university city to a dominant, almost obsessive, role in Peruvian life and politics. By placing this extraordinary phenomenon in its broader historical and social context, it provides the best, most up-to-date guide to the labyrinth into which Peru has been plunged in a few short years.

Colin Harding

September 1992

Preface

Today, Peruvians are living through a crisis of seemingly insurmountable proportions. A bloody war begun over twelve years ago by the Maoist Communist Party of Peru *Sendero Luminoso* ('Shining Path') has taken over 27,000 lives and caused billions of dollars of destruction. Despite the arrest of Abimael Guzmán in September 1992, this war seems set to continue. Within hours of his capture, a series of shootings and car bombs in Lima demonstrated that Sendero intends to continue its 'people's war'. Although politically disastrous for Sendero, Guzmán's removal does not necessarily affect its capacity for violence.

This violence takes place against a background of poverty and neglect. One out of four Peruvians receives food aid from international donor organisations. Over ninety per cent of the population is under-or unemployed. In the countryside, severe droughts together with reduced government assistance and credit have devastated agricultural production. In Lima, poor planning and rapid urban expansion have led to shortages of water and electricity. Recent deregulation measures have raised electricity prices among the highest in the world.

Deregulation and cutting social assistance programmes are just some of the ways in which the current government of President Alberto Fujimori has contributed to the hardships of the Peruvian people. Rather than look for economic recovery, Fujimori's administration has privileged international debt payment and privatisation of state-owned enterprises and social services. Following the 'self-inflicted coup' of 5 April 1992, which closed the national Congress and dismantled the judiciary, the technocrats in charge of economic policy have now almost unlimited power. Fujimori has paved the way for an unprecedented concentration of wealth, unbridled speculation and corruption.

Most recently, Peruvians have been scandalised by government measures favouring banking institutions in which friends and close associates of Economy Minister Carlos Boloña have direct finanical interests. In contrast to their own 'free-market' ideology, Boloña and Fujimori have also used government funds to purchase uncollectable debts from large banks while allowing smaller financial and business institutions to succumb to the 'invisible hand of the market'.

Fujimori's supposed crusade against corruption and inefficiency in government is also belied by the prominent role played in his administration by a close circle of military and intelligence officers, relatives and cronies. Many have proven records of human rights violations and involvement in drug trafficking. With virtual autonomy in carrying out its counter-insurgency campaign against Sendero, it is unlikely that the military will soon withdraw from politics. For many observers, a full-blown coup by one of the several factions within the military seems the inevitable outcome of Fujimori's attempts to harness the military to his own quest for power.

This book offers an examination of the principal actors and institutions that have shaped Peru's current crisis. Among the most important are Sendero Luminoso and the peasant and working-class movements and left-wing parties that are its principal declared enemy. Unlike the Latin American guerrilla movements of the 1960s and 1970s, Sendero Luminoso has sought to enforce its own idiosyncratic vision of world revolution by attempting to eliminate other left-wing forces. Perhaps one of the most serious consequences of Sendero's war has been a weakening of the popular grassroots organisations and opposition at precisely the moment Fujimori's economic offensive is taking its toll on the Peruvian poor. Other important actors include the international financial institutions which broker Peru's large foreign debt and the new elite of neo-liberal technocrats with ties to both these institutions and Fujimori's government. A final actor is the US government with its ongoing 'war on drugs'. As the most important source of foreign exchange in Peru, the cocaine industry is also the main factor determining how the US government will respond to Fujimori's record on democracy and human rights.

The particular dimensions of Peru's crisis emerge from the interaction of national history and the changing international political climate. The possibilities for finding a solution to this crisis will in turn also depend on our ability to understand the complex set of historical, political and economic factors determining the actions of the different actors. While Sendero's strategy, goals and ideology emerge from the histories of class formation and left-wing politics in Peru, they are also inextricably intertwined with trends in international Maoism. Similarly, although the resurgence of right-wing populism under Fujimori has roots in Peruvian history, his authoritarianism is also an ideological legacy of the conservative era of Reagan, Thatcher and Bush. Finally, neo-liberal technocrats such as Carlos Boloña, move in international circles and maintain allegiances to the same IMF and World Bank programmes that have 'restructured' the economies and societies of Chile, Brazil, Mexico, Poland, and, now, the former Soviet Union.

With this book, we hope to contribute to an understanding of the complexity of the Peruvian situation, the range of solutions open to Peruvians in fighting both Sendero and the military, and the possibilities for formulating a democratic alternative to Fujimori's economic policies and authoritarianism. Although to many the problems facing Peru today may seem insurmountable and far away, a careful consideration of the ways in which the international context has nurtured both Peru's 'dirty war' and its economic collapse helps to bring these problems closer and to make their solution more urgent. It is only by understanding the interaction of Peruvian political history and the international context that we will be able to formulate effective expressions of support and solidarity with the the Peruvian people.

Deborah Poole
Gerardo Rénique

September 1992

1
War Against Democracy

As dawn broke on the morning of 13 May 1991, six armed and masked gunmen waited outside a house in the southern Andean city of Juliaca. The gunmen were from the Peruvian Communist Party (PCP-SL), better known as *Sendero Luminoso* ('Shining Path'). The house belonged to Porfirio Suni, a peasant leader, elected representative to the newly created regional government in Puno department, and member of the left-wing United Mariateguista Party (PUM). Suni was an important figure in the local popular movement. Over the years, he had been active in land disputes and in the departmental peasant federation. As president of the regional human rights commission, he was also an outspoken critic of the military state of emergency which had been in force in much of the department since 1986. In May 1988 the police detained Suni, accusing him of terrorism. Following national and international human rights campaigns, he was released in early 1989. Having survived repeated torture, Suni was killed as he walked out of his house that morning by what Sendero calls an 'annihilation squad'.

Eight days later, a *Senderista* column entered the village of Huasahuasi in the central Andean highland department of Junín, demanding to see the 'Yankee' nun, Irene Teresa MacCormack. They claimed that Sister MacCormack, who was actually an Australian citizen, had corrupted the villagers and made them lazy by giving them free food and medical care. Ignoring the peasants' defence of the 52-year-old woman's community work with orphans, the *Senderistas* forced Sister MacCormack to kneel in the centre of the plaza. They then shot her at point-blank range along with a local schoolteacher, a former mayor, a former president of the district defence group or *ronda*, and the president of a committee to obtain a TV satellite antenna for the community. Before leaving, the guerrillas lectured the villagers on the need for a 'people's war' and painted the crumbling adobe walls of the plaza with party slogans and *vivas* to their leader, 'Presidente Gonzalo'.

Two days later, on the outskirts of Peru's capital, Lima, other followers of 'Presidente Gonzalo' ambushed Paul Loblet Lind, mayor of the community of Pachacamac. They accused him of covering up *Senderista* slogans which had been painted on the gravestones of party 'martyrs' in the local cemetery. In front of his family, they machine-gunned the mayor and then dynamited his body. Loblet was a politically independent leader who was particularly well-liked for his defence of the community's ecological and agrarian resources against urban developers. Moreover, it had been the army and not Loblet who had ordered the *Senderista* tombs to be painted over in military grey.

In the eyes of Sendero Luminoso, Suni, Loblet and Sister MacCormack were 'enemies of the people' because they were involved in grassroots political and social programmes not directly linked with the PCP-SL's political and military organisation. Since declaring the initiation of its armed struggle in May 1980, Sendero, which views itself as the revolutionary vanguard of the Peruvian people, has set itself apart from all other left-wing organisations, social movements and guerrilla groups in Peru. It differs from these other organisations in its refusal to recognise pluralistic cultural and political traditions, in its rejection of democratic decision-making, and in its exclusive emphasis on military action and violence as a means to gain power.

For Sendero, the only road to power is through armed struggle, and all those who do not cooperate are enemies who must be eliminated. As the pro-Sendero newspaper, *El Diario*, explains:

> On one side, [there is] the fascist government...its right-wing, centre and left-wing allies [and] on the other side, the PCP-SL, the working class, the peasantry... There is no room for intermediate positions. Either you side with the people and its struggles or you side with the reaction and its repressive apparatus.

Although the PCP-SL claims to side with the people, as an extreme vanguardist party it rejects dialogue with existing popular organisations or leaders. In Sendero's philosophy, the only way to achieve a revolution in Peru is through war and the militarisation of society. Rather than side with other political forces, it uses authoritarian means to destroy all established forms of organisation which it does not directly control. These include all forms of state organisation as well as those affiliated with the Left and opposition forces. Sendero targets provincial state functionaries, agricultural assistance workers, elected officials, development workers, church

'The Case of the Poles'

On 9 August 1991, Sendero Luminoso murdered two Franciscan missionaries from Poland in a raid at Pariacoto, Ancash. *El Diario* explained their deaths as follows:

'The forces of reaction have tried to show through their hack journalists that those two characters, Zbigniew Strzalowski and Michal Tomaszek, were just two good Franciscan missionary priests working on behalf of the poor. But nothing could be further from the truth.

The Party's thousand eyes and ears proved beyond a shadow of doubt that both of them were agents of imperialism, camouflaged as priests and involved in *asistencialismo*† as a means of controlling the masses as well as laying foundations and forming a spearhead for a new experiment: the penetration of imperialist forces through the clergy.

Apart from their repulsive trade in the people's beliefs, it was also proven that these individuals were spying for the Yankees. (It is well known that of all countries, Poland, or more precisely the Polish clergy, is the most obliging servant in the plans of the CIA, with the result that one of its bosses now heads the Vatican).'

El Diario, Lima, 29 August 1991

†Creating dependence on aid.

---

people, and left-wing peasant and union leaders, as well as police and military personnel. By eliminating all competing political actors, Sendero hopes to polarise Peruvian society to fit its distinct vision of political struggle. As seen by its founder, Abimael Guzmán ('Presidente Gonzalo'), the PCP-SL 'is not a mass party. It is a party of militants, of leaders, a war machine.'

In left-wing circles outside Peru, the PCP-SL tries to cultivate an image as the anti-imperialist revolutionary vanguard of the Peruvian people. Few of those who receive this version of events, however, are aware that Sendero's 'war machine' has been directly responsible for the deaths of many Peruvian union and peasant leaders in the past decade. This war against the Peruvian people results from Sendero's attempt, as a vanguardist party, to occupy a political space already filled by mass organisations, the legal Left and the progressive Church. In order to assert its claim over this space, the PCP-SL has tried to reverse the advances in popular power and democratic organisation which Peru's social movement has been building over the last thirty years.

Victim of a Sendero Luminoso 'annihilation squad', Mantaro Valley.
(Alejandro Balaguer)

The Dirty War

Since Sendero began its armed insurrection in 1980, Peruvians have faced a seemingly endless series of economic and political crises. The mounting foreign debt, declining international trade prices, raging hyper-inflation and escalating unemployment which affected all Latin American countries in the 1980s, hit Peru particularly hard. While the World Bank reported that the average annual growth rate of gross domestic product (GDP) for Latin America fell from 5.9 per cent in the 1970s to 1.1 per cent in the 1980s, Peru's GDP growth decreased even more precipitously from 3.5 per cent to a negative 0.6 per cent. The country's gross domestic investment between 1980 and 1989 decreased at an equally alarming annual average rate of 5 per cent. Inflation grew apace, increasing steadily from an annual average of 31.9 per cent during the 1970s to 665.9 per cent in 1988. In 1989, it skyrocketed to 3,400 per cent and in 1990 reached almost 8,000 per cent. Stifled by uncontrollable prices and declining wages, total national consumption remained stagnant throughout the 1980s. As prices soared and wages lost their value, Peruvians were forced to cut their standard of living to levels unheard of since the early 1960s.

Together with Sendero's war, these long-term economic woes have dominated the agendas of the democratically-elected governments of presidents Fernando Belaúnde (1980-1985), Alan García (1985-1990) and Alberto Fujimori (1990-). Under pressure from international lending agencies, each of these presidents has granted his economic teams considerable control over the lives and economic welfare of the Peruvian people. On the military front, each of these governments has outdone its predecessor in ceding responsibility for the confrontation with Sendero to the armed forces. The establishment of emergency zones and the resulting expansion of military rule has severely curtailed the power of democratically-elected officials.

Ironically, this increasing military power owes much to the Belaúnde government's initial reluctance to take Sendero seriously as a political-military force when it started operations in 1980. During his earlier term in office from 1963 to 1968, Belaúnde had faced both a left-wing guerrilla war and a highland peasant movement which continued, even after the guerrillas' defeat, to carry out widespread land invasions. Just when the peasants' actions seemed to promise a *de facto* agrarian reform, the military took over the government in 1968. Led by General Juan Velasco Alvarado, the reformist military government then set out to co-opt the peasant movement by declaring a state-led agrarian reform.

Although the society which Belaúnde inherited after twelve years of military rule was substantially different from the Peru he had governed between 1963 and 1968, the sudden appearance of a highland-based guerrilla group must have seemed threatening. Eager to avoid a replay of his earlier experience, Belaúnde dismissed the strategic and political importance of Sendero's activities, describing the guerrillas as a fanciful fabrication of Lima's sensationalist press and their bombings as childish acts of delinquency. Later, when Sendero's existence had become impossible to ignore, President Belaúnde attempted to explain away the armed attacks and sabotage as part of a 'plan set up, directed and financed from abroad'. As a result, for the first two years of its self-proclaimed 'people's war', Sendero was permitted to act virtually unchecked by military or intelligence operations. Rather than run the personal risk of giving increased powers to the military, Belaúnde vacillated while Sendero gained strength.

While part of the Belaúnde government's reluctance to confront Sendero's early actions was political, its attitudes were also coloured by cultural factors. Historically, Lima, as the seat of government, trade and industry, has exercised almost unlimited political control over Peru's highland provinces. This relationship of political patronage has been justified in terms of the cultural divide which is perceived to separate Peru's highland and coastal areas. Although in reality the two regions are linked culturally and demographically by centuries of migration and intermarriage, most non-Indian Peruvians still think of the Quechua- and Aymara-speaking peasants who make up the majority highland population as culturally and racially inferior to the coastal Spanish-speaking mixed-blood *mestizos* and *criollos*. Such was the strength of these cultural prejudices that, even after the turbulent experience of peasant mobilisation in the 1960s and 1970s, Belaúnde and many *criollo* politicians in Lima had difficulty taking seriously any political or military initiative coming from what was commonly referred to as the *mancha india* ('Indian stain') of Andean Peru.

Together with Belaúnde's fear of the military and the secretive underground nature of Sendero itself, this cultural contempt for the highlands helps to explain why Sendero was allowed to act virtually unimpeded for so long. Although the PCP-SL had, from the beginning, carried out armed actions in nearly every department of Peru, it was seen by the government in Lima as a problem restricted to the highland department of Ayacucho, where it had its strongest base.

Finally, on 26 December 1982, Lima was forced to react. Sendero had recently intensified both the number and geographic spread of its attacks. President Belaúnde declared a state of emergency in the city of Ayacucho and eight other provinces in the departments of Ayacucho, Huancavelica and Apurímac and gave the military extraordinary powers to deal with the situation. All citizens in these provinces suddenly found their constitutional rights of liberty and freedom of movement suspended.

For the next two years Ayacucho was the scene of the dramatic events which set off Peru's 'dirty war'. Building on counter-insurgency theory and anti-communist security doctrine, the military targeted the civilian population and popular organisations from which they wrongly believed Sendero drew its support. General Clemente Noel, the officer in charge of the emergency zone, openly advocated a scorched earth, no-prisoners policy. All Quechua-speaking peasants were suspected of being either terrorists or terrorist sympathisers. Thousands were killed; thousands more fled their villages to live in the slums of far-off Lima.

For the first time, Peruvian human rights organisations reported disappearances and extra-judicial executions. According to a 1989 Amnesty International report, 'presumed subversives were routinely disappeared, a majority of whom were civilians unrelated to the conflict, detained by the Peruvian armed forces. These victims were often found dead, with signs of being tortured, in the "cadaver dumping grounds" located on the outskirts of villages and small cities in the region.' Undaunted by accusations of human rights abuses, the Minister of Defence, General Luís Cisneros, declared that 'for the police force to succeed they would have to kill both *Senderistas* and non-*Senderistas*... They kill sixty people and at best there are three *Senderistas* among them.'

This combination of counter-insurgency doctrine, *criollo* racism and disdain for human rights characterised the escalating militarisation of Peruvian society over the following decade. Since Belaúnde's 'dirty war' of 1983-4, each of Peru's democratically elected presidents has given an increasingly free rein to the Peruvian military. By January 1985, the number of provinces under military control had grown from nine to 27. That same month, Amnesty International reported over 1,000 disappearances. A Peruvian senate commission on human rights reported 2,507 civilians and 4,428 'presumed subversives' killed in 1983 and 1984. During this same period 191 police and military were killed.

While most atrocities were attributed to the military, others were carried out by Sendero as acts of punishment for presumed peasant collaboration with the state. On 3 April 1983, for example, a force of 100 *Senderistas* staged 'people's trials' in the Ayacucho towns of Huancasancos and Lucanamarca, charging the townspeople with having resisted their presence on several previous occasions. They ended the trials by executing 45 peasants in Lucanamarca and 35 in Huancasancos. During the following two weeks Sendero killed 50 more peasants in punitive actions against the villagers of Chuschi, Juquisa, Carhuanca and Llusita in the neighbouring province of Cangallo. Sendero leader Abimael Guzmán later justified the killings in Lucanamarca and Huancasancos as excesses which had been necessary in order to 'make them understand... that [the PCP-SL] would stop at nothing, absolutely nothing. It was the party's Central Direction who planned the action and arranged everything.'

Repression and Paramilitaries

On 28 July 1985, the young and charismatic Alan García took office in a climate of great public enthusiasm. With García, the oldest nationalist political party in Peru, the American Popular Revolutionary Alliance (APRA), had won power for the first time since its founding in 1924. García's promises to confront Sendero's insurgency through social programmes, economic development and respect for human rights, raised Peruvians' expectations that the dirty war could be ended. In his inauguration speech, García vowed that his government would 'not accept the use of death as an instrument of the democratic system. The law will be severely applied to those who violate or who have violated human rights through death, extra-judicial executions, torture and abuse. The fight against barbarism', he proclaimed, 'does not require a fall into barbarism.'

García's good intentions were short-lived. Soon after the young president took office, the difficulty of controlling the military became evident with the revelation of extra-judicial executions in the Ayacucho communities of Pucayacu and Accomarca in August. In Pucayacu, the army executed seven schoolteachers, hiding their bodies in two unmarked graves. In Accomarca, 25 soldiers from the army outpost in nearby Vilcashuamán pulled peasants from their homes, tortured and beat men and children, and raped women. The villagers were then herded into a large house which, according to surviving witnesses, the soldiers then machine-gunned and set on fire. Thirty-nine adults and 23 children died.

Coming two weeks after García's inauguration, the Accomarca incident showed the shape of things to come. Parliament proved unable to enforce judicial proceedings against the military, in part because of García's inability or unwillingness to put his human rights promises into action. A parliamentary commission visited Accomarca to collect accounts from both peasants and army personnel. The officer in charge, army second lieutenant Telmo Hurtado, justified his actions to the commission as part of an overarching military strategy. 'I consider the decision I took to be correct', Hurtado testified. 'You cannot trust a woman, an old person or a child [because Sendero] begins to indoctrinate them when they are just two or three years old. Little by little, through trickery and punishment, they win them over to their cause.' In Lima, the commission recommended that those responsible for the massacre be tried in civilian as opposed to military courts, thus overturning long-standing traditions of military self-jurisdiction. In a highly publicised and bold visit to the emergency zone, President García himself descended upon Accomarca in a military helicopter and gave the peasants his word that justice would be done. In response, high-ranking military officers rallied to Hurtado's defence, proclaiming him a national hero. Hurtado was eventually turned over to a military tribunal and sentenced to ten days in prison. Since his release he has not been seen in Peru, and it is widely believed that he was promoted to lieutenant and sent to the United States.

García's proposals for social and economic development in the highland provinces also became mired down. By increasing state-sponsored credit and development projects in the most impoverished provinces of the southern highlands, he hoped to undermine Sendero's influence in the zone. Because of Peru's worsening economic crisis, however, García lacked the resources to carry out such ambitious programmes. Moreover, the APRA party apparatus through which he worked was unable to create viable programmes for social change due to its links with local elites more interested in safeguarding their own hold on power than in implementing reform.

García was also to blame as he sought to implement a *caudillo* (strongman) style of personal rule that circumvented both local party notables and local and regional organisations. Rather than work through the existing peasant federations, most of which were affiliated with opposition parties, García's much-vaunted *Rimanakuys* or peasant forums actually excluded delegates from these organisations. Similar problems plagued the new government's proposals for 'micro-regional' development. Provincial offices for the newly created micro-regions were staffed by local *Aprista* loyalists, or with party members from Lima totally unfamiliar with local problems and needs. Both types of party functionaries refused to work with elected municipal or community authorities from the opposition parties of the United Left (IU). Although APRA had at last captured the presidency and a parliamentary majority, its long-standing rivalry with the Left was exacerbated by the latter's control of many municipal and district level seats, particularly in the central and southern highlands.

In some regions *Aprista* enmities with the Left gave rise to paramilitary organisations. In early August 1986, unknown attackers bombed the offices of the Puno departmental peasant federation, a church-owned radio station and the homes of various left-wing leaders and church people. Although no one claimed responsibility at the time, it was widely believed that the bombings had been carried out by *Apristas* or military personnel. The discovery of three training camps and the formation of a security brigade linked with local *Aprista* militants, seemed to confirm suspicions of APRA's involvement.

In the following months, other paramilitary organisations appeared in different parts of Peru. In April 1987, the *Comando Anti-Senderista* claimed responsibility for bombings in Cusco. The next month, lawyers, journalists, congressmen and judges received threats signed by the *Pelotón Punitivo Peruano*. On Independence Day, 28 July 1988, Peru's largest paramilitary organisation made its appearance with the murder in Lima of Manuel Febres Cordero, a lawyer who had defended a PCP-SL leader, Osmán Morote, as well as several other *Senderistas*. In a note left on Febres' body, the *Comando Rodrigo Franco*, named after an APRA functionary killed by Sendero, stated that it was a 'group of citizens tired of the government's incapacity and of Alan García's demagogy.' It vowed to kill two *Senderistas* for every mayor, policeman or soldier killed by the PCP-SL. Subsequently the CRF targeted lawyers, journalists, judges, union leaders, church people and congressmen throughout Peru. In striking contrast to the massive roundups and punitive expeditions following even minor — or imagined — Sendero actions, no suspects were ever identified.

With Sendero in Lurigancho

'The country is seeing a campaign of genocide against us, the prisoners of war, and against the people. This campaign of genocide has increased with the government of Alan García, which is merely the latest stage of a reactionary power.

We have baptised 4 October† as Prisoner of War Day. We are undertaking a heroic struggle against genocide, transforming the massacre into a political victory for the Party. In six hours we showed that our morale was superior. The lives sacrificed and the blood spilt are banners which call for the rebellion to be continued.

We won't get out of here without leaving our dead behind, and our blood will stain those responsible. Through the Party's actions, these dungeons have become the glorious trenches of martyrdom.'

'Isn't it excessive to give up lives just to avoid being relocated to another prison?'
'The individual's life is worth nothing; what counts are the masses. When revolutionary blood is sacrificed, it isn't in vain. That blood brings forth new lives of struggle for the revolution.

The important thing is the masses; our individual lives are based and take meaning in them. And the masses, led by the Party, are daily winning new victories, fresh triumphs in this revolutionary war.'

'Doesn't this disregard that you have for your own lives amount to fanaticism?'
'Our morale is superior and we face death as a challenge. Fear can be overcome with ideology and in the contradiction between fear and bravery we turn fear into bravery. We love life, but because we love it we are willing to give it up. Take Chairman Gonzalo, he is the greatest expression of life's affirmation over death.'

Quehacer, Lima, June-July 1986

†On 4 October 1985, thirty Sendero prisoners were killed in Lurigancho prison while resisting their relocation to a new high-security prison.

In Lima, García refused to investigate the possibility of either military or APRA involvement with paramilitary activities. Concentrating instead on the more ethereal realm of foreign policy, García cultivated APRA's image as a progressive and anti-imperialist party through flamboyant speeches in the Non-Aligned Movement and through his activities in the Socialist International. The striking discrepancy between his nationalist posture and the increasingly repressive realities of Peru's domestic scene, were brought home by the events of 18 and 19 June 1986. On the eve of the Socialist International's Congress, which García had managed to host in Lima, Sendero prisoners in the penitentiaries of El Frontón, Lurigancho and Santa Bárbara staged coordinated uprisings. The Peruvian security forces reacted with aerial bombing and a massive use of force. In Lurigancho, all 124 mutineers were killed; according to Amnesty International, at least 100 of these were executed after surrendering to the security forces. Their bodies were later discovered in secret graves, some over 200 kilometres away.

Of the 154 *Senderista* prisoners in the island penitentiary of El Frontón, only 35 were acknowledged to have survived. Amnesty International reported that between 60 and 90 prisoners whom the army had claimed were killed in the initial attack on the prison, had actually been taken to a nearby naval base where they were 'disappeared'. The army tried to cover up the disappearances by returning to demolish those buildings left standing at El Frontón, and then claimed that the missing bodies had been buried in the rubble. Two women were killed in the Santa Bárbara prison and 62 removed clandestinely to an isolated prison in the southern department of Ica.

Shocked by the brutality of the prison bombings, several delegates to the Socialist International Congress left Lima or cancelled their visits. To save his international image and to allay Peruvian suspicions of complicity in the atrocity, García toured the prison and, amid the rubble, vowed that 'this crime will not remain unpunished... It will not be subject to a long and tedious investigation. We have clear and concrete evidence. Nor will those responsible for these crimes hide inside the barracks of any [military] institution.' García's sincerity was soon brought into question, however, by the speed with which his government allowed the matter to be passed over to military jurisdiction. In what was to become an increasingly common pattern, Peru's civilian judiciary was forced by the executive branch and an APRA-dominated parliament, to abdicate responsibility for protection of Peruvian citizens. Although some thirty security forces personnel were briefly confined to their barracks, they were released in November of that same year. A subsequent congressional investigation of the prison massacres suggests that President García himself may have participated in the planning and execution of the operation.

The prison incident gave Sendero the added momentum of revenge; to the military it gave the assurance of nearly guaranteed impunity; to the Peruvian people it meant escalating violence by both Sendero and the security forces during the remaining three years of García's presidency. Abuse, torture, disappearances and summary executions became daily occurrences. In 1988, the US human rights organisation, Americas Watch, found that, with the exception of pregnant women, virtually everyone they interviewed who had been detained by the investigative and anti-terrorist branches of the national police force had been tortured. For four consecutive years beginning in 1987, the United Nations Group on Forced Disappearances reported Peru as the country with the highest number of forced disappearances in the world. By comparison with the 17-year Pinochet regime when 2,500 Chileans were 'disappeared', over 3,200 people were 'disappeared' in Peru between May 1980 and July 1990 alone.

As the dirty war progressed, Peruvians became inured to the idea of a war with neither prisoners nor rules. Whereas in 1986 journalists and politicians had roundly condemned the killing of Sendero prisoners, by April 1989 few voices were raised to denounce the massacre of 63 people in the central highland town of Molinos. Just before dawn on the morning of 28 April, the army stopped two passenger trucks at a crossroads where peasants waited to board trucks and buses. They had been informed that the trucks were carrying guerrillas from the Revolutionary Movement — Tupac Amaru (MRTA), a rival political-military organisation to Sendero which started armed actions in 1984. Surrounding the trucks and without giving warning, they opened fire on the passengers, killing all of them. In a later communiqué following the incident, the MRTA claimed only 42 of the 63 victims as its combatants. Subsequent television and press coverage revealed that the guerrillas' weapons were hidden towards the front of the truck. The army, it was suggested, had massacred 63 unarmed people who could easily have been taken prisoner.

The Molinos incident coincided with the MRTA's efforts to consolidate its central highland front, opened in 1987. By early 1989, it was engaged in fierce competition for control of this area with Sendero, which regards its rivals as 'armed revisionists' allied with the government. Beyond their shared commitment to armed struggle, the MRTA differs from Sendero on virtually every ideological and strategic issue. It seeks to establish links with other left-wing groups and popular organisations and cultivate public support through the distribution of food and clothing captured from raids on large businesses.

Since the beginning of its insurrection in 1984, the MRTA has been an important presence in the north-east jungle department of San Martín, including the coca-producing Huallaga Valley, the central highland department of Junín, and along the north coast. After a series of military and political setbacks, including the Molinos incident, the MRTA captured national attention when, shortly before García left office in July 1990, its activists engineered a spectacular tunnel rescue from a high-security prison in Lima. More than sixty MRTA members, including national leaders, escaped through a 332-metre tunnel, lit and ventilated with electricity drawn from the prison's own lines and ending in a safe house just across the street from the prison watchtower. The much-publicised escape emphasised MRTA's differences with Sendero. Whereas *Senderista* prisoners see themselves as martyrs to the party and their highly disciplined prison community as 'the glorious trenches of martyrdom', the MRTA prisoners triumphantly wrote 'the Party wants us out' over the interior entrance to their tunnel.

As the MRTA expanded and Sendero intensified its activity in different parts of the country, new emergency zones were declared. By January 1989, 56 out of a total of 185 provinces, including Lima, were under military rule. More than half the Peruvian people were denied their constitutional rights. Between 1989 and 1990, one-third of Lima's population, or 2.5 million people, were subjected to forced searches by police or military; 9,000 people in Lima were detained under Peru's sweeping anti-terrorist laws. Migrants from the Andean highlands, street vendors, students, and any dark-skinned or Indian-looking people were especially subject to such abuses. Particularly targeted by the police were the tens of thousands of refugees from the highland emergency zones of Ayacucho, Huancavelica and Apurímac who had fled to Lima to escape both the military and Sendero.

Fujimori and the Military

Under the administration of President Alberto Fujimori, the situation has worsened dramatically. Despite election promises to put intelligence gathering before repression in the fight against Sendero, human rights abuses have increased. In 1991, 3,200 people died in political violence. During Fujimori's first 18 months in office, the average number of deaths from political violence per month climbed to 150, as compared to 140 during García's presidency. On 5 April 1992, Fujimori carried out an *autogolpe*, or self-inflicted coup, which closed Congress, disbanded the judiciary and gave nearly complete control to the military. At the time of the coup, more than half of all Peruvians were already living under a military state of emergency. With the nearly unlimited powers Fujimori has handed over to the military the situation is certain to grow worse.

Fujimori's ties to the military are not new. One of his first acts in office was to appoint two generals as Minister of Defence and Minister of the Interior. Three more cabinet posts were later turned over to the military. Following these cabinet appointments and Fujimori's unsuccessful attempts to decree judicial impunity for criminal acts performed by military personnel, the armed forces have been encouraged to unleash a no-holds-barred campaign against 'terrorism'. As a result, an even greater number of Peruvians have been subjected to different forms of repression by security forces whose activities increasingly penetrate every aspect of daily life. Under Fujimori, human rights abuses are no longer the exception but the rule.

The security forces' lack of accountability was brought home in late June 1991 when the police detained three students who happened to be passing by a raid on a suspected Sendero safe house in the Lima port of Callao. In front of national television news cameras, they were forced into the boot of a police vehicle and driven away. Within hours, their bullet-riddled bodies were dumped at the city morgue. The father of one of the students expressed the feelings of many Peruvians when he commented that, 'there is no difference between the police and Sendero Luminoso, when both of them kill us.'

Political projects which try to stake out a middle ground between the authoritarianism of both Sendero and Fujimori's counter-insurgency state have become increasingly difficult to sustain. Following its perceived strategic advances in militarising the state and polarising Peruvian society, Sendero announced in 1990 the initiation of a new phase in its military strategy, including an offensive against left-wing and popular leaders, NGO workers and development specialists. In mid-May 1991, Sendero killed four mothers, four children and one peasant man as punishment for their work with a local committee that distributes free milk to children. On 9 June, it executed six mining union members in the Huaura-Sayán valley in the province of Lima. A week later, *Senderistas* assassinated the president of the local committee of the Catholic Church charity, Caritas, in Ahuac. The same day in Lima they attacked two foreign relief workers from an international evangelical development agency. On 1 July, Sendero killed four agronomists and two peasants who worked for a programme to improve alpaca husbandry in Puno's peasant communities; on 12 July, it destroyed a sophisticated agricultural experimental station and murdered four Japanese horticultural specialists who worked for a technical programme sponsored by the Japanese government. By destroying these NGO and assistance programmes at a moment when the national economy had virtually collapsed, the PCP-SL had created a situation in which no resources could reach those sectors of the population most affected by the economic crisis. In Puno alone, the regional government estimated that Sendero's actions threatened to put an end to over US$100 million of economic and development aid.

Anti-terrorist operation, San Marcos University, Lima, 1990.

(Alejandro Balaguer)

The military, meanwhile, had launched a fierce campaign against all those who dared to speak out against Fujimori's militarised style of 'democratic' rule. On 19 April 1991, the military 'disappeared' the entire electoral slate of six left-wing candidates for the municipal elections in the town of Huancapi, Ayacucho. The six, all of whom were schoolteachers, had been in a bar celebrating the creation of a local left-wing alliance which they had christened United Socialist Left. When they left for home shouting celebratory *vivas* for their party, they were arrested by an army patrol. In front of protesting neighbours and relatives, they were then taken to the army barracks in Huancapi. During the night, residents heard shootings and grenade explosions. When their wives went to the barracks the following morning, the soldiers and officers denied ever having seen the six men. In response to a parliamentary committee's inquiries, the army has refused to release the name of the lieutenant, known only as *Centauro*, responsible for the arrests. Today all Peruvian military officers in the emergency zones act under pseudonyms such as *Búfalo*, *Lince* (lynx), *Baygón* (an insecticide), *Camión* (truck), *Rambo* or *Negro*. The use of such pseudonyms, which President Fujimori has legalised, makes it extremely difficult to prosecute those military personnel responsible for crimes and human rights abuses.

A number of human rights organisations are working to defend victims of military and police abuses and to publicise the atrocities committed by Sendero Luminoso and, to a lesser extent, by the MRTA.

Families of the Disappeared: Interview with Angelica Mendoza de Ascarza

'In 1983 disappearances and extra-judicial executions began to occur in those areas under a state of emergency. On 2 July a group of thirty hooded soldiers took my younger son, Artemio Arcasa, from my house. To this day he has never been seen again. In September, together with some other women, we formed a group to investigate what had happened to our disappeared relatives. Gradually more and more women joined, who were victims of the Los Cabitos barracks and the Lynx army patrol. On 2 September we got together forty women and formed the National Association of Families of the Kidnapped, Imprisoned and Disappeared (ANFASEP) to ask the military authorities and government to return our relatives alive.

Our Association has uncovered various secret graves. The bodies there carried the marks of torture and many of them were mutilated, without arms or heads. We have also found corpses up in the highlands and in streams. We have reported all these discoveries to the public prosecutor. The Association's other work is looking after the orphaned children who survive this war. We have been taking in hundreds of children who have lost their parents. Because of this situation, in 1985 we decided to set up the Casa de Maestro orphanage and soup kitchen for the orphaned children of Ayacucho... We have children from three to 18 years old.

I've been threatened a few times. Last year in Huanta when I was handing out toys, I was warned by soldiers to stop my work. Another time it was Sendero Luminoso. They came to see me and told me to show them who was giving us financial help. When they'd seen my papers they left.'

Grupo de Apoyo Peruano, *Informativo*, New York, 1991

These organisations work with parliamentary investigatory committees, church groups and international human rights organisations such as Amnesty International and Americas Watch. They denounce, publicise and investigate cases of forced disappearance, murder, torture and illegal detention. Among the more prominent national human rights organisations are APRODEH (Peruvian Pro-Human Rights Association), CEAPAZ (Episcopal Commission of Action for Peace), IDL (Institute for Legal Defence), and ANFASEP (National Association of Families of the Disappeared). Numerous other committees work at provincial and local level to assist families of the disappeared and victims of torture and abuses.

Church-sponsored *vicarías de solidaridad* (vicariates of solidarity) and social action committees have been especially active at the local level. The National Human Rights Coordinating Committee acts as an umbrella organisation for these different groups.

Their activities have made these organisations the target of death threats and bombings from paramilitary forces linked to the military and police forces. In early 1990, the Lima offices of both Amnesty International and the Andean Commission of Jurists were bombed. Although no organisation claimed responsibility, human rights sources suspect paramilitary groups. In a dramatic new development, a letter bomb was used for the first time in Peru in March 1991. The bomb was delivered to Augusto Zúñiga Paz, a well-known human rights lawyer. Zúñiga, who lost an arm in the explosion, had worked as legal adviser for the APRODEH and for PUM Senator Javier Diez Canseco. It is believed that the letter bomb, which was manufactured from sophisticated plastic explosives available only to special commandos of the Peruvian army and marines, was directly related to the disappearance of Ernesto Castillo Páez which Zúñiga was investigating. At the time of the incident, Zúñiga was on the point of filing a writ of *habeas corpus* attributing direct responsibility to the General Director of the National Police and the Ministry of the Interior. Paramilitary groups, sometimes posing as Sendero, have also attacked NGOs, research centres and church groups which work on human rights issues and on development projects with popular grassroots organisations. The International Commission of Jurists ranks Peru third in the world, after Colombia and the Philippines, in the incidence of violence against lawyers and judges.

Fujimori's failure to investigate these bombings is only the latest expression of a continuing pattern of government disdain for human rights work. In 1984, President Belaúnde unabashedly proclaimed that he had thrown Amnesty International's report on the 'dirty war' into the dustbin. In 1986, Alan García refused to meet a United Nations human rights delegation on an official visit to Peru. In October 1990, Defence Minister, General Jorge Torres Aciego and his right-hand man, General Alberto Arciniega, accused a human rights delegation sponsored by the World Council of Churches of acting as 'international missiles of Sendero Luminoso'. Such statements provide *carte blanche* for paramilitary attacks on human rights lawyers and activists. In late 1991, President Fujimori criticised both Amnesty International and Americas Watch, which he accused of belonging to an international campaign against Peru.

The paramilitary organisations, the military and their apologists share with their declared enemy, Sendero Luminoso, responsibility for the gruesome levels of political violence in contemporary Peru. Each

A Military Patrol in the Southern Highlands

On 20 April 1990, 26 military personnel, led by a lieutenant nicknamed *Negro*, arrived in the peasant community of Huacullo in the Department of Apurímac. They were accompanied by eight prisoners. Besides the lieutenant, known by his fellow officers for his reputation as a *loco* (madman), the patrol was made up of young soldiers. As one of the *patrullas ambulantes* (mobile patrols) sent out from regional headquarters in Antabamba, its mission was to round up 'subversives', locate arms caches and gather information on Sendero Luminoso's activities.

Calling the Huacullo peasants together, the soldiers arrested seven men without explanation, locked them in the community school building and forced the local women to cook for them. The next morning the prisoners were forcibly stripped, beaten and tortured by having their heads held under water in a nearby river. The soldiers accused them of having meetings with Sendero Luminoso, citing as evidence two recent religious meetings which had been held in the community. During the day another peasant, Víctor Huachaca Gómez, was arrested and killed during torture. His body was not handed over by the patrol, but was found six days later buried in the dirt floor of a house. The next day, the seven peasants were released.

Three days later, the soldiers arrived in Chuchumake, in the neighbouring department of Cusco. In response to their greeting of *'buenas tardes, compañeros'* — a common greeting in the area — a family replied with the same formula. Their use of the word *compañero* was then used as grounds for arresting five of the peasants on suspicion of subversion. The prisoners were taken to a nearby lake and tortured like those in Huacullo. They were then taken to a house, where their wives and a schoolteacher had also been imprisoned. The men were forced to strip naked; the women were made to cook for the soldiers and then raped.

On 26 April, eleven prisoners from various villages were taken to Ccapallullu hill and lined up. The soldiers machine-gunned them and dynamited their bodies. The corpses were left in caves on Ccapallullu and covered with dry grass.

'La Matanza de Chumbivilcas'. APRODEH and the Liga Agraria Arcadio Romero de Chumbivilcas. May 1990

of these political forces seeks to impose through authoritarian means its own solution to the problems confronting the Peruvian people. The extent to which the state has turned a blind eye to military and paramilitary violence raised serious questions about the democratic nature of Peru's elected government even before Fujimori's April 1992 coup. By capitulating to military counter-insurgency strategies and by demonising their political opponents and human rights critics as 'subversives', each government since 1980 has contributed to Sendero's goal of polarising and militarising Peruvian society. Those who have paid with their lives for this war have been the Peruvian people, the overwhelming majority of whom are opposed to the terror of both Sendero and the state.

Informales and narco-dollars

Arriving in Lima in early 1992, a visitor might not immediately detect any visible traces of the dirty war. Instead, what might first catch the eye would be the bustling life in the capital's streets. Hundreds of men and women line the curbs with piles of every imaginable item for sale. Others wander the streets, approaching cars and passers-by with cigarettes or chewing-gum. On street corners, money changers, holding fistfuls of dollars, wave calculators in the air. In an economy where hyperinflation has rendered the national currency worthless, dollar speculation and money-changing are thriving businesses.

Together with the smugglers and back-street manufacturers who supply their goods, these street vendors, or *ambulantes* make up the so-called 'informal sector' of the Peruvian economy. Because the majority of employed workers only work part-time, they have to supplement their low wages by selling in the street. Most *ambulantes*, however, have no other job at all and depend completely on their street work to support their families. Romanticised as 'grassroots capitalists' by champions of neo-liberal reform such as Hernando de Soto and Mario Vargas Llosa (see chapter 5), in reality the *informales* are products of an economy that has virtually collapsed.

Life in the informal sector is at best precarious in an economy where the real minimum wage in 1989 was less than a quarter of the 1980 minimum wage and where inflation in 1989 alone was over 3,000 per cent. Conditions are even worse in the countryside. Because of government neglect of agriculture, commercial farmers have reduced production drastically. Over the last two years alone, coastal and lowland farmers have been forced to plant fifty per cent less of both food and industrial crops due to lack of credit and a government-imposed freeze on crop prices. In Fujimori's first year in office, credit assistance was extended to less than forty per cent of the land which had been farmed with credit subsidies during the previous year. As a

Lima shanty town, largely populated by refugees from the highlands.
(Julio Etchart)

result, rice production in 1991 fell by 15 per cent, maize by 27.5 per cent, cotton by 22.4 per cent, and potatoes by 25 per cent.

Community-based agriculture in the Andes has also declined dramatically, threatening both urban food provision and peasant subsistence. Peasants have received no government assistance after the droughts and locust plagues of the last five years. In Puno, for example, potato production in the 1989-90 crop year declined to one-fifth of annual average production because of natural disasters and lack of credit. Even without such natural disasters, government-imposed consumer prices for food crops such as maize, potatoes and wheat are insufficient to cover the peasants' costs .of production and transport to the market-place. In response, peasants in many parts of the highlands simply ceased planting market crops, preferring to let their fields lie fallow.

In the military-controlled emergency zones conditions are even worse. Many fields are abandoned and villages are virtually deserted because of massive migration to Lima, Ica, Arequipa and the highland cities of Huancayo and Ayacucho. In the department of Ayacucho alone, land under cultivation fell by 56 per cent between 1981 and 1987, while production dropped by 78 per cent. As Peru's urban population continues to climb, the government has favoured increased imports of foodstuffs over promotion of domestic agriculture.

The only sector of the agrarian economy which has grown over the last twenty years is coca production (see chapter 6). Grown on the eastern slopes of the Andes, coca's production area spread from 33,000 hectares in 1979 to an estimated 200,000 hectares in 1990. In 1989, Peru produced around 300,000 tons, or 60 to 70 per cent of the world crop of coca leaves. This boom is particularly apparent in the Huallaga Valley, in the north-eastern department of San Martín. Because it is the only coca-producing area which is totally dependent on the illegal cocaine industry, the Huallaga Valley differs from other traditional coca-producing areas such as La Convención y Lares in the department of Cusco, where coca leaf is harvested as one of many cash crops and is sold legally on the national market. These legal markets for coca include the pharmaceutical industry and the highland peasants, who chew coca leaf as a traditional non-narcotic stimulant and use it as an important element in Andean religious rituals.

In the Huallaga Valley, by contrast, other commercial crops are less profitable and virtually none of the coca crop is destined for traditional legal uses. Growers instead sell their coca leaves to intermediaries of the Colombian cocaine cartels. The dollars which they receive fuel booming regional economies based on coca production. These 'narco-dollars' are also an important factor in the national economy. According to *Latin American Newsletters*, in 1989 the Peruvian economy took in between 1.3 and 2.8 billion narco-dollars, as compared to the US$3 billion generated by legal exports. Narco-dollars also fuel the parallel foreign currency market in Lima. A study commissioned by Alan García found that in 1988 around 360 million narco-dollars were exchanged on Lima's famous Ocoña Street, where the parallel foreign currency market is centred. Faced with the constant shortage of dollars created by debt repayment to international creditors such as the World Bank and International Monetary Fund, both García's and Fujimori's administrations have openly bought narco-dollars for debt service and other domestic needs on this parallel currency market. Narco-dollars are also an important source of hard currency for established businessmen, as well as for aspiring entrepreneurs in the informal sector.

Shock treatment

This chaotic economic situation set the tone for the 1990 elections, which pitted Peru's foremost literary personality, Mario Vargas Llosa, against an unknown agronomist of Japanese descent (see chapter 5). Fearing right-wing candidate Vargas Llosa's proposals for economic 'shock treatment' designed to lower inflation by freezing salaries, eliminating food subsidies, privatising state enterprises and reducing state payrolls, voters overwhelmingly turned to his opponent, Alberto

Fujimori. Fujimori, a former university professor who had never participated in politics before, campaigned on a platform of pacification and development without 'shock'. As he explained during his campaign, the neo-liberal shock formula:

> might work in the US or maybe in some European countries. But in Peru, the majority of workers earn 40 to 50 dollars a month and a school teacher with twenty years seniority makes barely US$60 per month. Do you believe that these miserable salaries could be lowered even more?

In order to contrast his own campaign platform with that of Vargas Llosa, Fujimori proposed instead to place the burden of economic recovery on the more privileged sectors of Peruvian society, and not on the poor.

The policies for which Peruvians voted were soon forgotten, however. One week after his inauguration on 28 July 1990, President Fujimori announced a package of economic shock measures designed to control inflation and to enable Peru to re-establish relations with international lending agencies, after President García's antagonistic stance had virtually severed contacts. In order to recover credit for debt payment, Fujimori put into effect a set of economic reforms identical to those which the Peruvian electorate had rejected when it voted against Vargas Llosa. These reforms called for restructuring the Peruvian economy so that a required US$600 million annual debt payment to the IMF, World Bank and the Inter-American Development Bank would be generated by cutting state and social services.

The resulting economic package, known as the 'Fujishock', lifted existing subsidies on basic foodstuffs and raised the prices of gasoline, electricity, transport, water and telephone calls. Overnight the number of Peruvians defined by UN criteria as living in absolute poverty almost doubled, from seven to over 13 million out of a total population of 22 million. With average household income below US$271 per year, sixty per cent of Peruvians were unable to meet the costs of basic subsistence. The number of soup kitchens organised by Lima's Church-sponsored charity, Caritas, doubled from 1,300 serving 541,000 people to 2,400 serving more than a million people.

The cumulative impact of the Fujishock on Peruvian society had become alarmingly apparent by the end of 1991. By simultaneously eliminating subsidies and price controls in all areas of the economy, Fujimori's anti-inflation plan started a seemingly uncontrollable spiral in prices. One week after the August package, the price of gasoline went up 3,039 per cent; propane cooking-gas went up from an equivalent of US$0.37 to US$3.61; potatoes, carrots, flour, milk and beans all went up by between 320 and 360 per cent. Total annual inflation for 1990 was 7,650 per cent, the highest in Peruvian history. Gross national product dropped by four per cent and Fujimori refused to adjust salaries to match real cost of living increases.

The effects on consumers were disastrous. In mid-1992 the minimum wage stood at US$72 a month while a poor household was estimated to require US$300-350 to satisfy its basic needs. By June, these same two minimum wage earners could only cover 19.8 per cent of their needs. Over ninety per cent of the working population, moreover, was classified as un- or under-employed, meaning that they did not hold even minimum wage eight-hour jobs or have access to social security and health care benefits. In a country where income distribution was already one of the most unequal in the world, the Fujishock has polarised the economic landscape even further. Even before the austerity measures, UNICEF reported that the poorest forty per cent of Peruvians accrued only seven per cent of gross national product. According to the Peruvian National Statistics Institute, between 1985 and 1989, the richest ten per cent of Peru's households received 30.5 per cent of the national income, while the poorest fifty per cent received only 19.6 per cent. With Fujimori's drastic reforms, the gap between rich and poor has become an insurmountable chasm. Whereas in 1975 profits accounted for only twenty per cent of Peru's gross national product, in 1990 profits had tripled to a scandalous sixty per cent of GNP. In a telling reflection on the worsening situation for Peru's majority, only 15 per cent of 1990 GNP went to salaries and wages, as compared to fifty per cent in 1975.

When the Fujishock hit, Peru's poor were already struggling to overcome deplorable economic and social conditions. As a result of continuing hyperinflation, shrinking salaries and unemployment, most Peruvians had trouble meeting minimum nutritional requirements. A study by the Peruvian College of Nutritionists found that spending on food in Lima's shanty towns dropped by 56 per cent between 1988 and 1989. For people living on the edge of subsistence, this meant eating roughly half the minimum amount required to maintain good health. Between 1970 and 1990, cases of chronic malnutrition jumped from 985,700 to 5,753,600 out of a total population of 22 million. Two out of five children under six years of age suffer from chronic malnutrition. Figures are even worse for the rural highland areas, where 75 per cent of children under five are malnourished. Eighty out of a thousand children die before reaching their first birthday.

These figures are matched by the government's neglect of public health care. Peru has only 9.8 doctors and 7.7 nurses for every 10,000 people. These medical personnel are distributed very unevenly by region. In the highland departments of Apurímac and Huancavelica, for example, there are only 0.4 doctors for every 10,000 people, in Ayacucho 0.6 and in Puno 0.9. The percentage of GNP invested in health dropped from an already low 0.99 per cent in 1985 to 0.85 per cent in 1989. Under Fujimori the figure has dropped still lower, as the government spends its scarce dollars on debt repayment rather than basic human needs.

Such chronically poor health conditions explain why easily-treated gastro-intestinal and respiratory infections have reached epidemic proportions in Peru. Tuberculosis, malaria, typhoid, yellow fever, dengue and cholera have all appeared in recent years, despite the existence of vaccines and medications to treat these diseases. Cholera is only the most publicised of these epidemics. When cholera appeared in January 1991, it was the first outbreak in the western hemisphere since the late 1800s. Given poor nutritional and health conditions in Peru, the disease spread rapidly. The situation was dramatically worsened by the shortage of proper sewage treatment facilities and deficient water supplies. Within a few weeks, cholera had spread from the northern coastal cities, where it first appeared, to Lima and to the highland and jungle provinces. By July 1991, there were 223,564 reported cases of cholera, 86,954 of which required hospitalisation. Over 2,000 people had died from the disease. By May 1992, the World Health Organisation reported a further 121,000 cases in Peru, with another 41,000 cases in Ecuador, Bolivia and Brazil.

Much like the scourges of economic 'shock treatment' and political violence, cholera affects primarily the poor. The disease is rarely fatal in a well-nourished population with proper access to medical care. Although cholera has been depicted as a medieval plague which has made a bizarre comeback in Peru, it is actually a very modern disease whose trajectory and distribution are determined by the epidemics of poverty, malnutrition and neglect now afflicting increasingly wide stretches of the Third World. Cholera has now expanded from Peru into nearly every Latin American country. The rapidity with which it has spread speaks for the years of indifference with which Latin American governments have treated their poor and Indian populations. It also speaks for the even more devastating hardship and economic austerity imposed on Third World peoples by the IMF and the World Bank.

Popular Resistance

When Sarita Colonia Zambrano died in 1940 in Callao, her fame as a spiritual healer and pious Catholic was already legendary. Seeking the

Children at one of the *Vaso de Leche* communal kitchens, Lima.

(Jenny Matthews)

famed *beata's* intervention in the problems of their daily lives, *ambulantes*, truck and taxi drivers, workers and poor housewives began to flock to Sarita's tomb in the cemetery of Lima's port city. Today her tomb has become a national shrine and her image, which hangs on the mirror of nearly every Peruvian taxi, bus and truck, is a pervasive presence throughout Peru. The interior walls of her shrine are covered with plaques expressing the gratitude of her many devotees. Outside the tomb, men and women from Lima's shanty towns exchange stories about Sarita's miraculous ability to find jobs, cure diseases, help troubled marriages and provide food for their children.

Although not recognised by the Catholic Church, Sarita Colonia is clearly the most popular saint in Peru. The poor are no longer able to wait for the occasional miracles of the official saints who intervene in such extraordinary events as epidemics, earthquakes, accidents and incurable disease. They need miracles for even the most basic human needs. In the aftermath of the Fujishock, it has become even more difficult for the poor to provide for themselves. As the prospects of receiving even minimal state services grow dimmer, new images of the Virgin Mary which weep tears of blood have appeared in several working-class neighbourhoods in Lima. These proliferating images reflect a pressing need for local forms of support to confront the seemingly insurmountable problems of daily life in 1990s Peru.

There have also been more aggressive forms of local response to the economic and political crisis. Over the last few decades, an amazing variety of grassroots organisations have emerged to address every imaginable social and political need. Survival organisations such as communal soup kitchens, childcare centres, communal stores, health care brigades, water supply committees, and construction and manufacturing cooperatives are just some of the forms through which people deal with the lack of state services and the economic crisis. Other popular organisations represent responses to problems of criminal and political violence. In the countryside, community-based peasant *rondas* (patrols) have successfully deterred livestock rustlers. Miners and peasants have formed self-defence committees to protect their communities from both Sendero and the military. Urban migrants' associations help refugees from the emergency zones. Traditional organisations, such as peasant federations, miners' unions, labour federations and professional associations mobilise their members against economic policies and militarisation. Broad-based regional movements have coalesced around issues concerning the control of resources and revenues which, because of Peru's highly centralised government, have traditionally benefited Lima.

Although a characteristic feature of national politics for much of the 20th century, self-help and grassroots organisations have flourished most dramatically in the last decade in the shanty towns or *pueblos jóvenes* ('young towns') of Lima and other major urban centres. In Lima alone, over a third of the population lives in *pueblos jóvenes*. Older settlements created in the 1940s and 1950s, such as El Agustino, Comas and Independencia, have become recognised municipalities. Physically, they have been transformed from improvised shanties to permanent structures of brick and mortar. Newer settlements founded in the 1970s, such as Villa El Salvador and Huaycán have pioneered new forms of community urban development based on self-management and self-government.

In their struggle to obtain legal recognition as well as such basic services as water, electricity and transport, *pueblos jóvenes* in Lima, Arequipa, Trujillo, Cusco and other cities have become major forces in the political arena. They raise local and community grievances as well as broader issues, such as the external debt, national sovereignty and increased participatory democracy. Given their strategic location on the outskirts of the cities, the poor outlying working-class districts and *pueblos jóvenes* played an influential role in the 1977 national strikes which helped bring an end to the military government in 1980.

Another dimension of political struggle is that of local and municipal elections. In Lima, more than half of the electoral districts contain a majority of their population in *pueblos jóvenes*. These districts have consistently supported left-wing candidates for local office. In the 1980 municipal elections, all but two of the twelve poorest districts in Lima elected candidates from the United Left (IU) coalition of legal left-wing parties. In the 1983 elections, IU took all twelve councils. In 1986, seven municipalities voted for IU and five for APRA, the governing party of recently-elected Alan García. In the 1990 elections, IU again won seven of Lima's poorest districts. Because of this electoral support for left-wing local and national candidates, the right-wing press began to refer to the poor neighbourhoods surrounding Lima and other cities as the *cordones rojos* ('red belts').

Organised labour is a further important element in the popular movement, although a shrinking formal sector means that union membership has declined. The principal national labour federation is the General Confederation of Workers of Peru (CGTP). Founded in 1929, the CGTP has a membership of over 800,000 workers from traditional sectors of the economy, such as mining, manufacturing, energy, fishing, metallurgy and sugar. While the CGTP represents general labour interests, unions from different sectors reflect more specific issues. Because of the historical importance of foreign capital in Peruvian mining, the 45,000-member National Federation of Miners, Metalworkers and Steelworkers (FNTMMSP), for example, has played an important role in rallying opposition to foreign control of parts of the Peruvian economy. Because of their focus on educational issues, the 200,000 members of the Union of Peruvian Education Workers (SUTEP), created in 1971, have provided an important link between the provincial and urban middle classes and Peru's working-class and peasant movements. The Interunion Confederation of State Workers (CITE), with 300,000 members, has introduced the social movement's concerns into state offices across the nation. These and other unions maintain close relationships with left-wing parties and provide the traditional political leadership for the social movement.

One of the most effective tools used by the social movement to press their demands on a reluctant government is the national strike. Since 1977, unions within the CGTP have organised 18 national strikes against state-imposed austerity packages. These strikes are visible reminders to the government of the strength and presence of a broad-based popular opposition which has historically refused to carry the burden of government austerity programmes. They are also highly charged political debates within the social movement itself.

Peasants were among the most active participants in the national strikes. Organised into two major national confederations, the peasant movement includes community-based peasants, as well as independent farmers and agricultural wage labourers. The Peasant Confederation of Peru (CCP), established in the late 1940s, acts as a national union for Peru's many departmental and provincial peasant federations, as well as for local committees of independent agricultural producers. The National Agrarian Confederation (CNA) was created in 1972 by General Velasco's military government in an attempt to counter the growing influence and left-wing tendencies of the independent CCP. Following the demise of Velasco's reformist faction in 1975 and the initiation of the conservative 'second phase' of the military government in 1975 (see chapter 4), the CNA acquired its own voice and autonomous identity. Today, with a large membership among peasants and small producers on the coast and north-eastern jungle departments, the CNA works closely with the CCP in pressing for credit, technical assistance, guaranteed prices for crops and the restructuring of government-managed agricultural cooperatives.

The range of issues addressed by peasant organisations and other social movements has made them a force to be reckoned with by both the government and opposition parties. Political parties of both Right and Left eagerly attempt to link themselves with these movements, in order to gain both votes and credibility. The state appeals to these sectors for its legitimacy and, when faced with the threat of opposition from them, often resorts to repression. Their central role has radically altered the nature and terms of political debate in Peru.

In recent years, however, it has become increasingly difficult for these popular movements to defend their political terrain. With their very survival under siege from Fujimori's economic shock policies and authoritarianism and their voices silenced internationally by more powerful images of Peru's dirty war, the poor have been transformed by press and academic coverage alike into passive statistics in a social and economic catastrophe about which they have little to say. Yet despite their depiction as passive victims of economic circumstances or as individualist entrepreneurs in the informal sector, the poor have a collective voice and history of their own. Through organisation and mobilisation, they are laying the groundwork for an alternative democratic solution to Peru's many economic and social problems.

Working-class and popular organisations are also commonly written out of accounts of Peru's dirty war. Yet precisely because of their capacity to propose alternative forms of politics, these organisations have in fact played a major role in the dirty war as the victims of both Sendero Luminoso and the Peruvian security forces. Although professed enemies in war, both the military and Sendero coincide in their desire to silence the voices of opposition coming from the legal Left, elected authorities, the social movements, organised labour, and church and human rights organisations. Hundreds of elected mayors from APRA, IU and other parties have been assassinated by Sendero. Between 1987 and 1989, it killed five leaders of the miners' union. Between 1980 and 1990, Sendero murdered more than a 100 agronomists, development specialists and NGO workers. PUM, the most radical member of the United Left coalition, claimed that by late 1990 more than forty of its militants had been gunned down by Sendero.

Most of Sendero's victims, however, are peasants and peasant leaders, particularly those affiliated with the CCP. In 1990 alone, over sixty per cent of Sendero's 1,249 recorded victims were peasants. Nearly 27 per cent were slumdwellers. Fewer than five per cent were police or military personnel. In Sendero's world view, the Left, organised peasants and NGOs are all indiscriminately perceived as government collaborators. Whoever is not with the PCP-SL is an enemy. 'Execution of these elements', according to Luís Arce Borja, editor of the pro-Sendero newspaper *El Diario*, 'is not like killing ignorant or innocent people':

> Their activities are financed by the state and by foreign powers because they all live on NGO money. Selective executions of United Left, police, members of paramilitary groups, government functionaries, foreign officials, yes, all that happens. There is no alternative... Whoever thinks that a war can be fought with rose petals is wrong.

As Arce Borja made clear in an earlier interview, however, the problem is less the 'collaboration' of these 'elements' with the state than their presence as an alternative political force to both Sendero and the state. As Arce explains, 'the political work that the United Left is doing in peasant organisations is to try to take away [potential] peasant bases from Sendero.'

By silencing these alternative political voices, Sendero's violence together with that of the military has helped consolidate the repressive state apparatus. Repression worsened following the military-backed coup of April 1992 when President Fujimori closed Congress and dismantled the judiciary. However, both the powers of this authoritarian state and its *raison d'etre* extend well beyond the war with Sendero. Although justified by the need to fight the 'terrorism' of Sendero Luminoso and instrumental in the capture of Guzmán in September 1992, the emergency powers assumed by Fujimori have also enabled him to move swiftly to impose the harsh economic programmes and privatisation measures demanded by the international lending institutions and financial capital. In their struggle to define a solution to their country's many-faceted crisis, Peruvians will have to steer a course between the competing authoritarian projects of Sendero Luminoso and a state willing to sacrifice democratic principles and the welfare of the majority to the debt payments and profits demanded by a handful of multinational banks.

2

The Shining Path

On 19 April 1980, Abimael Guzmán Reynoso, Secretary-General of the Communist Party of Peru — *Sendero Luminoso* (PCP-SL) gave a speech at the closing session of the party's first military school. 'We are the initiators', he proclaimed:

> We began saying that we were the initiators and we finish saying we are the initiators. Initiators of what? Of the people's war, of the armed struggle, which is in our hands, which shines in our mind, which palpitates in our heart, which stirs irrepressibly in our wills. This is what we are. A fistful of men, of communists, obeying the command of the party, of the proletariat and of the people.

Inspired by Guzmán's oratory, the graduating class of Sendero Luminoso's first military school went on to fight a war marked by the combatants' determination to make this singular vision of revolutionary struggle come true. Twelve years after the beginning of Sendero's armed struggle, it is no exaggeration to say that the forced migrations, material destruction, political upheavals and unfettered violence unleashed by the PCP-SL's party-led 'people's war' have changed forever the political and social landscape of Peru.

The party which Guzmán led into the 'grandiose armed struggle' in 1980 and which by 1992 had an estimated 5,000 combatants and many more supporters, had its rather inauspicious beginnings in the factional in-fighting of the 1960s Maoist Left. During these years, the schism in the international communist movement between the Soviet Union and the People's Republic of China was played out in fierce debates among Peruvian communists regarding the role of the party and the nature of the revolution. Maoist tendencies within the Peruvian Communist Party (PCP) accused the party leadership of abandoning a revolutionary strategy in favour of Moscow's new policy of a 'peaceful transition to socialism'. As a result of these disagreements, the Peruvian Communist Party split in 1964 into pro-Soviet and pro-Chinese parties. Named after their newspapers, these parties became known respectively as the Peruvian Communist Party 'Unity' (PCP-U, *'Unidad'*) and the Peruvian Communist Party 'Red Flag' (PCP-BR, *'Bandera-Roja'*). The majority of the national leadership, party finances and resources went with the PCP-U. Joining the PCP-BR were most of the party's youth, several regional committees and the core of the party's peasant base.

Bandera Roja took shape with a Maoist-inspired analysis of the 'semi-feudal' and 'semi-colonial' nature of Peruvian society, and championing a 'protracted people's war' which would move 'from the countryside to the city'. Its thesis was that Peruvian society, like the Chinese society analysed by Mao Tse-tung in the 1930s, was a predominantly rural or agrarian society in which the landlords or *gamonales* exercised absolute power over the peasantry. The landlords, in conjunction with 'the imperialist-dominated comprador and bureaucratic bourgeoisies', constituted the basis of state power and, as such, were to be singled out as principal targets in the revolutionary armed struggle.

Heading *Bandera Roja* was Saturnino Paredes, a lawyer who had worked as a legal counsellor for peasant communities and organisations, and who had played an important role in the creation of the Peasant Confederation of Peru (CCP) in 1947. In 1965, Paredes' leadership was questioned at the fifth party conference, where he was accused of embezzlement and, more seriously, of failing to construct the military apparatus necessary to carry out the armed struggle proposed in the party line. As a result of the disputes over these and other issues, the party became severely split. Three years later, the party's Bureau of Communist Youth led a splinter group to form the Peruvian Communist Party — 'Red Nation' (PCP-PR, *'Patria Roja'*). Declining the youth group's invitations to head their struggle against the national leadership of Paredes, Abimael Guzmán remained in the party as head of the *Bandera Roja* Special Work Commission in charge of military affairs. For Guzmán, the youth who went on to form *Patria Roja* had been overly influenced by the *foco* theory of guerrilla warfare and, in particular, by the ideas of Régis Debray. Three years later, in 1970, Guzmán led his own splinter group out of the PCP-*Bandera Roja* to form the PCP-Sendero Luminoso.

Guzmán's political career and its culmination in Sendero Luminoso have unfolded against this backdrop of Maoist political party manoeuvring. Himself a protagonist in the history of first the Peruvian Communist Party and then the PCP-*Bandera Roja*, Guzmán's considerable political energies have been devoted to perfecting an ideological position purged of what he views as the 'deformations' or 'deviations' of 'revisionist electoral opportunism and parliamentary cretinism'. Whereas other Peruvian Maoists merely talked about the need to wage a 'people's war', it was Guzmán who forged the political will and organisational prowess to lead his party into war.

From Mao to Mariátegui

Born in 1931, Guzmán grew up in the southern cities of Mollendo and Arequipa, where he went to university in 1953. There he obtained degrees in both philosophy and law, with theses on the 18th-century German philosopher Immanuel Kant's theory of space, and the state and bourgeois law. While at university, he helped to organise a study group which met weekly to discuss philosophy and culture. In the group's short-lived journal, *Hombre y mundo* ('Man and World'), Guzmán published a brief review of a physics text. This interest in the relation between science and philosophy would later surface in his thesis on Kant, as well as in the theoretical formulations which sustain Sendero's peculiar brand of 'scientific Marxism'.

Along with Kant, Guzmán also began to study the works of Lenin and Stalin. His interest sparked by the dramatic strikes and uprisings in Arequipa against the Odría dictatorship and by the debates and confrontations between Peruvian Communists and *Apristas*, Guzmán began to develop a more active interest in politics and joined the Peruvian Communist Party. In his recollections of these early years, he emphasises the extent to which he was influenced by Stalin. In the 1988 'Interview of the Century', in which Guzmán talked 'for twelve hours' with the pro-Sendero Lima newspaper, *El Diario*, he recalls that, 'those [of us] who became close to communism and who attained militancy, were educated with [Stalin's] *Foundations of Lenininism*. It was our guidebook. I was interested in Stalin's life, for us it was an example of the revolution. I participated in Stalin's defence, to take him away was like losing our soul.'

In 1962 Guzmán went to Ayacucho to take a teaching position at the University of San Cristóbal de Huamanga. An old colonial university, Huamanga had reopened in 1959 as a model of the new type of reformed university combining academic research with extension programmes in agriculture and rural development. By the early 1960s, several of the extension programmes were being run under the auspices of the United Nations, international development agencies and foreign governments. Upon arriving in Ayacucho, Guzmán was placed in charge of youth work in the Communist Party's 'José Carlos Mariátegui' regional committee. It was during these early years in

Ayacucho that Guzmán first become convinced of the political importance of the peasantry and Mao's writings. 'Ayacucho allowed me to discover the peasantry', he recalled in his 1988 interview. 'At that time Ayacucho was a very small town, mostly countryside. If you go to the *barrios*, even today, there are peasants, and if you go fifteen minutes out of town, you are in the country. It was there', he continues, 'that I began to understand President Mao Tse-tung.'

Determined to remake the party in Mao's image, Guzmán dedicated himself 'to work in the Party and to wiping out revisionism'. By 1964 when *Bandera Roja* broke away from the Communist Party, Guzmán and his comrades had successfully imposed their Maoist ideas on the Ayacucho party committee. Within *Bandera Roja*, Guzmán and the group with whom he worked in Ayacucho became identified as the Red Fraction because of their intransigent demand that the party take immediate steps towards military organisation. This intransigence eventually created tensions between the national PCP-BR leadership and Guzmán's Red Fraction, which considered itself to be applying 'the purest principles' in the 'worldwide fight between Marxism and revisionism'.

Some time in the mid-to-late 1960s, Guzmán travelled to the People's Republic of China. Although the circumstances surrounding his journeys are unclear, he recalls his experiences at a cadre school where he received training in politics, international affairs, Marxist philosophy, and military strategy and tactics. It was the practical training he received in ambushes, assaults, and demolition, however, which Guzmán remembers most fondly in his 1988 interview:

> When we handled volatile chemicals they advised us always to keep ideology in mind, and that this would enable us to do everything and to do it well; and we learned to make our first demolition charges... When we were finishing the course in explosives, they told us that anything could be exploded. Then, in the last class, we each picked up a pen [and it] blew up. We sat down, and [the seat] also blew up. It was a sort of general fireworks display. These things were perfectly measured to make us see that everything could be blown away if you put your mind to it.

It was also through his trip(s) to China that Guzmán discovered the influential Peruvian Marxist, José Carlos Mariátegui, whom he would later claim as the political and intellectual mentor of the PCP-SL. 'I began to appreciate and value Mariátegui with the understanding of President Mao Tse-tung,' comments Guzmán in the *El Diario* interview. 'Because he [Mao] urges us to apply creativity, I returned to study Mariátegui and understood that we had a first-class Marxist-Leninist who had analysed our society in depth.' In an address to a 1979 party conference, Guzmán mythologises his personal discovery of Mariátegui as a collective experience in which the Peruvian people ('the Party') first had to transcend their own historical reality in order then to gaze down upon their country from the heights of Maoist truth:

> Our people were illuminated by the brighter light [of] Marxism-Leninism-Mao Thought. We were first dazzled; at the beginning [there was] a burst of interminable light, light and nothing more; little by little our retinas began to understand this light, [and] we lowered our eyes and we began to see our country, Mariátegui and our reality.

Guzmán's adoption of Mariátegui also served to establish the claim of his own branch of the Peruvian Communist Party as sole legitimate heir to the original Socialist Party created in 1928 by Mariátegui. To establish this genealogy, Guzmán had first to differentiate his interpretation of Mariátegui's ideas from that of the many other Peruvian parties who claimed Mariátegui as their mentor, as well as from the left-wing intellectuals who had written about him. For Guzmán, Mariátegui — who in fact never wrote about 'armed struggle' — was a Maoist *avant la lettre*. 'For me concretely', Guzmán tells his interviewers, 'Mariátegui today would be a Marxist-Leninist-Maoist; and this is not speculation, it is simply a product of understanding the life and work of José Carlos Mariátegui.' In this way, Guzmán dismisses the legitimacy of competing political organisations who have not seen 'the truth' of Mariátegui's call for armed struggle.

Building the Party in Ayacucho

Guzmán's and the Red Fraction's unique identity within the party was also shaped by events in their regional base of Ayacucho. The reopening of the University of Huamanga in 1959 helped to revitalise intellectual and political life in the provincial city of Ayacucho. The new extension programmes at Huamanga, in particular the Allpachaka experimental farm which Sendero later destroyed, generated renewed discussion of the possibilities and limits to regional economic growth in Peru's poorly developed Andean highlands. Along with the expanding university and student body, the departmental capital of Ayacucho underwent a demographic boom during the 1960s and 1970s. Between 1961 and 1972, the city's population grew by 4.5 per cent annually as a result of both the university and migration from the provinces. By 1970, 38 per cent of the city's population lived in the *pueblos jóvenes* on the outskirts of the old urban centre. Over the

JUNIN

DEPARTMENT OF AYACUCHO

HUANTA

HUANCAVELICA

LA MAR

CUSCO

Huancayo

Huanta

Huancavelica

HUAMANGA

Ayacucho

CANGALLO

Chuschi

OCROS

Cangallo

Vilcashuaman

Apurímac

VICTOR FAJARDO

Lucanamarca

Huancapi

Cusco

Huancasancos

APURIMAC

LUCANAS

Lucanas

Nasca

Puquio

PARINACOCHAS

Lima

Coracora

ICA

Lake Parinacochas

AREQUIPA

following decade, the city experienced an even more impressive annual growth rate of eight per cent.

The flourishing urban economy and demography of Ayacucho city contrasted with the startling poverty of the surrounding countryside. One of Peru's poorest Andean regions, the department of Ayacucho's population was over seventy per cent peasant in the 1960s and in 1972 had a per capita GNP of only 7,782 *soles*, as compared with the national average of 26,661. Between 1968 and 1980, the department received only 0.3 per cent of national public investment. In 1972 only 5.5 per cent of the department's households had electricity; 93.4 per cent had no drinking water. Over sixty per cent of the adult population was illiterate. As a result of extreme poverty and economic stagnation, Ayacucho also had the second-highest rate of migration in the country. Two-thirds of the 14,000 *Ayacuchanos* who left between 1967 and 1972 settled in Lima, where they formed the second-largest migrant community in the capital. Most retained close ties with their relatives and villages in Ayacucho.

Ayacucho's stagnating rural economy also meant that the department's traditional landowning elite was already in a steep decline by the time the PCP-SL emerged — an irony for a Maoist party which identified it as the main class enemy. Landholders gradually lost political and economic power to the new sector of merchants, bureaucrats and professionals which had grown up around Huamanga's new university-centred service economy. By the 1960s, many of the department's larger haciendas had already been either abandoned or broken up into smaller holdings. In some cases, they had been sold to peasant communities. As a result, by the time of General Velasco's agrarian reform, much of the department's land was either already in the hands of peasant communities or belonged to small independent farmers.

Ayacucho had also played a relatively marginal role in the peasant movements which shook much of the rest of the Peruvian highlands between 1956 and 1964. At a moment when peasant land takeovers, regional federations, and the CCP were taking hold in many other parts of the Peruvian highlands, the Ayacucho countryside remained calm. Hacienda Pomacocha in the province of Cangallo was the scene of the department's only prolonged peasant struggles. Following repeated attempts by Pomacocha's peasant tenants to expropriate the hacienda lands through legal channels, the peasants took over the hacienda from the religious order which owned it in October 1961. The takeover was carried out with the support of Pomacocha migrants in Lima and the CCP, who sent their first delegation to Pomacocha in January 1960. Acting with the support and advice of the CCP and the PCP-BR, the peasants held the lands for over a decade.

Besides Pomacocha, however, organised peasant politics were relatively weak or non-existent in Ayacucho. Peasant resistance to the state and to the dominant culture of the regional *mestizo* elites was grounded instead in the deeply-rooted community traditions and indigenous authority structures characteristic of Ayacucho's peasant communities. Because of this strong tradition of local community organisation and the relative weakness of the haciendas, the supra-communal organisations that sprang up in Peru's other highland departments failed to win ground in Ayacucho. The few peasant federations created in Ayacucho during the 1960s and 1970s were inspired more by the agenda of the PCP-BR than by the needs or initiative of Ayacucho's numerous peasant communities.

The centre of Ayacucho's social movement was instead to be found in the towns and capital city. In March 1969, the military government issued Decree 006, severely curtailing access to free public education. The response in the cities of Ayacucho and Huanta was dramatic. In the first and largest popular opposition to the decree to emerge anywhere in the country, students, peasants, workers, market women, and residents of Ayacucho city's *pueblos jóvenes*, banded together with professionals and teachers to defend the right to free education. Based around the People's Defence Front, student and popular organisations in Ayacucho city and nearby Huanta organised marches and demonstrations. On the morning of 21 June, 35 university professors, students and leaders of the Defence Front, among them Abimael Guzmán, were rounded up and detained by the police. Shortly afterwards, anti-riot police arrived from Lima. According to government sources, 14 people were killed and 56 wounded in violent clashes on 21 and 22 June between residents of Ayacucho and Huanta and the police. Two days later, the government rescinded Decree 006. That same day, General Velasco announced the land reform.

The fight against Decree 006 galvanised regionalist, anti-Lima sympathies, particularly among the Huanta and Ayacucho secondary school students who assumed a leading role in the marches and demonstrations. During the events of June 1969 many of these students first came into contact with Guzmán's Red Fraction which, along with the rest of *Bandera Roja*, played an active part in organising the Defence Front and demonstrations. In the 1970s and early 1980s, many *Ayacuchanos* and *Huantinos* continued to remember with sympathy the role which Guzmán and his followers had played in this important regional struggle for free education.

Following June 1969, tensions between the PCP-BR and Guzmán's Red Fraction peaked. Although both groups agreed that the military government was fascist, they disagreed over the nature and goals of their political work. The debates which finally precipitated the Red

Fraction's breakaway occurred in December 1969 at the congress of the Departmental Federation of Ayacucho Peasants and Communities (FEDCCA), one of the small, largely symbolic peasant organisations controlled by the PCP-BR. At this congress, Guzmán opposed *Bandera Roja*'s proposal to support peasant demands for an immediate implementation of the government agrarian reform in Ayacucho, arguing that such demands implied 'collaboration with the fascist government of Velasco'.

Faced with defeat within the FEDCCA and PCP-BR, Guzmán's fraction began its 'reconstitution' of the party in early 1970. According to Sendero Luminoso's official history, it was through this process that the Red Fraction 'assumed the defence of the Party against the perverse plan to destroy it' put forward by the 'right-wing liquidationism' of Saturnino Paredes. For the Red Fraction, Paredes's crime was his 'attempt to destroy the party by focusing on open mass political work and moving the party towards legalism'. It also accused Paredes of denying the 'fascist nature' of Velasco's military government and of supporting its agrarian reform. Having declared itself the true heir to Mariátegui's party, Guzmán's fraction broke definitively with the PCP-BR to become the PCP 'for the Shining Path of Mariátegui', a name it took from the masthead of a newspaper published by a pro-Guzmán faction of Ayacucho's Revolutionary Student Front (FER).

Following the split, Guzmán's newly-formed party concentrated on strengthening its position within the university. Guzmán, who had been provost of the university from 1968 to 1969, retained an important following among students and teachers. Antonio Díaz Martínez, a prominent PCP-SL leader — who was later killed in the June 1986 Lima prison massacres — also wielded important influence as Dean of Student Affairs. Until 1979, many other administrative and academic positions were occupied by Sendero sympathisers and militants, most notably in the education department which they controlled for a number of years. A majority of Sendero's original political cadres were trained in Huamanga's education department and in the secondary school that its students and professors ran. It was in large part through the work of these teachers and students trained at Huamanga that Sendero could create the bases for armed struggle in the Ayacucho countryside. Outside Ayacucho, Sendero's influence during the early 1970s was confined to a handful of universities, principally in Lima, where it maintained active student groups in the University of San Marcos, the National Engineering University and the La Cantuta National Education University.

In keeping with Mao's principle that 'the line determines everything', Guzmán and other party intellectuals used their university positions to construct and disseminate the authoritarian political line and totalising world view which has come to be Sendero's trademark. Particularly important in this respect was Guzmán's 'José Carlos Mariátegui Centre of Intellectual Work' (CTIM) in Ayacucho. At the CTIM, Guzmán and other Sendero intellectuals offered seminars and lectures on topics ranging from European philosophy to biology, physics and world history. Tying together these different subjects was Guzmán's unifying theme of a historical process in which all material facts, from the earth's geological formation to the 20th-century history of Peru, could be seen to lead to the inevitable emergence of the PCP-Sendero Luminoso and its programme for a 'people's war'. For many of the provincial university students who attended the CTIM classes, the appeal of Guzmán's oratory, accessible explanations and apparently universal truths led to militancy in the party.

The success of Guzmán's ideological work in the CTIM was not matched, however, on other fronts. During the mid-to-late 1970s, Sendero was forced to confront the growing presence in Ayacucho not only of other left-wing parties but also the wide variety of peasant and worker organisations that had expanded throughout the country in the 1970s. Faced with competition within Huamanga University from such New Left parties as the Revolutionary Left Movement (MIR), Revolutionary Vanguard (VR) and the Revolutionary Communist Party (PCR), Sendero lost control of Huamanga's student organisation in its 1973 elections. The following year, Sendero lost its majority on the university executive council and was also defeated in the union elections of the Huamanga University professors and lecturers. Shortly afterwards, as a result of growing opposition to its activities, the Ayacucho teachers' union dealt Sendero another blow by splitting into two factions. By 1975, Sendero's presence had also been weakened in Ayacucho's People's Defence Front.

These political setbacks reinforced Guzmán's arguments for distancing his party from both the 'revisionist' Left and the labour, peasant and urban popular organisations which Guzmán considered accomplices of the 'fascist' military government. Alone among left-wing parties, Sendero refused to participate in the 1977 and 1978 national strikes, which it labelled 'revisionist strikes' in the service of 'Soviet social imperialism'. During these years, the PCP-SL maintained that Peru's large trade unions and federations were contaminated by revisionism and needed to be 'reconstructed from their foundations'. According to Sendero, the masses had become confused by the military government's 'fascism' as well as by its reforms. Only through the guidance of the Party and its People's War could they be made to find the 'truth' of armed struggle.

'The Son of the Storm'

'The Party is everything' for *Senderistas*. Their party, the unquestioned and unquestionable culmination of world historical processes, is the natural expression of the proletariat and the only correct path towards the 'conquest of power in the service of the world revolution'. 'Class engendered the Party', Guzmán has said. 'The Party rose up and began to walk, it is the son of the storm. The Party can never be smashed or destroyed, the Party will necessarily triumph.'

In reality, however, Sendero's emergence and consolidation as a political party was the result of a decade of effort to forge an organisation capable of matching Guzmán's vision of a militarised society engaged in a permanent people's war. A first step in this process was to establish an absolute consensus within the party around the necessity of preparing for the war. Those who objected to Guzmán's plans for an immediate initiation of armed struggle were expelled.

Having 'purified' the party line, the PCP-SL next set out to establish the organisational basis for the war through the formation in 1973 of *organismos generados* ('party-generated organisms'). The *organismos generados* were defined by the party as 'natural movements generated by the proletariat in the different organisational fronts'. They included the Popular Women's Movement (MFP), the Class Workers' and Labourers' Movement (MOTC), the Poor Peasants' Movement (MCP), the Popular Intellectual Movement (MIP), and the Neighbourhood Class Movement (MCB) set up to act in Peru's urban shanty towns. The Popular Peru Movement was also created to attract international support for Sendero's armed struggle. Within Peru other important *organismos* were the Revolutionary Student Front (FER) and the Revolutionary Secondary Students' Front, active in universities and high schools.

Through such organisations Sendero began to build a base of support and a pool of young recruits. For provincial or highland youth whose only options for employment lay either in the informal sector and the drug economy, or as subordinate members of a military and government hierarchy dominated by coastal *criollos*, Sendero offered a unique opportunity for attaining some level of personal power and recognition. This was especially true for the many provincial women to whom Sendero offered leadership positions and militancy rather than demeaning domestic work in Lima and other cities.

Building on the networks and contacts provided by the *organismos generados*, Sendero established 'people's schools' for political education in 1975. They were set up in different parts of the country by the first Sendero cadres, a majority of them *Ayacuchanos* who had been taught at the University of Huamanga's department of education. These schools enabled Sendero to form a social base in the countryside and provincial towns, most successfully in the Ayacucho countryside, and in the neighbouring provinces of Huancavelica and Apurímac, where Sendero cadres had more personal contacts, and where independent and CCP-sponsored peasant organisations were weaker. Their principal constituency was among the young sons and daughters of peasants, many of whom had received secondary or university education. The same social aspirations and urban experiences which attracted this youth to Sendero's cause served in many cases to set them apart from the rural lifestyles, agricultural livelihoods and community-based identities of their parents. This youth's disdain for the traditional values and culture of their parents found an outlet in the 'scientific Marxism' through which Sendero proposed to transform the backward or 'archaic' traditions of rural Andean society into a harmonious and ordered society.

In 1977 Sendero's central committee decided that the party's reconstitution had entered a final phase in which it would be necessary to establish party bases for the initiation of the armed struggle. The 'national plan of construction', approved that year, gave priority to sending cadres to consolidate the party structure in the countryside and to prepare the conditions for armed struggle. By 1978, the central committee had formulated a blueprint for the 'People's War'. A year later, at the June 1979 central committee plenary, Guzmán proclaimed in an impassioned speech entitled 'For the New Flag', that the reconstitution was complete and that the armed struggle was now a reality:

> Why look backwards? We must look forward, to see that the dawn which rises is the fire of revolution. The revolution. We will carry out the armed struggle, that is what we have to do, let us repeat it: that is what we will do! We will do it! We will! And it will be done because it is necessary and nothing can stop us, absolutely nothing can stop us. We have taken the three theological virtues to interpret them. Paul said, man of faith, hope and charity. Alone one is worth nothing; the mass is everything. Why speak of our individual glories? Our love, our faith, our hope are collective; they are realisable, they are three in one flag.

By the end of the year, the party created a military school to train the first company of Sendero's army. 'To forge in actions the First Company! [So] that concrete violence may flower in the initiation and development of the armed struggle', announced an internal party directive. 'Let us open [this new stage] with bullets and let us offer

Images of 'Chairman Gonzalo', discovered by police after raid on Sendero safe house in Lima, 1990.
(Alejandro Balaguer)

our blood to write the new chapter in the history of the Party and our people.' By May 1980, the first graduating class of Sendero's military school was ready to launch the armed struggle.

The consolidation of Sendero's party structure and plans for armed struggle coincided with debates within the Peruvian Left over the 1978 elections for a national constituent assembly. The PCP-SL rejected all electoral politics as 'parliamentary cretinism'. Several factions within other small left-wing groups which also rejected electoralism left their organisations to join forces with Sendero. Along with them came several grassroots leaders, such as Julio César Mezzich and Félix Calderón. Mezzich had significant influence among the peasants of Andahuaylas in Apurímac, where he had led a wave of land takeovers in 1974. Calderón was an experienced peasant organiser from the northern department of Cajamarca. Other groups brought with them union organisers from the mining camps in the central highland departments of Pasco and Junín.

These years also saw Sendero build up a party organisation suited to the clandestine and hierarchical military command structure needed for the armed struggle. At the apex of Sendero's pyramidal structure is a central committee headed by a general secretary. As the day-to-day decision-making body in the party, the central committee gives all strategic, military and political orders. Many of the central committee's members began their political careers in the late 1960s in Guzmán's Red Fraction. Most of this 'old guard' are professionals or intellectuals from Ayacucho's provincial elite, and others have long-standing ties to the University of Huamanga. Among them, a small nucleus — known as the 'holy family' for their intimate links with Guzmán and Sendero's Ayacucho elite — wield particular influence within the party.

Immediately below the central committee are the regional committees for the five strategic zones into which Sendero has divided Peru. The regional committees coordinate the small cells in which the majority of Sendero militants are organised. Each cell is led by an experienced cadre who receives his or her orders from the regional committee. Other cell members have little or no contact with Sendero members outside their cell, and none has contact with higher levels within the party.

Finally, in addition to its party cells, Sendero also depends on a network of sympathisers who provide party members with information, refuge, services and support. This periphery of sympathisers, together with the party's secretive and highly centralised chain of command, facilitated Sendero's growth and survival through the many years of armed struggle. Built on Guzmán's five 'organic needs' of centralism, clandestinity, discipline, vigilance and secrecy, Sendero Luminoso's party structure has survived infiltration as well as the detention and death of important cadres and leaders. How well it will cope with the arrest of Guzmán, however, remains to be seen.

Until his capture, Guzmán was the party's single most important source of theoretical and tactical authority. The high degree of discipline and centralism which unites its militants around the armed struggle is directly related to the extraordinary personality cult which grew up around Guzmán. For *Senderistas*, every command and action has been an expression of the will of Guzmán, known to party members as 'Presidente Gonzalo' (Chairman Gonzalo, after Guzmán's *nom de guerre*). In the 1988 *Bases of Discussion*, Guzmán's leadership is presented as absolute:

> It is the obligation of all militants to struggle permanently to defend and preserve the Party leadership, especially the leadership of Chairman Gonzalo, our chief, against any attack from within or outside the party, and to subject ourselves to his leadership and personal command raising the slogans 'Learn from Chairman Gonzalo' and 'Incarnate Gonzalo's Thought'... who knows revolutionary theory, has knowledge of history, and a profound understanding of practice (*movimiento práctico*); who... has overthrown revisionism, right- and left-wing liquidationism, right-wing opportunism and right-wingism (*derechismo*); [who] has reconstituted the Party, leads it in the people's war and has become the greatest living Marxist-Leninist-Maoist, great political and military strategist, philosopher, master of communists, centre of party unification.

The mystique surrounding Guzmán was long heightened by his seemingly supernatural ability to escape state surveillance and arrest. Following his disappearance underground in 1979, he was an object of intrigue for the press and the Peruvian popular imagination. Sightings of Guzmán were printed in the Lima papers, next to speculation about his death, illness or sightings overseas. When in 1990 Peruvian intelligence forces captured his headquarters in a wealthy residential neighbourhood of Lima, television and press focused their coverage on details of Guzmán's bed, spectacles and other personal belongings. A video captured in the raid showed Guzmán attending the funeral of his wife, presiding over a central committee meeting, and, finally, dancing to 'Zorba the Greek' at an inner circle party. Aired repeatedly on television and analysed by Sendero 'experts', the video provided undeniable evidence of Guzmán's ability to evade the Peruvian intelligence and security forces. This ability was to prove short-lived.

Abimael Guzmán at funeral of his wife, 'Comrade Nora', in November 1988.
(Alejandro Balaguer)

The Fourth Sword

Nine years after the start of the armed struggle, Abimael Guzmán gave his first extended interview to the pro-Sendero newspaper, *El Diario*, in July 1988. In the 48-page special edition, Guzmán assessed his party's historical importance, reasserted its intention to seize power through armed actions, and clarified the unequivocally authoritarian nature of his organisation. At a time when rumour was rife that Guzmán had died or was soon to die from an incurable disease, the interview served to confirm the fact of Gonzalo's clandestine survival. It also provided proof of his seemingly inexhaustible will to transcend mortality as the 'Fourth Sword' of Marxism, the title Guzmán uses to situate himself as the direct intellectual and political heir to Marx, Lenin and Mao.

Guzmán's ambitious claims to a place in the pantheon of world communist thinkers are tied to the party's campaign to enshrine his military and political rhetoric as a new form of political doctrine known as '*Pensamiento Gonzalo*', or 'Gonzalo Thought'. Breaking with the traditional Maoist formula of 'Marxism-Leninism-Mao Tse-tung Thought', the First Congress of the PCP-SL held in 1988 moved, on the one hand, to 'elevate Mao Tse-tung Thought' to 'Maoism', and, on the other, to expand the triumvirate to include 'Gonzalo Thought'. Justification for this move lay in the equation of 'Gonzalo Thought' with the incontrovertible 'material' fact of the armed struggle and hence, through a bizarre twist of what Guzmán considered 'materialist thought', with 'truth' itself. As Guzmán himself explained:

> It is the application of Marxism-Leninism-Maoism to the Peruvian Revolution that has generated 'Gonzalo Thought', in the class struggle of our people, principally the proletariat. 'Gonzalo Thought' was moulded by applying the universal truth [of Maoism] in the most faithful manner possible to the concrete conditions of our country. This was previously called Guiding Thought, and if now the Party Congress has sanctioned 'Gonzalo Thought', it is because this Guiding Thought has made a leap, precisely in the development of the People's War.

The decision to enthrone Guzmán in the communist canon sparked an ongoing, pedantic debate among the several small Maoist parties which, together with the PCP-SL, form the Revolutionary Internationalist Movement (RIM). Based in London, the RIM, which held its first international conference in autumn 1980, is devoted to the creation of a new Communist International based on 'Gang-of-Four' Maoism. Its founding membership included parties from India, Ceylon [sic], Italy, New Zealand, Colombia, Iran, Haiti, Bangladesh, the US and Britain. The RIM and its member parties are a crucial source of support and propaganda for the PCP-SL, whose armed struggle the RIM considers the centre of the 'strategic offensive of world revolution'. While they uncritically support Sendero's armed struggle, many members of the RIM are reluctant to embrace Guzmán as 'the fourth sword of Marxism'. Sendero also keeps a critical distance from the RIM's formulation of 'Marxism-Leninism-Mao Thought' by declaring itself a 'fraction within the RIM' devoted to making 'Marxism-Leninism-Maoism the rule and guide of world revolution'. More than esoteric squabbles over vocabulary, Sendero's discussions with the RIM reveal the importance of ideology or 'guiding thought' to the Maoist conception of political praxis. For Sendero, as for other Maoist parties, a correct or 'pure' ideology is the indispensable means to achieve victory and the conquest of power. Debates over the semantics and basic principles of revolutionary theory thus acquire a transcendental importance for each party's political identity and revolutionary strategy. They also provide an important means of deciphering the strategy, actions and world view of parties such as Sendero Luminoso.

While 'Gonzalo Thought' builds on a general Maoist concern with ideological purity, its specific propositions for the correct road to communism differ from other varieties of Maoism. It draws on Maoism principally in its concern with ideological purification and its identification of revisionism as one of communism's foremost enemies. For the PCP-SL, explained Guzmán in his interview, 'the problem is to fight revisionism and to fight it implacably. It is not possible to fight imperialism without [also] fighting revisionism.' From the time that the Maoist PCP-BR first expelled the pro-Soviet 'revisionists' of the PCP-U, continued Guzmán, 'we have continued to fight revisionism and not only here but also abroad. We fight Gorbachev's Soviet social-imperialism, the Chinese revisionism of the wicked Deng Xiao-Ping, the Albanian Revisionism of Ramiz Alia, follower of the revisionist Hoxha; just as we fight all the revisionists who follow the orders of social-imperialism or of Chinese or Albanian Revisionism, or whoever else.'

Since the PCP-SL's armed struggle against revisionism is carried out neither in Albania nor in China, but in Peru, the principal targets of its crusade are the 'false Communists' on the Peruvian Left who do not endorse the 'all powerful ideology' of Maoism and 'Gonzalo Thought'. For Sendero, revisionism is a natural waste product of a class struggle which unfolds without guidance from the true Party. 'A decades-old [social] movement, such as the proletarian movement in our country', claims Guzmán, 'generates garbage which has to be continually swept away bit by bit.' The most important and dangerous form of this contemporary revisionism is the 'parliamentary cretinism and pacifism' of the Peruvian Left. In Peru 'the right is secondary, our problem is not with them', Guzmán wrote in 1979, one year before the initiation of his party's 'people's war', in which the Left would be the principal target. 'The problem is the Left because [the PCP-SL] is The Party, the salt of the earth, the living tree, the others are parasites. The Left must burn the useless, it must bathe itself, wash itself, remain clean, clean the [parliamentary] stable we have, remove the scabs directly, truly, cleanly, honourably; this is our problem.'

The language of purification common to much Maoist discourse is taken to extremes in Guzmán's speeches and writing. The Party is repeatedly described as a body which must be cleansed and purified of the 'cancer' and 'filth' of revisionism, or of any influence which questions the inevitability of the Party's armed struggle. In March 1980, faced with criticism that his military strategy put too much weight on urban actions and hence neglected the countryside, Guzmán accused his critics of wishing to postpone the armed struggle. 'Will [anyone] begin to make use of our Party to defend treason and cowardice?', he asked the party's central committee:

> No. We must uproot the weeds, that are pure poison, cancer of the bones, [and] would corrode us; we cannot permit it, it is rottenness and evil pus, we cannot permit it, especially now... We must banish those sinister vipers, those noxious vipers, we can permit neither cowardice nor treason, they are asps. [...] We must begin to burn, to uproot that pus, that poison, to burn it is urgent... We must forge ourselves in another temple, in another spirit. Those [of us] who are in this [other temple] are the first that have to brand [the traitors] by fire, to uproot, to burst the boils. Otherwise the venom would spread. Poisons, purulences, [we] have to destroy them; the body is health, if we do not destroy them its vigor will cease.

Guzmán's metaphors of disease and purification convey a world view which has proved compelling for the predominantly young and provincial militants and sympathisers who back Sendero's armed struggle. As a world view which divides all things neatly into absolute good or absolute evil, it provides simple answers to the complex problems of Peru and its largely futureless youth. Its conception of the armed struggle as a purging mechanism for the attainment of absolute purity, perfection and truth also provides a means to intervene in the cosmological battle between good and evil. More than a simple quest for power, the PCP-SL sees the armed struggle as an Olympian battle between good and evil which is fought at all levels of existence, from the universe to the individual soul. 'The problem', says Guzmán, 'is

Sendero's Programme

'The Communist Party of Peru is based upon and guided by Marxism-Leninism-Maoism, principally Maoism and, specifically, by Gonzalo thought as the creative application of universal truth to the concrete conditions of the Peruvian revolution as made by Chairman Gonzalo, leader of our Party.

The Communist Party of Peru, organised vanguard of the Peruvian proletariat which is an integral part of the international proletariat, particularly adopts the following basic principles:

★ Contradiction, single basic law of the endless transformation of eternal matter;

★ The masses make history and 'rebellion is justified';

★ Class struggle, dictatorship of the proletariat and proletarian internationalism.

★ The need for the Marxist-Leninist-Maoist Communist Party to defend its independent decision-making and self-support with firmness;

★ Fight imperialism, revisionism and the inseparable reaction implacably;

★ Conquer and defend Power with the people's war;

★ Militarisation of the Party and the concentric construction of the three instruments of revolution;

★ Struggle on two fronts as the driving force of the Party's development;

★ Constant ideological transformation and always putting politics first;

★ Serve the people and the world proletarian revolution; and

★ Absolute and fair disinterestedness and correct style of work.'

Luis Arce Borja (ed), *Guerra popular en el Perú: el pensamiento Gonzalo*. Brussels, 1989

the [presence] in each soul of two flags, one black and one red. We are [the] left, let us make a holocaust with the black flag; it is easy for each one to do it, and if not the rest of us will do it for them.'

Since Guzmán believes the opposition between the contrasting red and black poles within each being to be irreconcilable, the 'black' or impure pole must be totally annihilated, leaving no remains. It is the mission of the PCP-SL, and its leadership, to carry out this task of excising the impure through a process which to which Guzmán refers repeatedly as 'sweeping' or 'burning'. Led by its revolutionary party, the people must then eradicate all physical trace of the 'revisionists' so that the 'cancer' will not once again reproduce itself. 'The people', writes Guzmán, 'will tear the reactionaries' flesh, convert it to shreds and sink the black scraps of meat into the slimy mud; what remains, [they] will burn and scatter to the winds of the earth so that nothing remains except the evil memory of that which must never return because it cannot and must not return.'

This black-and-white vision of political struggle derives from Guzmán's idiosyncratic (and Kant-influenced) understanding of the Maoist and Marxist concept of contradiction. According to Marx, contradiction is manifested through the struggle between opposing classes in society. In capitalist society, the principal contradictions are those between wage labour and capital, and between money and the commodity form. The fundamental characteristic of these contradictions is that they are dialectical because both terms of each contradiction existentially presuppose the other. As such, social contradictions imply a form of inclusive opposition which must be worked out through the concrete actions and struggles of human beings. It is this human agency and struggle which is, for Marx, the motor force of history. All ensuing Marxist tradition follows Marx's interpretation of contradiction as a unity of opposites.

Guzmán departs from the Marxist-Leninist tradition in assuming that *all* contradiction is antagonistic. Rejecting the basic Marxist principle of the unity of opposites, Guzmán instead constructs his theory of contradiction on Kant's concept of real or exclusive oppositions. Kant suggests that these oppositions are resolvable only through the intervention of a suprahuman agency (the divine). In this conception, the two poles of a contradiction remain in essence different from and external to each other, rather than being viewed, as in the Marxist dialectic, as two aspects of one and the same force which are resolvable through human agency. Guzmán concludes that the necessary and only resolution to the antagonism or contradiction existing between such irreconcilable (because exclusive) poles is through eradication of one of the poles.

It is this conclusion which leads to his conception of the 'armed struggle' as a universal purging mechanism — the suprahuman force — which will rid both society and the party of all traces of the evil pole of revisionism and 'the reaction'. Because its goal is to eliminate all traces of its opposite, the inevitable outcome of the armed struggle will be a society from which all antagonism, contradiction and difference has been purged; it will be what Guzmán calls the 'society of great harmony'. According to Chairman Gonzalo:

> communism [is] the only and unsubstitutable new society, without exploited or exploiters, without oppressed or oppressors, without classes, without the State, without parties, without democracy, without arms, without wars. [It is] the society of great

'Gonzalo Thought'

This Alone is the New

Los comunistas	Communists
deben estar muy claros	must be quite clear
que es lo nuevo	what the New is
y que es lo viejo.	and what the Old is.
Lo nuevo es la lucha armada,	The New is armed struggle,
es el acero mas fino,	is the finest steel,
aguda espada,	a sharp sword,
punzante lanza para herir	a piercing lance to wound
las entrañas de la reacción.	the entrails of reaction.
Eso es lo nuevo	That is the New.

Abimael Guzmán, 'Solo eso es lo nuevo'. *Sí*, Lima, 2 December 1990

harmony, the radical and definitively new society towards which fifteen billion years of matter in movement, of that part which we know as eternal matter, is directed necessarily and irrepressibly, [and] to which humanity must arrive only by passing through the highest expression [*potenciación*] of the class struggle...and [through] the shadow of the rifles of the invincible people's war.

As the inevitable outcome of this Olympian struggle between the antagonistic forces of good and evil (the red and black flags), the PCP-SL's armed struggle is presented by Guzmán as an act of destiny. Building on Kant's theory of causal necessity, Guzmán sees the party and its armed struggle as the necessary consequence of all past events leading up to this moment. For Guzmán, as for Kant, there is no need to look back into history and question why, or what if. 'The done is done, it cannot be reopened [*replanteado*]. Are we to revoke written time, the fact engraved in matter?', inquires Guzmán. Nor is it possible as individuals to shape or change the course of history. 'How can the grains detain the millstone?', Guzmán asks. 'They will be reduced to dust.' Throughout Guzmán's speeches and writing, history is presented as an inexorable material force devoid of human agency. 'One [person] is worth nothing, the masses are everything, if we are to be something it will be as part of the masses.' Devoid of human agency or will, the historical movement towards the armed struggle is consistently and graphically depicted in Guzmán's fiery rhetoric as a 'storm', 'bonfire', 'earthquake' or other natural force which the individual is unable to resist.

The main inexorable force moving history forward is violence. Guzmán understands violence as a natural and universal fact which must be elevated into the guiding principle for political action, revolutionary praxis and the reorganisation of a 'new society'. 'We reaffirm ourselves in revolutionary violence as the universal law to take Power and as the essence (*médula*) for substituting one class for another', proclaims Guzmán in *Bases of Discussion*. 'We will attain communism only with revolutionary violence and while there remains a place on Earth in which exploitation exists, we will finish it off with revolutionary violence.' For this reason, the document continues, 'we communists must empower ourselves ideologically, politically and organically to assume [violence] properly.'

The Storm Approaches

As the 'Fourth Sword' of international communism, Guzmán extends his theories beyond Peru. Believing that in any new order Marxism-Leninism-Maoism must first be purged completely of the evils of both 'Soviet revisionism' and the 'arch-revisionism of the crafty Deng Xiao-Ping', Guzmán sees the armed struggle as universal. In Peru, Guzmán wrote in a 1986 party document, 'the proletariat, represented by its Communist Party, leads the democratic revolution which once triumphant will open the doors to socialism and, continuing with cultural revolutions forged in the epic of world revolution, will go into the future: communism, humanity's only goal — necessary, inescapable and unrenounceable.'

Since it believes itself to lie at the apex or centre of the 'strategic offensive of world revolution', 'Gonzalo Thought' claims to have made several specific advances over the political and military thought of Marx, Lenin and Mao. These improvements on Marxism-Leninism and Maoism are the products of Guzmán's 'scientific' application of the 'universal laws' of violence and contradiction to the analysis and guidance of the world revolutionary process. A first such contribution is Guzmán's contention that the principal contradiction in today's world is that which exists between the oppressed nations and the world powers. According to Guzmán, this contradiction generated conflicts between the US and Soviet Union and among the lesser imperialist powers in strategic regions of the world such as the Middle East, South Africa, Afghanistan, Central America and the Caribbean. Since any such conflict could lead to World War III, Guzmán warns that 'the world people's war is the adequate response which serves to impede imperialist war, or if this occurs, to transform it into the people's war'. The PCP-SL's armed struggle, stated Guzmán in 1988, together with conflicts in Nicaragua, the Iran-Iraq war and the Afghanistan conflict, constituted the 'spark' with which to start the 'strategic offensive of world revolution'. This final stage of the resolution of the universal contradiction between revolution and counter-revolution 'is inscribed', he explains, 'in the next fifty to one hundred years; only after that will the contradiction between capitalism and socialism unfold, the resolution of which will take us to communism.'

Guzmán's vision of Sendero's armed struggle as part of a global revolutionary movement also underpins his reinterpretation of Mao's concept of bureaucratic capitalism. Whereas Mao used the concept to analyse a particular phase of capitalist development in China, Guzmán affirms that 'bureaucratic capitalism is not a process which is particular to either China or Peru'. Rather, he considers it to be a generic and all-inclusive form of capitalism which the West imposes on all 'the oppressed nations of Asia, Africa and Latin America which have neither destroyed feudalism nor reached their own national capitalist development.' As such, it encompasses all forms of capital including 'the capital of large landlords, large bankers and magnates of the capitalist class.'

On the basis of his understanding of the universality of bureaucratic capitalism and the inevitability of its domination and demise, Guzmán rewrites in *Bases* the history of contemporary Peru in three stages. The first stage is from 1895 to 1945, when the Communist Party supported the presidential candidacy of reformer José Luís Bustamante. In this period, he observes, 'bureaucratic capitalism developed, the PCP was constituted, and the path to encircle the cities from the countryside was revealed and outlined.' In the second phase from 1945 to 1980, 'bureaucratic capitalism took root, the PCP was reconstituted, and the path to encircle the cities from the countryside established.' In the third and present stage, 'bureaucratic capitalism enters a general crisis, the PCP assumes leadership of the people's war, and the path to encircle the cities from the countryside is applied and developed.' Since, according to Guzmán, bureaucratic capitalism 'is born sick, rotten, tied to feudalism, and subjected to imperialism', its destruction is inevitable.

From this reading of Peruvian history, Guzmán draws two conclusions with important repercussions for Sendero's military strategy. The first is that Peruvian history has always been determined by violence as a means of bringing about political change. 'Violence', he writes:

Mural of 'Chairman Gonzalo', Huancayo, 1990.   (Alejandro Balaguer)

is inscribed in the deepest core of our history. The conquistadors used violence to subject these lands and to submit them to colonial domination; Tupac Amaru unleashed violence in defence of rights and demands which mobilised hundreds of thousands of indigenous peasants; yesterday and today violence is the peasantry's usual medium in its unfinished struggle for land... Violence is in the centuries of history of our society.

The second is that this violence has not brought significant change because it has lacked the direction and theoretical guidance of a 'true' Communist Party. 'The [Peruvian] people have always fought, they are not peaceful and they apply revolutionary violence with the available means; the peasant struggles are the ones that have most shaken the foundations of society, but which have been unable to triumph because they lacked the leadership of the proletariat represented by the Communist Party.'

Guzmán proposes to systematise the force of violence in Peruvian history through a military strategy which Sendero claims has made several specific contributions to revolutionary military theory. First, according to Guzmán, the party should recognise armed struggle as the principal aspect of its work. Military actions must precede political change. While it proclaims itself a party in the service of the people, Sendero considers popular organisations as merely convenient 'conveyor belts' for furthering the party's armed struggle. The struggle for specific objectives such as land, wages and state services is a secondary form of mass work which should be subsumed to the needs of the people's war. For this reason as well, all established popular and political organisations are old forms which have been contaminated by revisionism and which must therefore be eliminated. 'All these political and union organisations and their leaders', argues Guzmán, 'do not represent the people but rather the scab (*costra*) of the labour aristocracy, union bureaucracy and bourgeois workers' parties who always attempt to deviate the masses from their path, and who are nothing more than part of that colossal pile of garbage which must necessarily be swept away.'

Guzmán's second contribution is to modify Mao Tse-tung's principle of 'encircling the cities from the countryside' to elaborate the concept of a 'unitarian people's war'. Drawing on Mao's military theories, the PCP-SL seeks to develop armed struggle in two interrelated theatres of operations: the countryside and the city. However, whereas Mao prioritised rural actions and saw the urban insurrection as a final step in the overthrow of the old regime, Guzmán sees military actions in the city and the countryside as parallel and simultaneous arenas of military manoeuvre. In Guzmán's own words, 'it is a specification of the people's war in Peru to make the countryside into the principal theatre of actions, and the cities into the necessary complement.' According to this vision of complementary theatres of operations, the peasantry can only be an effective political actor in alliance with the urban proletariat. Even then, it can only act under the leadership of the revolutionary party in its capacity as the ideological and political vanguard of the proletariat.

A third contribution claimed by Sendero is Guzmán's doctrine of the militarisation of the party and the concentric construction of the three instruments of revolution which are the Party, the Popular Army and the New State. Using Lenin's and Mao's military writings, Guzmán has developed the concept of militarisation to fit his world view. The process of militarisation begins with the Party in its capacity as leader of both the war and the construction of the 'New State'. It then proceeds in concentric stages extending out from the Party to encompass the Popular Army and the embryonic basis of Sendero's New State or New Democracy. The Party's purpose is therefore to promote the formation of a totally militarised society, an 'armed sea of masses that guards the conquest and defence of Power'. In this vision the armed masses, organised as a Popular Militia, are considered the sole guarantors of the installation of the New Democracy, its successful transition to the dictatorship of the proletariat, and its final transformation into a communist society. Through successive 'cultural revolutions' under communism the armed masses will prevent the restoration of capitalism or any deviation from the true revolutionary path.

Guzmán ultimately sees militarisation as the task of all true revolutionary communist parties the world over, and justifies it as a necessary response to the violence of the 'Old States'. 'Revolution and counter-revolution lend themselves to violence', exhorts Guzmán. 'They [the 'Old States'] in their old and bloody violence, in their peace of bayonets. [...] This evil violence today has met its match. The revolution's violence prepares to define its battle with arms... the masses rumble, the tide swells, the storm approaches.'

3

Time of Fear

In the early hours of 17 May 1980, five masked youths broke into the offices of the local election board in the remote Ayacucho village of Chuschi. After tying up the startled attendant, they proceeded to burn the district voting register and ballot boxes which were to be used in the next day's national presidential elections. Within hours the municipal authorities had located and arrested four secondary school students from Chuschi and the neighbouring community of Quispillacta. They had been identified by the attendant, who recognised them as the same young students who had been threatening for some time to destroy the electoral office. The fifth attacker, who managed to escape, was later identified as a teacher at the local secondary school. The following day, new ballots were delivered from the provincial capital of Cangallo and the elections went ahead as planned.

Eclipsed by the news of Fernando Belaúnde's election, the events in Chuschi went largely unnoticed in the Peruvian press. Only four days later was the break-in first mentioned in an Ayacucho newspaper, and the Lima press later picked up the piece simply as a filler about curious happenings in the far-off Andean highlands. The levity with which it was treated reflected most journalists' and political analysts' belief that the students' exploit in Chuschi, and the group in whose name they acted, were just another passing fad in left-wing student politics.

Within a few months, however, the small village in Ayacucho's far-off Cangallo Province had become a household name throughout Peru. Evoking long repressed colonial fears of the highland peasantry's legitimate claims for justice, Chuschi came to stand for coastal Peruvians as a symbol of Sendero Luminoso's roots in Ayacucho. For Peru's highland citizens, it resonated as a metaphor for all the frightening implications of the 'ILA', Sendero's acronym for 'Initiation of Armed Struggle'. As the years went by and Sendero's armed struggle intensified, the nature and scope of its early exploit in Chuschi were magnified accordingly. By 1988, the influential Peruvian magazine *Sí* was simply repeating what had become accepted historical fact when it described the students' action as a full-scale military 'occupation' of Chuschi by 'armed graduates of Sendero's first military school'.

In fact, Chuschi was one of many symbolic actions with which the PCP-SL launched its armed struggle in 1980. The following day, its militants sabotaged the air control tower in the departmental capital of Ayacucho. A month later, others attacked the police infirmary, a government-sponsored tourist hotel, and the political headquarters of the then governing Popular Action Party in the same city. In their most spectacular action, on the night of 16 June, 200 youths encircled the municipal building in the working-class Lima district of San Martín de Porras, half a mile from Peru's presidential palace. Yelling the party slogan 'People's War — From the Country to the City', they threw molotov cocktails at the building, destroying it completely. In the leaflets which they left behind, the attackers identified themselves as members of the Class Workers' and Labourers' Movement (MOTC), one of Sendero's 'party-generated organisms'.

In the remaining months of 1980, the PCP-SL bombed banks and public offices, electricity pylons, and police posts throughout Peru. At the same time, Sendero also targeted numerous mining camps in the highlands where they procured dynamite, and stepped up assaults on policemen from whom they could then seize arms.

By the end of the year, it was no longer possible to ignore Sendero's armed campaign. In late December 1980, Interior Minister José María de la Jara announced that over 200 terrorist acts had occurred in the six month period since Sendero's first actions in May, and that more than a hundred suspected· terrorists had been detained. By early January 1981, the Belaúnde administration had hesitantly decided to take action. A detachment of 150 specially trained police was dispatched to Ayacucho and to the five Ayacucho districts most seriously affected by Sendero's attacks. Thirty special counter-insurgency troops of the Republican Guard were stationed in the city to guard public offices and services. The other 120 were made up of the special anti-terrorist unit of the Peruvian Civil Guard, formed after the 1960s guerrilla war with the assistance of US Green Berets and the CIA. Aptly christened by the Peruvian military as *sinchis*, a Quechua word which as a noun means 'valiant one' and as an adjective means 'excess', these special troops were already notorious for their brutal repression of strikes and demonstrations in the 1970s. By 22 January, the first reports of abuses and excessive force by the *sinchis* had begun to emerge from peasant communities in the province of Cangallo.

While Belaúnde concentrated on Ayacucho, Sendero expanded into the rest of the country, tripling its attacks nationally in 1981. Significantly, over a quarter were carried out in Lima. Among the more dramatic were several attacks on foreign embassies and US interests, including the Chinese and US embassies, the Ford Motor Company's assembly plant, the Sheraton Hotel, the Lima offices of Bank of America and the Coca-Cola bottling plant.

By March 1981, the government had become sufficiently alarmed to issue Legislative Decree 046, which defined terrorism as a special crime subject to military jurisdiction and relaxed criteria of legal proof. Any perceived act of 'apology or support' for terrorism was prosecutable as terrorism. Within a week, the dangers implicit in DL 046 became dramatically evident with the arrest of several grassroots leaders, including elected municipal officers from the United Left (IU) who had been accused of terrorism. The stage was set for an undeclared war in which Sendero's violence would be used by the armed forces and the police to strike back at the dark-skinned 'cholos', 'indios', 'communists', 'red priests' and 'subversives' whom they saw as a threat to the established social order.

Over the next decade, Sendero's 'people's war' prised open even further this Pandora's box of racial violence and political conflict. For people in the cities, the war meant adjusting their daily lives to the nearly constant bombings, blackouts and police round-ups. For Andean peasants caught between Sendero's authoritarianism and the military's retributive violence, the PCP-SL's 'glorious armed struggle' ushered in a new chapter of their history which they aptly called the *manchay tiempo*, the 'time of fear'.

The New Democracy

Sendero approached the second anniversary of its armed struggle with an expanded military capability and a proven ability to incite government reaction and public fears. Confident of its growing strength, in early March 1982 Sendero carried out one of its most sensational actions, the main objectives of which were to liberate jailed cadres, 'to annihilate the enemy's forces and to provoke the First Repression'. In a well-planned operation, more than a hundred *Senderistas* attacked the prison in Ayacucho, freeing over 250 inmates. Among them were many party members including such prominent figures as the writer Hildebrando Pérez Huaracca and Edith Lagos Sáenz. The next day, as police declared a state of emergency, a group of police and Republican Guards entered the Ayacucho central hospital and summarily executed three interned prisoners who had been accused of terrorist activities. *Ayacuchanos* reacted with outrage to the atrocity, whose senseless brutality seemed to diminish the seriousness of the jail break and even to heighten public admiration for the audacity with which a local student-based guerrilla group had defied the national police from Lima.

Following the operation, the PCP-SL central committee issued a 20-page document entitled 'Let Us Develop Guerrilla Warfare', containing its first public assessment of the military campaign. The document claimed responsibility for over 2,900 armed actions intended to 'inflame the peasantry, teach the people and alarm the reactionaries'. Boasting 'four great conquests', it asserted that the operations had established 'the temper of the Party' in the form of 'leaders, cadres, militants and combatants forged in the crucible of the armed struggle', marked 'the formation of armed forces led by the Party', produced 'an increased quantity and quality of armed actions' and led to 'the emergence and development of seven guerrilla zones and eight zones of operations.'

The central committee also announced the formation of the People's Guerrilla Army (EGP). As described later by Guzmán in *Bases*, the EGP was 'a new type of army which fulfils the revolution's political tasks as established by the Party'. Separate from, yet dependent on the party, the EGP has three responsibilities, which in order of importance are: (1) combat; (2) mobilisation, politicisation and arming of the masses; and (3) food procurement and production. The EGP is made up of different levels of combatants. The 'principal force' consists of mobile columns of experienced fighters with no specific territorial base, which are dispatched to different fronts according to strategic goals defined by the national party leadership. In carrying out specific operations, the principal force depends on the support of 'local forces', made up of local party members, sympathisers and, at times, forced recruits. As well as providing military support and intelligence for the principal force, the local forces also carry out their own actions. These include assassinations, expropriations of arms and explosives and 'armed propaganda'. Unlike the principal force columns, most members of the local forces are not full-time combatants. A final level of Sendero's military organisation are the 'annihilation squads' (*comandos de aniquilamiento*) and 'special squads', which act on directives from the national central committee and the various regional committees.

Together with the formation of the EGP, the central committee announced the close of the first military stage of 'initiating and developing the guerrilla war'. Following Mao's scheme of 'prolonged people's war', in the second stage the party would now concentrate on 'conquering bases of support' upon which to begin building the 'New Democracy'. This war was to be fought through four methods:

Sendero Luminoso graffiti claims responsibility for destroyed electricity pylon, 1990. (Jacinto Crita/Ayaviri/TAFOS/PANOS)

guerrilla warfare, sabotage, selective 'annihilations' and armed propaganda. In accordance with these party directives, in the months following the prison attack, *Senderistas* all over Peru stepped up the campaign of armed propaganda and the sabotage and bombing of public offices, railways, banks and electrical installations.

In Ayacucho itself, armed propaganda and sabotage were complemented by intensified political work in the countryside. Party work there had begun in 1977 and 1978, when Sendero first moved cadres into the countryside. Over the following three or four years, primary school teachers, theatre groups and students affiliated with the PCP-SL tried to teach peasants their vision of class struggle and Peruvian history. During this period the party recruited many of the rural youth who made up its local forces over the following years. The majority of these new recruits and sympathisers — some as young as 13 — were sons and daughters of peasants. Many came across Sendero in secondary school or while finishing primary school in the provincial or district capitals. Unwilling to continue living in rural poverty and disillusioned with the lack of opportunities awaiting them after graduation, these students saw the party and its armed struggle as both an adventure and a way to fight back at a system which was not working for them. 'They were adolescent kids and they were desperate to learn about arms, a submachine gun for example. For them, handling dynamite was a big thing', a young man from a community in Cangallo explained in an interview with Carlos Iván Degregori:

[The *Senderistas*] told them that Ayacucho was going to be a liberated zone in 1985. It was a grand illusion which they planted in the kids' minds... One kid asked me, 'Don't you want to be a minister? Don't you want to be a military leader? To be someone? In 1985 the revolution is going to triumph and then those of us here in Sendero, those who have more time as militants in Sendero, we are going to be ministers.'

Sendero also began to reorganise communities to conform with the strict moral and social dictums of Guzmán's 'New Order'. In order to curtail food supplies to the cities, militants tried to close weekly markets and annual fairs and to force peasants to cut back or eliminate production for the market. In many towns they banned the celebration of religious fiestas and rituals which they considered 'archaic superstitions' (as well as events in which drinking and satirical dances might embolden critics of the 'New Order'). They also attempted to disband the traditional political-religious authorities known as *varayuq* ('staff-holders') and replace them with party-sanctioned governing bodies called 'Popular Committees'.

Much of the PCP-SL's emphasis was on enforcing a new moral order in the countryside. Theft, adultery, wife-beating, corruption, failure to cooperate in communal work projects and other moral infractions were severely punished by flogging and occasional executions. Schoolteachers were forced to respect their classroom duties and work schedules. Finally, armed cadres provided security from rustlers, and punished bandits and abusive authorities and merchants. During these early years many peasants viewed the PCP-SL positively as a source of the moral order and security which the Peruvian state had for centuries failed to provide.

There were limits, however, to the power which peasants were willing to concede to the party. Most communities rejected Sendero's authoritarian interventions into their systems of production and marketing, its dismantling of the traditional authority hierarchies based on age and experience, and the imposition of moral strictures on religious fiestas, rituals and festive drinking. They particularly resented the replacement of elected or traditional authorities with the Sendero-controlled Popular Committees.

The peasants' rejection of these aspects of the fledgling New Order reflects Sendero's troubled relationship with Andean peasant culture. While Sendero's military and political work relies on a certain relationship with the Andean countryside and, in particular, with rural youth, the party has consistently dismissed the communal and cultural traditions of indigenous Andean society. Indeed, a good deal of its appeal to rural Andean youth has been its emphatic celebration of 'progress' and its disdain for the 'backward' cultural traditions and religious beliefs that some rural youth blame for the poverty in which their parents have always lived. In the party's 'scientific' ideology of revolution and progress, such important bases of community organisation as fiestas and traditional political-religious authorities are condemned to extinction as 'archaic' folklore. According to PCP-SL spokesperson Luis Arce Borja, Andean religious practices are 'irrationalities which continue to have influence over the most backward inhabitants of Peru. This [Andean] cultural tradition has absolutely nothing to do with the war and the revolutionary struggle.' Intellectual or political programmes which take account of Andean peasant traditions have been similarly disparaged by the pro-Sendero newspaper, *El Diario*, as 'magical whining nationalisms' which are condemned to extinction as the 'residue of a moribund bourgeois ideology'.

Such statements contrast sharply with Sendero's image outside Peru as an 'Indian' or ethnically based revolutionary movement. Contrary to this image, the historical vision, political philosophy and military strategy of the PCP-SL as a Maoist-inspired political party, posits class as the sole form of social contradiction driving the 'people's war'. This view of Peruvian society ignores completely the importance of ethnic and racial ideologies as forms of social and cultural oppression. No party document mentions the ethnic, racial and cultural discrimination that Andean peasants face.

For most Andean peasants, however, ethnicity, race and cultural difference remain the most visible markers around which relationships of power and domination are played out in daily life. For centuries, Andean religious and cultural practices have been suppressed and devalued by Peru's dominant *criollo* society. As Sendero's authoritarian and paternalist nature became increasingly evident, peasants began to see it as another expression of this historical legacy of discrimination. Indeed, the *Senderistas'* attitude of moral and cultural superiority has made them synonymous in many peasants' eyes with the ruling elites known throughout the Peruvian highlands as *mistis*. As used in contemporary rural Andean society *misti*, derived from the Spanish *mestizo* or 'mixed blood', is a term of ethnic differentiation which has no basis in skin colour or 'racial' differences, but is a derogatory word used to describe individuals such as landlords, merchants and local state functionaries. The defining characteristics of *mistis* are, on the one hand, their refusal to undertake physical labour, and on the other, their use of authoritarian violence to support their claims to cultural and moral superiority.

Sendero's claims to teach the peasants a superior or 'true' form of politics and morality resound with the authoritarianism, racism and paternalism associated with *mistis*. Sendero views its relationship with the 'masses' as a hierarchical one in which, in the words of Guzmán, the party 'through forceful actions keeps pounding ideas into the minds of men, who little by little begin understanding their only true road, thus developing their political consciousness. The masses have to have ideas hammered in ... the masses need the leadership of a Communist Party.'

Despite Sendero's authoritarianism, the urban population of Ayacucho and Huanta had some sympathy for Sendero's militant stance against the central government, based on long-standing regionalist antipathies towards the coast and especially towards Lima, where economic resources and political decision-making have traditionally been concentrated. These sympathies grew in direct relation to repeated 'terrorist' round-ups, special states of emergency and police abuses.

In September 1982, public frustration with the police forces sent from Lima climaxed in the burial of Edith Lagos, a well-known *Senderista* who had been killed by the police in Andahuaylas. Thousands of people attended the funeral. The contradictory elements at play were graphically symbolised by the contrasting images of the PCP-SL party flag which covered Edith Lagos's coffin and the ultra-conservative and staunchly anti-communist bishop of Ayacucho, Federico Richter Prada, who presided over the funeral. While Lagos's funeral has been taken as a massive show of support for Sendero Luminoso, in fact emotions were far more complex. As the daughter of a wealthy Ayacucho merchant, as a law student at the Lima University of San Martín de Porras, and as a woman guerrilla, Edith Lagos meant many different things to many different people. Many *Ayacuchanos* saw in her the romantic image of a local woman who had had the courage to fight against Lima. Others admired her courage as a woman and, by extension, Sendero's willingness to flaunt Peru's dominant patriarchal values by accepting women as leaders and combatants. Still others saw the familiar face of their own brothers, sisters, cousins, aunts, sons or daughters who had also joined Sendero. Finally, for an important sector of the public, solidarity with the many *Ayacuchano* victims of Sendero's war took precedence over Edith Lagos's identity as a *Senderista*.

Sympathies for Sendero were soon tempered by the escalating wave of violence. Following the gruesome execution of the director of the Ayacucho branch of the National Institute of Culture in December 1982, President Belaúnde issued a stern reprimand. 'Stop the wave of foolishness which you have unleashed, and give yourselves up to the authorities within 72 hours.' The following day, Sendero responded in a communiqué published in *El Diario*: 'More repression will be met with more guerrilla action.' Later the same day, the President ordered the military into Ayacucho.

With the troops' arrival, *Ayacuchanos* lost even the limited rights they had enjoyed under police jurisdiction. Civilian authorities surrendered power to the Political-Military Command created to preside over the emergency zone and to conduct the counter-insurgency campaign. Citizens' rights were suspended, while under the leadership of General Clemente Noel the military launched the dirty war described in chapter 1. For the PCP-SL, this war has been both a test of Guzmán's military prowess and a chance to further the goal of 'deepening the contradictions' in Peruvian society.

The People's War

When the military arrived, Sendero pulled out of the communities. While some cadres remained in Ayacucho as mobile military columns, others — including the political command — were removed to other parts of the country. Many local sympathisers and youth left behind felt betrayed by the withdrawal and by the way in which the remaining Sendero combatants retreated after their clashes with the military, leaving the communities defenceless. 'They told us to be prepared for war, to defeat the enemy, and we believed them', reported one young sympathiser from Huanta. Later, however, 'they escaped through here and we were screwed (*jodidos*). They had handed us over; they had practically sold us out. They didn't act like real men.'

Sendero's tactical retreat affected everyone in the areas in which it had been operating. In many communities, Sendero left behind local younger party members in charge of the Popular Committees. Their ability to govern was undermined by their status as junior members of communities in which age was an important element in traditional conceptions of authority. Their personal connections also made them interested parties in the many different family rivalries and animosities characterising every Andean peasant community. According to a schoolteacher and former Sendero sympathiser interviewed by Carlos Iván Degregori, 'the worst thing Sendero did was to rely on very young kids... they left young sons of the community in charge. Perhaps one of their fathers had a dispute with another's father over property boundaries, animals, theft, domestic fights. Since Sendero had left local kids in charge, they began to take reprisals, to take revenge.' With this abuse of authority, the party began to lose its credibility as an enforcer of moral and political order. According to a peasant from the Province of Huamanga interviewed by Ponciano del Pino, 'the *jefes* (leaders) were kids, know-it-alls. Then the Party themselves began to lose out. Then the people began to pull back from those [party] affairs.'

This local dynamic was made worse by the cycle of punishments and revenge set off by the Peruvian military. In accordance with its counter-insurgency doctrine, the military, which was often unable to keep up with Sendero's highly mobile columns, focused its efforts on the civilian peasant population who, it believed, supported Sendero unanimously. Reinforced by racist perceptions of highland peasants as inferior *indios* or *cholos*, the military — in particular the marines and army rangers — practised indiscriminate exemplary punishment. In Chuschi, troops who arrived shortly after Sendero had retreated seized four elderly men and blew one of them up in the central plaza using a home-made *Senderista* bomb which they had found in the village. 'When the army began to patrol the communities', reports a former Sendero supporter from the province of Cangallo:

> they inflicted massacres and assaults on the communities, they even took livestock such as bulls [and] pigs... They began to break down doors, demolish houses, to beat peasant men and women, to take them prisoner to the provincial capital and make them disappear. It was then that the peasants became scared.

According to the same witness, local Sendero supporters had been told by the party that the army's arrival would advance the struggle. 'Our idea was that, with the arrival of the army, we were going to have more support, because all those [soldiers] in the army were also sons of poor, hungry and miserable people.' In fact, Sendero's failure to provide protection from the army's abuses lost the party the support of all but the most committed younger recruits. Claiming that Sendero had betrayed them, peasants in Cangallo and other provinces began to abandon their communities. Between 1981 and 1985, over 3,000 families (nearly half the total) moved out of the 32 peasant communities most affected by the war. Some towns were virtually deserted. In others only the elderly and orphans remained to guard the houses and fields. Many of the families who remained slept in their fields or in caves for fear of night-time incursions by Sendero or the military. Those who left went to live in the *barrios* of Lima, Huancayo, Pisco and Ayacucho.

During this period Sendero, too, began to use exemplary punishments to retain control over communities in which its support was fading. Following in the wake of the army, *Senderista* columns visited the ravaged communities in search of 'stoolpigeons' and 'collaborators', whom they executed. Since the Popular Committees had ceased to function in many communities, it was often no longer possible for Sendero to allot punishment behind the facade of 'people's

Trained to Kill: Interview with a Sendero Cadre

Isidoro Santiago Nunja García, alias 'Enrique', 34, was arrested in May 1988, following a Sendero attack on the agricultural cooperative at Andahuasi. The complex was destroyed, and the cooperative manager and a plumber murdered.

Why were you arrested?
For terrorism.

For the attack on Andahuasi?
Yes. I placed a bomb. It was my job to put it in the control room. That was all I did.

Why was the plumber, a man of humble background, murdered?
Sometimes things don't happen the way they're planned.

And the engineer?
He was the functionary representing the government. He put the government's policies into practice. But they're not killed just like that. They're given warnings and they're only killed if they don't obey them.

Have you taken part in other actions?
Yes, blowing up electricity pylons.

How long have you been in Sendero?
A year and a half.

Have you been active in the Left?
I was never a member, but a sympathiser, close to small political parties. At that time I thought that the United Left was the most correct. With time and getting to know the three luminaries [Marx, Lenin, Mao], you realise that things aren't like that, that all that is revisionism and opportunism, and you drift apart.

Have you taken part in assassinations?
Anybody can take part in 'liquidations'. The leadership just has to give the order and one acts.

Is there any training before actions and in order to be promoted?
You learn to fight through fighting and to lead by leading.

When a Senderista is guilty of something or makes a mistake, how is he punished?
It depends. First, he submits to self-criticism. Then he is judged and may be punished. The maximum punishments are expulsion from the party and even death.

You murder them?
They're executions.

Why are you a Senderista?
I think it's the way to make sure that all Peruvians have everything that they need.

Caretas, Lima, 30 May 1988

trials'. Now crimes against the party were to be judged by cadres and punished through execution. When one Ayacucho community opposed an execution a *Senderista* responded, 'You peasants still have those archaic ideas of defending yourselves. From here on we are not going to ask you... because if we pardon the bad weeds, we're never going to triumph'. According to a peasant from Huancasancos interviewed by Degregori, peasants had supported Sendero's authoritarianism before the dirty war, saying that they could 'punish but not kill'. Later, however, 'the people were unhappy because the *Senderistas* committed many stupidities. They killed innocent people saying they were stoolpigeons. I think that if someone has made mistakes they should be simply punished, they should be whipped or have their heads shaved... but not like Sendero has done — killing [the mayor of our town] like a pig.'

In many cases, anger at Sendero led the peasants to adopt more aggressive means of keeping it out of their communities. In early 1983, following a punitive expedition in which 200 *Senderistas* sacked and burnt the village of Chuschi and executed the mayor and four peasants, community members took action, demanding a police or military post in the village and agreeing to participate in a military-organised civil defence patrol. In the nearly communities of Lucanamarca and Huancasancos, peasants took similar actions against Sendero. In reprisal Sendero killed eighty peasants in Lucanamarca in April 1983. In other regions, such as the province of Huamanga, peasants began to form *rondas* to defend themselves from Sendero. The *rondas* later spread to incorporate highland herding communities, and by 1984 they had evolved into a regional network. All decisions regarding their actions are decided in community assemblies, as well as in inter-community assemblies which discuss regional organisation. In this area of Ayacucho, the emergence of the democratically organised and independent *rondas* has undermined even further the Popular Committees and authoritarian command which Sendero had earlier set up.

In other regions of Ayacucho, Apurímac and Huancavelica, the army formed mandatory 'civil defence' groups and camps or 'strategic hamlets', in which entire communities were resettled. Unlike the autonomous peasant *rondas*, the civil defence groups answer directly to army commanders. Community members have little or no say in their organisation, and participation is compulsory. The hamlets and civil defence groups are integral parts of a two-pronged counter-insurgency strategy of *peinados* (combings) meant to rid villages and communities of 'terrorists' and the formation of anti-Sendero organisations among the peasantry. Although the civil defence groups are asked to take a front line position in the fight against Sendero,

Peruvian military trainer with 'civil defence' patrol, Ayacucho.

(Alejandro Balaguer)

until very recently they have been expected to do so armed only with slings, sticks, knives, and the single-shot homemade rifles called *tirachas*. When the Fujimori government finally decided to provide them with arms, they were given single-shot hunting rifles.

The civil defence groups and hamlets have created widespread discontent among the peasantry. Peasants are forcibly relocated and made to abandon their livestock and fields. They are often made to perform unpaid domestic services for the military and to provide them with food. To return to their communities for harvest or other agricultural chores, the peasants must obtain passes from the military post in their hamlet. When they do so, they run the risk of being punished by Sendero for 'collaborating' with the military. Some communities have simply refused to take part in the military's schemes. Others attempt to negotiate their way through the conflicting demands placed on them by the military and Sendero by playing to both sides. As one community president from Parinacochas Province explained to Luís Montoya Canchis:

> if we allow the *compas* (*compañeros* or comrades) to come and set themselves up here, we will be the target of the *sinchis*, because they will accuse us of being terrorists and helping the *Senderistas*. By the same token, if we let the military in, first they will abuse us and second, when they've gone, the *terrucos* (terrorists) will accuse us of being stoolpigeons and they might even kill us. The

best thing is to be in the middle, with neither one. Because otherwise either one can shoot and both can kill.

Forced relocation and mandatory civil defence patrols have created a complex scenario in which Sendero and the military must compete for control over the factional disputes that can be used to generate violence between, and within, the communities. Following the logic of counter-insurgency strategy, peasant civil patrol groups are made to 'comb' the surrounding villages in search of *Senderistas*. Frequently, they direct these *peinados* at communities with which they have had long-standing disputes over boundaries or animal thefts. In some cases, the patrols have used the military authority conferred on them to steal animals and crops from other peasants, or to punish those they suspect once stole from them. This problem has become most severe in areas where independent community-based *rondas* have refused to submit to the authority of the military. Since the military's strategy depends on incorporating all peasant communities into their hamlets and patrols, it has encouraged rivalries and vendettas between the *rondas* and its own civil defence patrols.

Sendero, meanwhile, sees both types of peasant militias as collaborators or *mesnadas* (feudal retinues) which must be eliminated. Although glossing over the important differences between the two types of peasant groups, Sendero has also exploited conflicts between them to exacerbate existing tensions, rivalries and confrontations between communities and generations. Peasants who have had animals stolen or relatives harmed by either the independent *rondas* or the civil defence patrols often turn to Sendero for revenge. Sendero has also been able to organise peasants opposed to the relocation of their communities to strategic hamlets. Acting under cover of night when the civil defence groups were patrolling the countryside, 300 Sendero-led dissidents killed forty people in an attack on a relocation camp in Pampacancha in April 1984. The dissidents belonged to four of the communities which had recently been relocated by the navy to the strategic hamlet of Pampacancha. Driven to side with Sendero by the military's destructive policies, the peasants had attacked and killed their own neighbours and relatives in an attempt to recover their old lands, communities and freedom.

Conquering Bases of Support

Over the four years following the military's arrival in Ayacucho, the average annual number of terrorist incidents in the department diminished from 460 to 354. Over the same period, incidents in the department of Huánuco rose from 13 in 1983, to 84 in 1985 and 55 the following year. The Department of Junín experienced a similar trend, from 68 incidents in 1983 to 169 in 1986. The most dramatic increase, however, occurred in the Department of Puno where terrorist actions jumped from 25 in 1983 to 277 in 1986.

Sendero sees the department of Puno as an area of strategic geographic and political importance. Located in southern Peru, Puno provides access to the much-crossed border with Bolivia. Known for its active contraband economy and arms smuggling, the Peru-Bolivia border also offers obvious advantages to a political group interested in moving people, arms and munitions in and out of Peru. The principal roads and railways connecting Cusco with Bolivia, Arequipa and the coast run through Puno.

With its large peasant population and active peasant federations, Puno also offered Sendero an important political front. Situated in Peru's southernmost high *altiplano*, its predominantly rural population is also one of Peru's poorest. The Quechua- and Ayamara-speaking peasants who live in its many communities maintain close relationships with the thriving market towns and commercial centres of Juliaca and Puno. Known for its buoyant commercial economy and large merchant class, Puno has since the early 19th century been the principal centre for alpaca and sheep wool marketing in southern Peru. Both haciendas and peasant communities produced wool for the export market and large commercial houses in Arequipa.

Puno was also prominent in the national debates over agrarian reform and rural development. In many ways Puno seemed to epitomise the contradictions of General Velasco's agrarian reform politics. Although a large percentage of Puno's total agrarian lands were affected by the land reform, only 2.5 per cent of these lands were given directly to the peasant communities. In comparison, ninety per cent of the land was constituted into large 'associative enterprises'. These combined different forms of partnership between technicians, administrators, workers and peasants, and were managed by state-appointed bureaucrats. In many cases, the administrators were former hacienda foremen or relatives of the same hated *hacendados* who had formerly owned the land. Because the 'new' administrators maintained close ties to local elites, the structure of social and political power in Puno remained largely intact following the agrarian reform.

Challenging the new elite of bureaucrats and administrators, Puno's peasant movement also gained momentum with the agrarian reform process. During the 1960s, provincial and district level peasant organisations grew up around the various land takeovers which occurred in different parts of Puno. Only in 1977-8, however, did these organisations coalesce into the Departmental Peasant Federation of Puno (FDCP), affiliated nationally with the Peasant Confederation of

DEPARTMENT
OF PUNO

Peru (CCP). The local federation played a pivotal role in the mobilisations and strikes against the government of General Morales Bermúdez. In the early 1980s, the United Peasant Federation of Melgar Province (FUCAM) emerged as the centre of Puno's peasant movement. In opposition to Belaúnde's plan to dismantle and privatise the associative enterprises, the Melgar peasants proposed a 'democratic restructuring' to benefit the peasant communities. The failure of Alan García's APRA administration to honour its pledge to assist the restructuring merely worsened tensions between local *Apristas*, bureaucrats and the peasant federation, allied with the Church, NGOs and left-wing parties.

The Left had kept a significant presence in Puno's politics since at least the mid-1970s. Throughout the 1980s, the IU in particular had dominated municipal elections. In a blow to APRA, the IU had also won the 1985 parliamentary elections by a relatively wide margin. Within the IU, PUM had played a particularly important role in the land takeovers in 1985 and the movement for democratic restructuring. Another of the peasants' most powerful supporters was the Catholic Church. Following the theological reforms of the Medellín Episcopal Conference of 1968, the Church in Puno has been highly committed to support for grassroots organisations and the poor.

Sendero's immediate aims in 1985-6 were to challenge PUM's leadership of Puno's grassroots peasant movement and to exploit animosities between the pro-peasant front and APRA. Its eventual objective was to provoke militarisation in the department, on the basis that the army's presence would both strengthen its base of support and put an end to the activities of Puno's powerful peasant federations. To obtain these objectives, the PCP-SL counted on a local network of party militants and sympathisers active in the department since the early 1980s, when *Senderista* teachers first set up Popular Schools in the province of Azángaro.

Sendero's 'principal force' for the offensive was made up of trained combatants from the coast and from the Ayacucho province of La Mar. In the early months of 1986, the 'principal force', in coordination with local forces, attacked a number of police posts and partially or completely destroyed installations, livestock and buildings on associative enterprises in the provinces of Azángaro and Melgar. On several occasions, livestock belonging to the enterprises was forcibly distributed to peasants from surrounding communities. Far from being a reward, the improved and imported breeding stock which the Sendero cadres forced upon the frightened peasants could easily be traced by police searching for the 'terrorists' who had stolen them. As a result, many of the valuable breeding animals were slaughtered or sold on the black market.

Voting at FDCP congress, Puno.　　　　(Marcelo Quispe/Ayaviri/TAFOS/PANOS)

Killings in Puno also increased during this period as Sendero singled out local *Aprista* leaders and managers and technicians on the associative enterprises, hoping to convince the peasantry that the land problem could only be resolved through the total destruction of the enterprises. Both the 'pacifist' land takeovers organised by the FDCP and the government's bureaucratic restructuring were equally ineffective, Sendero told the peasants. The only means to achieve a victory over the enterprises, they preached, was through 'armed takeovers within the [final] aim of seizing power'.

Unable to erode the FDCP's organisation and public appeal through violence, Sendero adopted an even more aggressive strategy for confronting the federation. In June 1986, a Sendero column stopped various trucks on the road to the weekly market in Ayaviri and rounded up some 200 peasants. All of them were from Macarí, the community which had initiated decisive land takeovers at Kunurana in December 1985, and which, as a result, occupied an important position in the FDCP. The Macarí peasants were taken to Kunurana and forced by the *Senderistas* to loot and then burn the installations. At the same time, seven Kunurana workers were killed and mutilated by Sendero.

Despite the wave of terror unleashed by Sendero and the APRA-sponsored paramilitaries which emerged in response, the FDCP continued to organise communities around its platform of democratic restructuring. At the regional level, it successfully pushed for a project to place peasant communal enterprises at the centre of Puno's regional development. Nationally as well, the FDCP became involved in the leadership of the CCP and in the organisation of the May 1987 national peasant strike. During this strike, 211 peasant communities took over almost 400,000 hectares of land from several associative enterprises in Puno. The peasants met heavily-armed special police and counter-insurgency forces, and one was killed and several others arrested. But even with police support, the administrators were unable to stop the largest land takeover in Puno's history.

Predictably, the FDCP also met with opposition from Sendero. On 8 April 1987, a few days after the FDCP had met in assembly to decide on the May actions, a *Senderista* column entered the FDCP stronghold of San Juan de Salinas. At gunpoint they held a 'people's trial' in which the accused was Zenobio Huarsaya Soncco, a founding member of the FDCP and community organiser who had recently been elected as the town's mayor. Despite pleas for clemency from the assembled peasants and an impassioned speech by Huarsaya himself, the *Senderistas* shot the mayor in the head. At Huarsaya's funeral, hundreds of peasants joined the national leadership of the CCP in condemning Sendero's authoritarian violence.

The conflict between Sendero and its perceived competitors gradually developed into a war of attrition. After the setback of losing its 'principal force' in 1987 in a fight with police, Sendero gradually recovered ground. Bombings, murders and destruction of property increased steadily. In line with objectives defined in Sendero's first national party congress held in early 1988, the target of this renewed wave of violence in Puno was the Left, the progressive Church, grassroots organisations, NGOs and other pro-peasant forces.

In March 1988, Sendero was again challenged by Puno's dynamic peasant movement which called a strike demanding that the government declare Puno a disaster area (because of recurring droughts), speed up the restructuring process, guarantee crop prices, increase wages, respect human rights, free peasant leaders detained as terrorists, and, finally, grant regional autonomy to Puno. During the strike which began on 1 March, peasants held demonstrations in the provincial capitals, as well as in the departmental capital of Puno, supported by workers, students, and urban grassroots organisations. Finally on 19 March, the García government agreed to form a commission to discuss the peasants' demands.

Faced with mounting support for the FDCP's strike, Sendero attempted to recover political ground by calling its own 48-hour 'armed strike' in Azángaro to coincide with the peasant strike. The armed strike was neither successful in provoking a military state of emergency, nor in deterring the peasants from their own course of

Sons of the War

'Everything was well organised. For example, one attack took place at the Allpachaka cattle ranch (the university's experimental farm). The planning took two months. Some comrades took care to work out how many people worked there and whether there were any police. They worked on it for six weeks. Afterwards they called [Sendero's] military and political leaders together and told us that they needed support from all the communities and that all militants should take part, and that even non-militants should be involved in the attack, since there were no police and nothing to be afraid of. That's what they told us and we agreed...

At Allpachaka we went in during the daytime. At 5 am all those from the party surrounded the community, stopping anyone from leaving Allpachaka. Other groups went in and took all the peasants to one area, threatening anyone who tried to stay in their house. When everyone was there, the political chief from Cangallo and Huancapi district made a speech. In those days I didn't really understand how much of a debt Peru owed to the US. When he said 400 million dollars or something like that, I didn't really understand what it meant. And he told us that in Lima there were top government officials, like bulls which don't produce anything, like bullocks. A bullock isn't worth anything in the *sierra*, if a bull is worth anything it works, but a bullock is just fat, no good even for ploughing. He said there were many like that, in the ministries, and that the people paid for this bureaucracy in ministries like Education and Health. Because of this, Sendero Luminoso was fighting and the goal was to win power through guerrilla warfare from the countryside to the city...

We took the ranch because the workers there didn't even get to taste the cheeses they made. The party found out that these cheeses weren't eaten in Peru, but were exported to Holland, I think, and that using the name of the university had created the ranch, but in reality the university got nothing out of it. That's why we decided to act.

There were four bulls, they were enormous. We killed them straightaway and began to cut them up. As there were pots, we began cooking. We cooked meat and potatoes, made soup and handed it out to everybody and we told the women to bring their big pots and wood for cooking. Everybody ate. There was a lot left over. And old women from other communities who'd heard about it, came to ask for meat, potatoes or anything...

There were beds, tables, cheeses, wine, everything in Allpachaka. So we had to take it all out, sort it out and destroy what nobody could take with them. There were huge stocks, at least eight large yards full. We were there on Saturday, and on Monday they were due to send out all the cheeses, so we arrived just in time. We burnt where they kept the oats, broke down the doors, smashed the walls, and we released the pigs and guinea pigs.

We killed what cattle we could. But when we were slaughtering, the women began to cry, asking what the cattle had done. They were crying, asking us to stop, but we'd already killed about a quarter of the cattle. We had intended to kill them all, but we couldn't once the women started crying.'

Carlos Iván Degregori et al, Tiempos de ira y amor. Lima, DESCO, 1990

action. Unable to compete with the peasant strike, Sendero once again resorted to a campaign of bombings and murders against the Left, the Church and the NGOs which supported the strike. In separate attacks, they also destroyed three of the most important experimental farms in the region managed by the Church and the university. For the remainder of 1989, it brought terror to peasant communities. In a single night in early December, in Orurillo, Sendero killed the mayor and secretary of the district peasant federation, the general secretary of the local teachers' union, a primary school teacher, the director of the agricultural secondary school, the deputy governor and the justice of the peace. By the end of 1989, Sendero had carried out more than 200 armed operations in Puno, nearly half of which involved assassinations.

Following the death of its regional commander 'El Gringo' Olivares, in an attack on a police post in Sollocoto in early January 1990, Sendero's actions once again declined until the reconstruction of its principal column in March. Reinforced with new cadres from Cusco and Apurímac, Sendero renewed its efforts to capitalise on the tensions that were slowly building within the peasant movement as a result of the terror campaign. Fearful of Sendero's reprisals, nearly three-quarters of the elected peasant and municipal authorities in Azángaro Province had already resigned by September 1989. 'With the violence, the organisations built up by the people are being weakened', reported the new mayor of Azángaro in September 1989. 'Azángaro was one of the strongest bases of the FDCP, but in the last six months this level of organisation has been shaken. We are operating in very difficult conditions, they do not even allow us to go to the districts... to support the communities' demands, because we run the risk of being shot down.'

The frustrations caused by Sendero's campaign to undermine the FDCP were further aggravated in July 1990 when Sendero successfully infiltrated peasant land takeovers at the associative enterprise of Quisuni. In the midst of the FDCP-led takeover, a Sendero column intervened, killing six workers from Quisuni and proclaiming that destruction and armed takeovers were the only correct revolutionary strategy. The violence incited a wave of accusations of complicity with terrorist actions against the FDCP and its supporters in PUM and the Church. Ignoring the subtle dimensions of Sendero's campaign against the peasant organisation, the national press and departmental authorities chose to focus only on the fact that the murders had take place during an FDCP event. These accusations reiterated long standing charges that PUM and the 'communist priests' had been working with Sendero all along.

The expanding cycle of recrimination, threats and counter-threats provoked by the Quisuni killings provided an opening for renewed military intervention in Azángaro and Melgar Provinces in October 1990. With the military came yet more violence. But, supported by the bishopric of Puno, a department-wide network of local human rights activists has effectively monitored the military's activities. In large part through their work, it has been possible to prevent the recurrence of the widespread abuses and killings which accompanied military intervention in Ayacucho.

The Lima Corridor

Located in the hinterland of Lima, the central highland departments of Pasco and Junín are the site of some of Peru's richest mineral deposits, most productive agricultural lands, and liveliest peasant and labour movements. Within this region, the rich Mantaro valley of Junín has historically been the breadbasket of urban Lima. Besides its thriving peasant agriculture and livestock raising, the region is also home to Peru's largest hydro-electricity plants and most important mining complexes. Workers at the mines, smelters, railways, and energy plants in Junín and Pasco form some of the most important centres of organised labour in the country. A short distance to the east of the Mantaro valley and easily reached by the Central Highway which passes through Junín, lie some of Peru's best lowland agricultural and coca-producing lands.

The central highlands' proximity to Lima and concentration of wealth have given them a unique historical and cultural identity. Unlike other parts of the Peruvian highlands, the independent peasant communities which line the rich agricultural lands of the Mantaro valley have always overshadowed haciendas. Since colonial times, these communities have prospered from the commercial opportunities offered by Lima's ever growing demand for food. Their role as a reservoir of migrant labour for the large mines of Junín and Pasco has

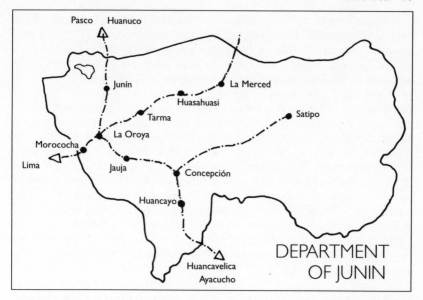

also given the central highland peasants a distinctive identity, rooted in the countryside, yet closely linked to Peru's national labour movement.

Physically as well, the Mantaro landscape contrasts with the dispersed communities and dilapidated transport networks to be found in the southern highlands of Puno, Apurímac, Cusco and Ayacucho. Along the Mantaro valley, peasant communities have expanded into urban centres connected by a constant flow of trucks, buses and taxis. Rural literacy rates and education levels are much higher than in other areas of the highlands. Strong community organisation has allowed peasants to develop their own forms of communal and inter-communal enterprise for livestock fattening, public transport, fisheries, hydro-electric plants and the marketing of agricultural products. Community-based peasant organisations maintain close ties with the thriving provincial clubs of migrants in Lima and other coastal cities.

The political character of these communities has also been shaped by their close historical ties to the miners' unions, and by the relative lack of ethnic division between workers and peasants in a region where peasants only rarely speak Quechua. Throughout the central highlands, peasants and miners have experienced the effects of migration, as well as joined in opposing landgrabbing, ecological destruction and labour exploitation by the large US-based mining enterprise, Cerro de Pasco Mining Corporation.

Foreign and *Limeño* capital has also fuelled the development of the central highlands' livestock, dairy and wool economy. Until the agrarian reform of 1969, the high prairies, or *punas*, above the Mantaro valley hosted some of Peru's largest and most technologically advanced cattle-raising and wool-producing haciendas. Their presence in the area has been contested by the surrounding peasant communities. During the 1960s, some of these communities invaded and took back land from several of the haciendas. With Velasco's agrarian reform, a special form of associative enterprise known as the Agrarian Society of Social Interest (SAIS), modelled on Yugoslav self-management enterprises, was developed for this area. In this model of the SAIS, peasant communities participated as full partners in the associative enterprises created out of the haciendas. While participation brought some benefits such as new roads, schools and technical support, conflicts later developed between the peasant communities and the administrators and technicians. When Sendero began its expansion into the central highlands in 1987, these conflicts were reaching a peak.

Both its geo-political and social characteristics make the central highlands a key piece in the PCP-SL's strategy to sabotage the national economy, disrupt provision of food and energy to Lima and undermine the viability of independent peasant and labour movements. Sendero began activity in the central highland cities and mining camps with its armed struggle in 1980. By 1983, it had sharply stepped up political work in the region in preparation for an offensive which would come in 1988-9. This has entailed armed incursions into towns and villages, where residents are forced to attend assemblies held at gunpoint. In these assemblies, *Senderistas* lecture the population on the armed struggle, distribute literature and collect 'quotas' of money for the armed struggle. In one such assembly in the village of Cochas, the villagers were told that anyone found removing the party's graffiti and flags from walls would be killed. The villagers were then reminded that 'the Party has a thousand eyes and a thousand ears', so that, as one man later reported, 'we feel under surveillance even though we do not see them.' As a reminder of the omnipresent party apparatus, Sendero also stops buses and cars along country roads and city streets to collect 'quotas' from passengers whose electoral identification cards are then stamped with the PCP-SL's hammer and sickle symbol.

Railways, mining installations and productive infrastructure throughout the central highlands were also singled out in the offensive. In 1988 alone Sendero carried out 18 bombings of the Central Railway which connects Lima with the mines of Junín and Pasco. In December 1988, *Senderistas* destroyed one of Peru's largest milk and dairy processing plants. Located in Concepción, this cooperatively-owned plant had provided jobs for over 800 workers and was the principal supplier of milk for Huancayo and Lima.

Sendero has also threatened and killed elected authorities throughout the central highlands. By murdering mayors in Pasco, Junín and the highland provinces of Lima, Sendero has created a climate of fear in which 195 out of 298 mayors have resigned. These resignations have seriously weakened state representation in an area which Sendero hopes eventually to control.

The party's ambitions for the region ultimately depend, however, on its ability to control the strategic high plains or *puna* above the Mantaro valley. This *puna* offers access to the intermontane valleys that descend from the western Andes to the coast and to the neighbouring departments of Huancavelica and Pasco. Such territorial corridors are crucial for a military strategy premised on the use of highly mobile columns. Sendero's expansion into this area began with attacks on police posts in the communities of Chongos and Yanacancha in May 1988. Three months later, it destroyed a Jesuit development and educational centre in Jarpa and the communal farms of Yanacancha and Cachi. They then began their siege of the associative enterprise, SAIS Cahuide.

With over 270,000 hectares of land, seven productive units, 120,000 sheep, 9,000 head of cattle and 600 horses, Cahuide was the largest SAIS in the Peruvian highlands. Its associates included 29 affiliated peasant communities and a large cooperative formed of the SAIS's workers, technicians and shepherds. At the time Sendero began to attack Cahuide, its affiliated communities were active in the struggle for the SAIS' democratic restructuring. As in Puno, peasants were dissatisfied with the administration and organisation of the associative enterprise and sought to transform it into a multi-communal enterprise directly controlled by their communities.

As support grew for the restructuring project, Sendero increased its attacks on the SAIS. In November 1988, PCP-SL columns destroyed the installations at three of Cahuide's seven productive units. Targeting the nine communities of the Canipaco valley which had led the restructuring movement, Sendero next killed Víctor Lozano, a peasant organiser from Canipaco, and Manuel Soto, a university professor who had been working with the Canipaco peasants on the restructuring project. As in Puno, Sendero opposed restructuring in favour of a total dismantling of the SAIS and its productive infrastructure, followed by the distribution of livestock and land to the peasants. Defying Sendero's threats, in December 1988 Cahuide's general assembly approved the final dissolution of the SAIS and the creation of a new multi-communal enterprise from its installations and land.

In reprisal, Sendero destroyed Laive, the most technologically advanced and productive of Cahuide's seven production units. After demolishing the buildings and installations, Sendero distributed 5,000 head of cattle and 40,000 sheep to the surrounding peasant communities. The peasants were prohibited by Sendero from keeping this improved breeding stock for themselves or for the benefit of their communal herds, and were told instead to sell the valuable animals immediately for slaughter. Laive's 200 resident workers were ordered to return to their communities. In one move, Sendero had deprived the peasant communities of installations and livestock which had once produced over 5,000 litres of milk a day and 150 metric tons of wool annually. In the slogans painted on Laive's ruins, the *Senderistas* wrote, 'Total destruction of the SAIS, work of the people, under the direction of the PCP'.

Following the destruction of Laive, Cahuide's extensive pasture lands were left intact and unclaimed as a virtual no-man's land through which PCP-SL columns could now move with impunity. Control of this strategic territorial corridor was assured by the imposition of party-generated Popular Committees in several of the former communities of the SAIS. Those communities which refused to accept Sendero's rule were threatened or punished. In one such incident, on 12 April, a *Senderista* column stopped a bus travelling through the highlands of the Mantaro valley and forcibly removed twenty passengers from Chongos Alto, a community which had attempted to recover lands taken by Sendero. Other Sendero cadres rounded up peasants from neighbouring communities. 'So you want to organise peasant *rondas* and communal enterprises?' the *Senderistas* demanded of the peasants. 'You are with the Old State, with the wretches of the CCP, the United Left and Alan García. We are going to kill all the representatives of the Old State.' Reading from a list of names, the *Senderistas* then shot twelve of the prisoners.

Miners and mining unions have also been the victims of Sendero's central highlands offensive. Historically, miners have formed the core of the Peruvian labour movement. Since its formation in the early 1930s, the Peruvian National Federation of Mining, Metallurgical and Steel Workers (FNTMMSP) has represented Peru's many different company and regional miners' unions. Of these, the unions from the large central highland mining towns of Morococha, Casapalca, La Oroya and Cerro de Pasco have played a particularly important role against foreign-owned corporations and in supporting the peasant movement for land.

In 1989, in the midst of Sendero's campaign, the FNTMMSP came under fire from various quarters. Faced with the possibility of a general strike in support of a new union contract, mine owners, APRA government functionaries and the right-wing press began accusing FNTMMSP leaders and rank-and-file members of terrorism in the hope of provoking military intervention in the mining camps which supported the strike. After months of such attempts to discredit the union leadership, in February 1989 the right-wing paramilitary *Comando Rodrigo Franco* assassinated Saúl Cantoral, the FNTMMSP General Secretary, and Consuelo García de la Cruz, a women's organiser in the mining camps. Over the following four months, Sendero followed suit with the murders of three prominent union leaders. Several other union activists and organisers of miners' wives also received death threats.

At its 1989 congress, the FNTMMSP approved the creation of miners' self-defence brigades and called a national strike for 14 August in anticipation of the management's refusal to recognise the new union contract. In preparation for the strike, miners from the central highlands held a regional congress in Morococha in late July. Several days before the event, Sendero destroyed machinery and installations at the Morococha mines and threatened union leaders. At the congress, which was also attended by representatives from peasant and women's organisations, the delegates agreed to support the strike and to oppose Sendero's efforts to provoke military intervention in the mining camps.

Amidst proliferating accusations of terrorism, the military intervened during the miners' strike. In Morococha, Casapalca and La Oroya, striking miners were arrested, and union offices were raided and documents were seized and destroyed. While the miners successfully carried on their strike and even won some of their original demands, the PCP-SL had succeeded in creating an atmosphere in which all union activity was increasingly difficult. Under siege from both Sendero and the right-wing paramilitaries, the miners' unions have not only lost some of their best leaders. Today they also confront a situation in which Sendero and the military can act with virtual impunity.

The Iron Belt

On the afternoon of 29 August 1991, as trucks and porters were loading and unloading their wares in Lima's busy wholesale produce market, three gunmen entered the storefront handcart rental shop of Virgilio Ramírez Huaranga and, without saying a word, shot him dead. To his family and those who knew him, the motive for Ramírez's execution was obvious. On two previous occasions, he had ignored Sendero's orders to stop renting handcarts in the market during armed strikes called by the party. The handcarts which he rented to porters and stevedores were a vital link in a market which provisioned the whole of urban Lima. Without them, trucks would be unable to unload their produce and retailers would be unable to supply the grocers and neighbourhood markets of Lima. Like others in the wholesale market, Ramírez had chosen to ignore Sendero's threats, with the result that business went on as usual during the days of the armed strikes.

Following Ramírez's murder, his 22-year-old daughter, Teresa, and her brother-in-law, Walter Huillca, decided to continue with the handcart business. When Walter and Teresa refused to comply with Sendero's demands that the family drop the business altogether, they too were killed, exactly a month after the shooting of Virgilio. This time the assassins left a note: 'This is the way stoolpigeons and massacrers [sic] of the people die. Ramírez Family, get out of the market. The People's War will destroy you. Long live Chairman Gonzalo.'

From the beginning of its armed struggle, the PCP-SL has considered the cities an important theatre of operations. 'In the cities,' Guzmán explained, 'there are the *barriadas* (shanty towns), the immense shanty-town masses. Since the year 1976, we have had a plan for work in the cities. To take neighbourhoods and shanty towns as the base and the proletariat as leader. That is our plan and we continue to practice it... To which masses do we point? The immense masses of the neighbourhoods and shanty towns which are like an iron belt that will encircle the enemy and contain the reactionary forces.'

As the centre of economic and political power, and as home to over a third of Peru's population, Lima has been a crucial arena for propaganda, sabotage, recruitment and consolidating a support network. In a 1986 interview with *El Diario*, Guzmán stressed the importance of Lima. 'As the capital, Lima allows for actions of great impact [because they produce] an immediate sharpening of contradictions in the heart of the reaction.' In keeping with the capital's political and military significance, the party committee for Lima is one of the most powerful of Sendero's regional committees. Known as the 'Metropolitan Committee', it was set up even before the initiation of the armed struggle. The Metropolitan Committee, which is divided into six subcommittees in charge of different zones, is entrusted with providing security and protection for the national leadership's headquarters in Lima and with punishing party dissidents or 'traitors'. Because Lima is home to all Peru's major governmental and civil institutions, the Metropolitan Committee is also responsible for intelligence gathering and infiltration in ministries, left-wing parties,

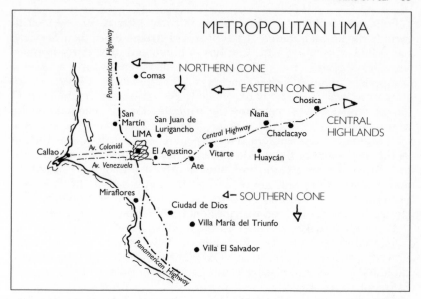

labour unions, and the military establishment. In January 1981, the PCP-SL central committee ordered the Metropolitan Committee to set up 'action groups', in charge of bombings, arson, sabotage, and graffiti, and 'special squads' for assassinations and more technically specialised forms of sabotage.

Spanning all Peru's urban centres is the *Socorro Popular* (Popular Aid), a party-generated organism created in 1982. Organised in geographically defined committees, *Socorro Popular* coordinates the work of intellectuals, lawyers, university and school students, workers and professionals in logistical support for the armed struggle. *Socorro Popular* members provide legal defence for prisoners and detainees, security and housing for party cadres, economic and medical assistance for party members and their relatives, and support for the families of prisoners and 'fallen heroes' of the party. *Socorro Popular's* work was severely damaged in 1985 and 1985 by the capture in Lima of important members of its coordinating committee. Following the arrests, the party's central committee reorganised *Socorro Popular* to conform with the general strategy of attaining the total militarisation of the party and its affiliated organisms. Action Committees were formed within Socorro to carry out agitprop and sabotage. After 1987, members of *Socorro Popular* also began to kill selected businessmen, factory managers and public officials, including the director of Peru's social security administration.

Following Sendero's first congress in early 1988, it was decided to step up the urban initiative through armed strikes. Since then, Sendero has called at least ten armed strikes in Lima, and over thirty in other provincial towns and cities. These armed strikes are a crucial component in the PCP-SL's concept of 'complementary theatres in the prolonged war from the countryside to the cities'. As described in *El Diario*, armed strikes 'combine the struggles for the demands of the masses with the struggle for political power. They have the strategic goal of training the workers and the people for the urban insurrection as the final stage of the people's war'. They also offer an opportunity to train sympathisers and militants in armed propaganda, sabotage and assassination, and act as a constant reminder of the PCP-SL's presence in the cities and of its ability to intervene and disrupt such strategic activities as food distribution, transport and energy supply.

The armed strikes are also meant to show Sendero's advances in constructing the 'People's Republic of New Democracy' (or 'New Power') as a counterforce to the 'Old State' dominated by bureaucratic capitalism. 'The armed strikes, and particularly those in Lima', writes *El Diario*, 'have served so that two states can express their existence and measure each other's strength as enemies.' As such, they fall within the party's third strategic stage of 'developing bases of support'. This stage, which follows the previous two stages of 'developing the guerrilla war' and 'conquering bases of support', began in 1987 with the establishment of Open Popular Committees in some areas of the countryside. Defined in *El Diario* as committees which 'function in broad daylight as state and government', the Open Popular Committees differ from the earlier, clandestine, Popular Committees. As public organisms created by the party, they operate only in those isolated pockets of the countryside where the party has managed to eliminate the presence of state agents, traditional community authorities, and other organisations not affiliated with the PCP-SL. 'In the countryside', Guzmán wrote in *Bases*, 'we make all the masses participate armed, organised in the Party [and] the Army. If all the masses are not organised, the New Power cannot sustain itself for long. There is no room for amorphous masses or for Power without organised masses under the leadership of the Party.'

In the cities as in the countryside, Sendero works through 'people's schools' and party-generated organisms. However, given the greater difficulties of carving out areas of total party control in the cities, Guzmán specified that 'the Party applies this strategy in one fashion in the countryside, given that it is there that the New Power is constituted, and in another fashion in the cities...[where] we use the double strategy of developing our own organisms... and penetrating all types of organisations.' The party's different strategies for city and countryside reflect Guzmán's particular understanding of the New Democracy and how it will be achieved through armed struggle. Whereas Mao foresaw the establishment of a New Democracy only after the final seizure of power, Guzmán has proclaimed its existence wherever the party has taken control through the creation of Popular Committees and bases of support. In the countryside, 'the Popular Committees', he explains, 'are concrete expressions of the New State... led by Commissars with state functions... They apply the people's dictatorship, coercion and security, exercising violence with firmness and decision in order to defend the New Power against its enemies.' In the cities, where total party control can only be attained after the final insurrection, Guzmán has specified that the party should establish 'Centres of Resistance' and party-generated organisms under the umbrella of the Revolutionary Movement for Defence of the People (MRDP), a multi-class organisation, 'formed with the aim of the final insurrection'. In Lima, the party-generated organisms which make up the MRDP include the Neighbourhood Class Movement (MCB), the Class Workers' and Labourers' Movement (MOTC), *Socorro Popular* (Popular Aid), the Popular Women's Movement (MFP) and the Revolutionary Student Front (FER).

The task of establishing these party-generated organisms in Lima is complicated by the city's immense urban sprawl and deeply-rooted traditions of neighbourhood organisation, as well as by the presence of established labour unions and left-wing parties, including the MRTA. While the PCP-SL retains its military goals of preparing the terrain for the urban insurrection, it has encountered different social and political conditions in the various zones of metropolitan Lima. In older working-class municipalities such as San Martín de Porras, El Agustino, Villa María del Triunfo and Comas which started as migrant settlements in the 1940s and 1950s, Sendero has had to confront established municipal governments with long histories of involvement with left-wing parties. The mature neighbourhood and grassroots organisations which support these governments have years of accumulated political experience. In addition, as full-grown urban communities, with permanent buildings of brick and stone, police posts and transport systems, these neighbourhoods also offer different physical conditions for developing clandestine or illegal activities.

Interspersed with the older communities, are the rapidly growing *pueblos jóvenes* or shanty towns, in which live nearly a third of Lima's total population of eight million. Home to Lima's many street vendors, domestic servants and labourers, these precarious settlements frequently have no police stations nor any other state representatives. In most *pueblos jóvenes*, people have to organise their own security, food distribution, water supply services, and construct their own schools and public buildings. NGOs, development agencies and church organisations play an important role in providing financial and technical support for such grassroots community development projects.

Geographically, Lima's poor neighbourhoods are concentrated in three triangular zones or 'cones', whose tips converge on the downtown area. The 'northern cone' contains the working-class municipalities of Comas and San Martín de Porras, as well as the newer neighbourhoods and *pueblos jóvenes* made up of migrants and street vendors who live around the municipalities of Carabayllo and San Juan de Lurigancho.

Fanning out from the municipality of San Juan de Miraflores, the 'southern cone' stretches into the dunes of the coastal desert. The biggest settlement here is the Urban Self-Managed Community of Villa El Salvador (CUAVES). Created in the 1970s by survivors of an earthquake that devastated the Callejón de Huaylas in 1970, CUAVES has grown into a town of over 300,000 with paved streets, municipal gardens, schools, and electrical, water and sewage systems created through the efforts of its residents. CUAVES is also home to an impressive variety of grassroots organisations, ranging from mothers' clubs and youth organisations to Christian base communities and political parties. In 1988, CUAVES, with the support of the United Nations and development agencies, created an industrial park, where factories were to be run as cooperatives or as self-managed enterprises. Because of its success as an independent citizen-managed community, CUAVES has been recognised internationally as an exemplary alternative model of Third World urban development.

Extending east of Lima along the Rímac river valley, lies the third or 'eastern' cone. Known as the 'Carretera Central' after the strategic Central Highway which passes through on its way to Junín and the jungle, this region contains Lima's oldest and largest industrial belt as well as some of its newest *pueblos jóvenes*. The core of this area lies in the municipal district of Ate Vitarte, Lima's oldest working-class neighbourhood and home to many labour unions. Many more recently established *pueblos jóvenes* ring the outskirts of the urbanised area of Ate Vitarte. Principal among these is the community of Huaycán, created in 1984 under the auspices of Lima's left-wing municipal government. Following the example set by CUAVES, Huaycán's 70,000 inhabitants have decided to build their community through self-management, communal administration and grassroots organisations.

Mirroring the Carretera Central region on the west side of central Lima and along the principal thoroughfare to the port of Callao, is the capital's other industrial belt, named after Avenida Argentina which passes through its heart. Many industries line Avenida Argentina, as well as some of Lima's oldest poor neighbourhoods. All traffic to and from Lima's port and airport passes through this strategic and densely populated area. The factories situated along the corridor formed by the Carretera Central and Avenida Argentina account for over seventy per cent of Peru's total industrial output.

As elsewhere, Sendero's strategy for Lima's poor neighbourhoods and industrial areas must be understood in military terms. Its goals are to provoke repression and to build a base of support through armed propaganda operations such as bombings, armed incursions into schools and markets, leafleting and graffiti. These activities train new recruits and announce the party's presence in the communities. Other forms of agitprop are the dramatic bonfires in the shape of the hammer and sickle which *Senderistas* set ablaze on the surrounding hills. After some months, party members may be brought in to carry out military drills at night through the streets of the community. Accompanied by the chanting of party slogans, these drills imitate those of the Peruvian military and symbolise the party's resolution to open a front in the area. During daytime, *Senderistas* may also appropriate community loudspeaker systems to make speeches about the 'people's war'. In one neighbourhood in San Juan de Luringancho, a local leader was killed when he refused Sendero access to the community's megaphone system. At some point, party members will begin openly to collect contributions, sell literature and give speeches in markets and schools. 'They go to the neighbourhood markets', said a street vendor in San Juan de Lurigancho in the magazine *Sí*, 'and they ask us for a contribution for the trenches. We give them potatoes or a chicken wing. Whatever we can. They call it a voluntary donation. We feed others of them as if they were clients [at a restaurant]. We do it out of fear.'

Together with open activities, cadres work individually to develop the contacts necessary to set up a 'base of support'. Making use of family and community networks in the *pueblos jóvenes*, they visit the homes of new migrants and refugees from the emergency zones, asking for shelter or some other small favour. Eventually, such favours may escalate into more compromising activities, such as storing arms or giving space for meetings. Playing on the migrants' fears of the police, Sendero tries to coerce them into *de facto* collaboration with the party. Party recruiters also target left-wing activists who have become disillusioned with their parties, as well as school students who may then be used to compromise whole families in party-related activities. As one working-class woman from San Juan de Lurigancho recalls:

I was surprised one day when a stranger brought my son home. When I asked him who he was, he told me that he belonged to the PCP-SL and that I shouldn't be afraid because they were fighting for a new society. Days later, the same guy came back with my son. This time he acted differently. He acted arrogantly. He said that I had to cooperate with whatever the party said. I was with my husband. They asked us to let them use the house for meetings. They threatened us and our son. We had to agree.

Once people have agreed to allow a meeting to be held in their home, they become publicly compromised as party sympathisers in the eyes of their communities. Going door to door, *Senderistas* invite neighbours to the meeting to discuss community problems such as electricity or water supplies. Once at the meeting, the residents are instead lectured on the 'people's war' and told to keep the meeting a secret. Residents are likely to keep quiet about such meetings and activities, since they know that the police view any involvement with Sendero as terrorism. Many people also approve of Sendero's self-assumed role of moral guardian against the drugs, prostitution and petty crime found in all of Lima's poorer neighbourhoods. This process eventually culminates in the establishment of bases and contacts for the party-generated MCB.

A dramatic example of the advances and setbacks which Sendero has experienced in Lima's poor neighbourhoods is the case of Huaycán. Located in the Carretera Central region, Huaycán was set up in 1984 as a model urban settlement under the sponsorship of Lima's IU municipal government. From an initial population of 20,000 in 1986, Huaycán had become home to more than 70,000 people by 1990. By the end of IU mayor Alfonso Barrantes' term in 1987, substantial progress had been made in housing, road construction and water and electrical services in the older core area of Huaycán. Under the new APRA municipal government which took over in 1987 not only did all such work come to an abrupt halt, but the influx of new migrants from the emergency zones put an increasing strain on Huaycán's already overburdened public services and transport system. While the elected community authorities petitioned in vain for municipal support, the burdens of life in Huaycán began to fuel conflict between older members of the community and newcomers who settled on the fringes of Huaycán, far from bus routes and services. Sendero's activities in Huaycán played off these and other tensions within the community.

Huaycán offers Sendero several strategic advantages. Lying in the centre of the Carretera Central corridor with its factories and unions, Huaycán is also situated at the juncture of two ravines which provide easy 'backdoor' access to downtown Lima and the southern cone. By late 1985, Sendero had entered the marginal areas of Huaycán, bringing members and student recruits from other areas of Lima for drill training, indoctrination and agitprop activities. *Senderistas* also mounted armed patrols in the community with the double intention of deterring thieves, drug users and other criminals, and making public the party's presence. Around the same time, the MRTA also appeared in the community, like Sendero using Huaycán as a base from which to launch attacks along the Carretera Central. Within the community, the two armed groups engaged in heated competition, reflected in the profusion of MRTA and Sendero graffiti which covered all of Huaycán. By early 1986, the police and security forces had declared Huaycán a 'red zone', subject to continuous surveillance, searches, and round-ups of residents and community leaders.

Forced to compete with older, more established neighbourhoods for scarce communal resources, some residents in Huaycán's marginal areas found an answer to their grievances in Sendero's fiery denunciations of the corruption and 'revisionism' of community authorities. Sendero's advances in Huaycán were also due to the pluralist political traditions guiding the grassroots organisations and community assembly, where pro-Sendero delegates participated along with other delegates from a wide spectrum of political tendencies. Many Huaycán citizens tolerated Sendero's activities as long they did not interfere with the assembly's democratic procedures. Even those opposed to Sendero's presence often kept quiet out of well-grounded fears of both increased police repression and Sendero's notorious treatment of 'stoolpigeons'.

Sendero's main goals in Huaycán, however, remained military. In the absence of state authorities and police posts in the settlement, Sendero continued to use Huaycán as a base for attacks along the Carretera Central. It also used intimidation to persuade assembly delegates and committee leaders to give it support. Finally, Sendero tried to intervene in community marches and demonstrations to provoke confrontations with the police. Forced to suffer the consequences of the ensuing military raids, the residents of Huaycán had finally had enough. In 1989 they created their own *rondas* to deter both Sendero and criminals in the community. A final blow to Sendero came in an assembly held in May 1991 to decide whether the community was to adopt the legal status of a 'self-management community' along the lines of CUAVES. Sendero opposed the move on the grounds that self-management (and the financial assistance it brings from international development agencies and NGOs) is a diversionary 'imperialist' tactic to reinforce 'bureaucratic capitalism'. The assembly rejected Sendero's argument by a big majority and voted against its delegate slate for the community board. Six months later,

Sendero retaliated with the murder of Víctor Aguero, a leader of the self-defence committee which organises Huaycán's *rondas*.

For Sendero, communal work parties, food assistance programmes, cooperative workshops and self-management enterprises are all part of the 'revisionist' strategy of community leaders who, it claims, benefit through either electoral politics or illicit profiteering. Elected left-wing municipal governments such as those in El Agustino and Villa María del Triunfo are condemned in the pages of *El Diario* as 'demagogues' who corrupt neighbourhood organisations through their proposals for increased popular participation in municipal government. Such proposals, argues the newspaper, serve 'yankee imperialism's plans to fight the people's war through military aid and social development'.

In recent years, Sendero has directed its fire against leaders of the organisations it accuses of *asistencialismo*. The worst hit has been the Metropolitan Organisation of 'Glass of Milk' Committees and Soup Kitchens (*Vaso de Leche*), Lima's largest grassroots organisation, created in the 1980s by a broad-based women's movement in poor neighbourhoods. In 1991 alone, Sendero murdered five organisers from the *Vaso de Leche* Committees and other similar neighbourhood programmes. Other leaders, such as Michel Azcueta, the former mayor of Villa El Salvador, Pedro Zazzali, mayor of San Juan de Lurigancho, Esther Moreno, former mayor of Independencia, Humberto Paredes, the mayor of Comas, and Teresa Aparcana, leader of the Metropolitan *Vaso de Leche* Committee, have been constantly threatened in the pages of *El Diario*.

Among those whom the newspaper threatened was Maria Elena Moyano, a well-known feminist organiser, left-wing activist and Sendero opponent, who was also the Deputy Mayor of Villa El Salvador and a founder of the *Vaso de Leche* Committee. On 15 February 1992 Moyano was killed by a Sendero commando during a fundraising event for the Vaso de Leche Committee in Villa El Salvador. After firing two shots at close range into her head and chest in front of the many women at the meeting, the *Senderistas* dragged Moyano's body outside and blew it up with dynamite. The day before her killing, Moyano had led a peace march in Villa El Salvador against the armed strike which the PCP-SL had called for that day. 'We do not support those who assassinate popular leaders and massacre leaders of the soup kitchens and *Vaso de Leche*', she said in her speech that day. 'We do not support those who undermine the people's organisations and who wish to impose themselves by force and brutality.'

Sendero has also worked to set up party-generated organisms in specific parts of the labour movement. In its early years, the PCP-SL made limited advances in certain sectors of organised labour in the central highland mines and in the industries along the Carretera

La balearán, la dinamitarán...
¡Y NO PODRAN MATARLA!
Maria Elena M...
luchando...

Women from Villa El Salvador demonstrate against Sendero at the funeral of Maria Elena Moyano, 1992. (Alejandro Balaguer)

Central and Avenida Argentina. It also retained influence over some branches of the powerful teachers' union, SUTEP. By the late 1970s, however, Sendero had already begun to lose ground to the emerging coalition of left-wing parties that later became the IU. By May 1980, when Sendero launched the armed struggle, the party's union work had effectively reached rock bottom. Only in the late 1980s did Sendero manage to gain an entry into the unions of Lima's industrial corridor.

The renewed emphasis on union work coincided generally with the PCP-SL's military offensive in the cities and specifically with the goal of creating 'centres of resistance' in preparation for urban insurrection. This means that workers' specific economic demands must be subordinated to the aim of mounting an insurrection. With the slogan 'Combat and Resist', Sendero sees strikes, marches and demonstrations as 'glorious combat trenches' in which striking workers can be trained militarily to fight the 'henchmen of the reaction'. 'The struggle for wages, working conditions and other rights', states Guzmán:

is a guerrilla war in which [the proletariat] not only fights for a concrete economic or political demand. Rather, they are preparing themselves for the great moments to come. Our problem is to bring together the struggle for demands with the conquest of Power. This is what we call developing mass work in and for the people's war.

Since Sendero believes that demonstrations and strikes must be confrontational to be effective, *El Diario* presents sensationalist descriptions of even the most peaceful labour conflicts as violent conflicts. In accompanying photographs, workers are shown in violent street fighting, giving the impression that all strikes in Lima are controlled by the PCP-SL and close to full-blown insurrection. Following one such story in 1990, *El Diario* concluded: 'Today as never before demonstrations proliferate with such violent actions as barricades of burning tyres, lightning mobilisations with agitation and leafleting, even sabotage.' Such stories are presented as evidence that 'the masses are advancing using the people's war as a means of struggle.' What the newspaper does not report is that many of these strikes are led by organisations in which the PCP-SL has little or no influence.

In unions in which Sendero does have a presence, its militants encourage confrontations between rank-and-file workers, management and established union leaders by advocating impossible demands such as weekly, or even daily, renewable work contracts. They use every opportunity to urge wildcat and indefinite strikes, and reject less confrontational forms of negotiation or pressure. They accuse union leaders of selling out to management, and volunteer for strike committees on which other workers may be afraid to serve for fear of being fired. In the few unions in which Sendero has won control, it has fired legal counsellors and refused to negotiate at crucial moments in the strikes. They also promote confrontation through party-generated workers' organisations. In January 1989, Sendero-controlled organisations in the Carretera Central and Avenida Argentina called an armed strike in these two strategic industrial areas. Despite intimidation of factory and transport workers, the strikes were overwhelmingly rejected. Such activities are normally complemented by intimidatory bombings, killings of owners and management and destruction of factories. In the textile sector alone, Sendero has killed 21 plant managers.

Sendero also kills union leaders whom it accuses of revisionism. Between January and May 1989, Sendero murdered more than fifty union leaders nationwide. Union 'revisionism', stated *El Diario* in May 1989, 'tries to keep the Peruvian proletariat away from the people's war.' In order to combat this tendency the paper concludes, it is necessary to 'eliminate the revisionist, sell-out leadership.' By November of that same year, Sendero followed words with action by killing Enrique Castilla, general secretary of the labour federation representing the 4,000 workers of the La Unión textile factories. A veteran union and left-wing activist, Castilla was a key figure mediating between the competing political factions in the popular movements along the Carretera Central.

Strategic Equilibrium

Sendero's urban strategy entered a new phase of 'strategic equilibrium', according to an announcement in *El Diario* in May 1991, the llth anniversary of the armed struggle. Three months earlier, the central committee had met to evaluate the party's armed struggle and specifically the results of its campaign to consolidate its bases and strengthen the EGP. It decided that the successful creation of Open Popular Committees and the consolidation of the 'power of New Democracy' in certain parts of the countryside had laid the groundwork for the People's Republic of Peru. It also concluded that, in ten years of armed struggle, Sendero had maintained the military and political initiative and had begun to put the enemy on the defensive. Because the EGP had also gained in experience, discipline and firepower, it resolved that the party was ready to advance to the second phase in Guzmán's scheme of prolonged people's war. In this new phase, a 'war of movements', characterised by the deployment of larger military units in frontal engagements with the enemy, would establish a 'strategic equilibrium' between Sendero and the armed forces. The initiation of the 'strategic counter-offensive' — the third and final phase of the war — would, in turn, be followed by general urban insurrection, the retreat of the enemy and final victory.

The new offensive took dramatic form in the 'red month' of May to June 1991. During a period meant to celebrate the anniversaries of the initiation of the armed struggle (17 May) and the 1986 prison massacres (18 June), Sendero carried out its most intense wave of attacks to date. It called armed strikes in different cities and sabotaged electricity pylons, causing blackouts in Lima and other coastal cities. In a period of three days in late April, *Senderistas* launched a rocket at the presidential palace during a cabinet meeting, orchestrated simultaneous bombings of fifty banks in different parts of the city, set bombs off outside the right-wing think-tank, the Institute of Liberty and Democracy (ILD), and burnt a university preparatory academy belonging to Fujimori's Economy Minister. On the eve of 'Heroes' Day' (the anniversary of the prison massacre), bonfires were lit on hillsides behind Lima, and another blackout affected the city for several hours. *El Diario* headlined what it claimed as 1,600 successful military actions in May and June as 'The Growing Offensive in the War of Movements'.

Since 1987, the 'red month' has been an important date in Sendero's calendar. Through spectacular actions concentrated in a short period of time, Sendero skilfully reinforces its self-image as an invincible war machine in order both to heighten the climate of terror and to encourage increased militarisation. 1991's 'red month', however, was to be followed by a series of devastating blows which placed the concept of 'strategic equilibrium' and Sendero's claims to invincibility in some doubt.

During the preceding year, Sendero had already suffered a number of setbacks. The arrests in 1990 of several important cadres — including part of the *Socorro Popular's* Lima leadership — were the most significant blows to Sendero's security since the capture in 1988 of Osmán Morote, Guzmán's alleged right-hand man. There had also been fierce and potentially divisive debates within party ranks regarding Guzmán's emphasis on urban actions and the brutality of the offensive against popular leaders and grassroots organisations. Although the precise nature and extent of the internal dissent is unclear, rumours regarding the debate escalated in the Peruvian press to include accounts of an imminent split within Sendero.

1990 had also brought with it Fujimori's devastating economic packages and the new forms of grassroots organisation through which Peruvians were responding to the reforms. The unprecedented number of strikes, marches and demonstrations, together with the mounting momentum of the new regional governments and the MRTA's military and political advances, belied Sendero's claims to represent the popular classes. The widespread opposition to Sendero's authoritarianism and violence was also a challenge to Guzmán's proposition that once 'revisionist' leaders had been eliminated, the PCP-SL could then appropriate the energies of this popular 'insurrection' for its own ends.

Shortly after the announcement of 'strategic equilibrium', anti-terrorist police raided Guzmán's headquarters in a wealthy Lima neighbourhood, capturing a number of important party documents, including videotapes of 'inner circle' gatherings. These serious setbacks to the PCP-SL's security and party organisation were aggravated by exaggerated press accounts of the raid's significance and by ensuing arrests. Media and government assessments of the captured documents' importance were ridiculed in the pages of *El Diario*. Following the party's recent problems, the *Senderista* newspaper's scornful dismissal of the raid rang somewhat hollow:

> The extent to which the reaction lacks perspective in their fight against the People's War is revealed every time the strategists and ringleaders of the counter-revolution launch their repeated,

expensive and insipid campaigns of psychological warfare. In May 1990, they raised their humbug of 'division' within the PCP-SL and the 'surrender of the EGP', a sequel to the earlier fiasco of their psychological war alleging the 'strategic failure of Sendero'. Regarding the 'video of Chairman Gonzalo', the counter-revolutionary General Command pawned their souls to the devil in order to proclaim false triumphs and the 'imminent defeat of subversion', to the point of rejoicing that Chairman Gonzalo was alive and [that] they had captured him on a video. When the revolution begins to unfold in the STRATEGIC EQUILIBRIUM, Fujimori and his deputies in the Armed Forces, the pack of 'senderologists' and other yes-men will find that they have practically exhausted their catechism of lies.

Fujimori's April 1992 *autogolpe* was followed by another series of blows to Sendero. That month, police arrested several members of the Association of Democratic Lawyers, a group which provides legal help for *Senderistas*. Next, security forces rounded up 26 people working at the pro-Sendero *El Diario*, including important party members, and confiscated computers and printing equipment.

A further, and bloody, setback came in the four-day battle in May between *Senderista* prisoners and police commandos at Lima's maximum-security Castro Castro prison in the Canto Grande district. The prison housed 450 men and 180 women in two special cell blocks reserved for Sendero prisoners. Since their transfer there after the 1986 prison massacres, the *Senderistas* had been allowed virtual control of their cell blocks. Refusing prison food, they had daily visits from relatives and supporters who brought in supplies, including weapons. The prison came to function not only as a centre for political education and military training, but also as an unofficial base of communication with the press and other media. The intention of the police operation was therefore to remove the female prisoners to solitary confinement in a high-security jail in the southern city of Ica and to impose stricter control over the male prisoners.

It took 650 police four days to gain control of the prison. The *Senderistas* had built a network of tunnels and passageways between all levels of their cellblocks and defended themselves with home-made bombs, acid, crossbows and some firearms. The police, armed with tear gas, machine guns and explosives, finally blasted a large hole in the prison wall to gain entry. Fifty prisoners died in the fighting — or were killed afterwards — including leaders such as Janet Talavera (former assistant director of *El Diario*), Elvia Nila Zanabria (personal assistant to Guzmán), Yovanka Pardavé and Tito Valle Travesaño (founder members of the Association of Democratic Lawyers) and Hugo Deodato Juárez Cruzat (a possible successor to Guzmán).

The Canto Grande operation was a double-edged success. While costly to Sendero in terms of deaths, it also handed over more martyrs to an organisation which teaches its members that 'the road to revolution is paved with blood'. In each such battle, Sendero's well-organised support groups reap a harvest of new recruits drawn from relatives and friends of dead *Senderistas*. Even as the police stormed the Castro Castro prison, relatives and supporters gathered outside to sing party songs and chant slogans.

In response, Sendero organised its own show of force. In the first seven weeks after the coup, it was responsible for eleven car bombs and forty killings in Lima alone. One car bomb levelled the police station in the *pueblo joven* of Villa El Salvador; another destroyed the police station and church in Carmen de la Legua, near Callao. The biggest military successes were the car bombing of a police headquarters close to the presidential palace and explosions in the wealthy shopping district of San Isidro. The new wave of car bombs has involved large trucks, buses or vans carrying oil drums packed with dynamite and *anfo*, a powerful home-made explosive made from a readily available commercial nitrogen fertiliser.

In July 1992, Sendero carried out an even more destructive series of bombings leading up to an 'armed strike' called to coincide with Peru's national independence day celebrated in late July. The week-long wave of bombings, assassinations and random killings attacked civilians and private property in nearly all of Lima's neighbourhoods. In one of the most bloody incidents, Sendero set off a powerful car bomb in the early evening in a residential street in the upper middle-class neighbourhood of Miraflores, completely destroying several apartment buildings and killing over twenty people. Breaking with the previous pattern of late night and early morning bombings, it also bombed a high-rise gas company building at a busy Lima intersection during the early morning rush hour, and a primary school for army children during school hours. Other important targets included the Bolivian Embassy, the recently rebuilt police station in Villa El Salvador, a railway bridge on the line connecting Lima to the central highland mining centres, and numerous bank offices in different parts of the city. In an effort to enforce compliance with the armed strike, *Senderistas* killed several taxi and handcart drivers who had gone to work in defiance of Sendero's orders and tossed dynamite among shoppers and workers at Lima's largest wholesale food market.

Just as Sendero seemed to be regaining the initiative, it suffered its most unexpected and dramatic blow yet. Late on 12 September, DIRCOTE, the special anti-terrorist police unit, raided a house in the

Police display weapons captured from *Senderistas* during fighting at Castro Castro prison, 1992.

(Alejandro Balaguer)

middle-class Lima suburb of Surco and captured Abimael Guzmán. Along with Guzmán and in other simultaneous raids elsewhere in Lima, police also captured Laura Zambrano, head of Lima's Metropolitan Committee, Martha Huatay, a lawyer and European fundraiser for Sendero, Yanila Iparraguirre, reputedly second in command to Guzmán, and other central committee members. Guzmán surrendered without a struggle and was taken to DIRCOTE's headquarters, where hundreds of heavily armed police and soldiers guarded the building. The following day, President Fujimori made a special television broadcast, describing Guzmán as a 'monster who ordered the deaths of thousands of innocent people'. Referring to him as the 'chief hitman of drug traffickers in Peru', Fujimori likened Sendero to 'the fascist criminals of the Second World War'. While television news showed Guzmán shirtless, with a criminal identification number hung around his neck, Fujimori promised that Sendero's leader would receive 'the maximum punishment possible'.

Within hours Sendero retaliated with the shooting of a policeman and two car bombs, despite a massive security operation in Lima. The response suggested that while Guzmán's arrest was undoubtedly a huge political blow, it did not immediately affect Sendero's military capability. Analysts in Lima and elsewhere were also quick to point out that the arrest did not spell the end of Sendero's offensive and that, instead, it might lead directly to intensified violence from Guzmán's followers. As with the Canto Grande prison incident and other previous defeats, it is highly probable that Sendero will try to turn events to its advantage by stressing Guzmán's 'martyrdom' and the permanence of 'Gonzalo thought'. The tight and secretive nature of Sendero's organisational structure also means that the small cells in which militants operate need not be affected by Guzmán's removal. The regional committees which coordinate these cells are capable of functioning with a certain amount of autonomy.

It remains to be seen whether any individual can successfully replace Guzmán's pervasive personality cult with a new aura of leadership. Several high-ranking *Senderistas*, such as Osmán Morote and Hugo Deodato Juárez Cruzat who might have succeeded Guzmán are either already in prison or were killed in the Canto Grande violence. While the theoretical canon of 'Gonzalo thought' will continue to dominate Sendero's ideology, a new leader will have to win the respect of Sendero's cadres and sympathisers through successful military action. This will ultimately determine the direction, political and tactical, which Sendero takes over the coming years. In the meantime, it is reasonable to assume that the party will continue to wage its 'people's war' against the Peruvian state and its political rivals.

4

A Nation for the Few

To convey the depth and severity of the problems facing their country in the 1990s, many Peruvians compare their current situation to the aftermath of the 1879-1883 War of the Pacific. Following Peru's defeat by Chilean troops, the country was left in a shambles. It had lost territory and important economic resources to its neighbour to the south; its meagre state apparatus was demolished and its political elites in disarray. With no clear blueprint for the reconstruction of a nation state, different factions of the elites fought for the 'Throne of Pizarro' in Lima's presidential palace. Meanwhile, the Indian militias that had fought in the war with Chile turned their guns on the landlords. Land takeovers ensued in the central and southern highlands, as Indians sought revenge for the landlords' abuses and for the elite's betrayal of the nation in surrendering to Chile. Chinese labourers and black Peruvian sharecroppers seized the moment to challenge, and in some cases to overturn, the exploitative working conditions of the coastal plantations. More than any other time in Peru's short republican history, it became evident that the poor were unwilling to accept the elite's rule.

The analogies with today's situation are striking. The general crisis brought on by a failing economy and the political violence of the 1980s has highlighted the limitations of the political traditions and projects prevailing in Peru for most of the 20th century. During the last fifty years, Peruvians have lived through an impressive array of such projects, each promising a solution to Peru's problems. None of these diverse governments, whether democratic, authoritarian, civilian, military, populist or dictatorial, has been capable of bridging the widening gap between state and society. With the increasing class, ethnic and racial polarisation brought on by recent economic policies and counter-insurgency campaigns, this gap has reached critical proportions.

Oligarchy and Imperialism

Peru's recovery from the war with Chile coincided with turn-of-the-century global capitalist expansion. Because capitalist development in Peru was nurtured by pre-existing colonial forms of labour exploitation, it exacerbated the cultural, racial and geographic divides that were the legacy of colonialism.

The elites and the majority were separated by skin colour, class and culture. Coastal elites clung to European culture as a means to reaffirm what they perceived as their superior 'white' racial origins. Peru's majority identified with indigenous Andean and Amazonian cultures, as well as with the African and Chinese influences brought in by colonial slaves and indentured Chinese workers. The striking geographic and ecological differences between Peru's mountainous highlands and its desert coast strengthened the perception that the Quechua and Aymara-speaking Indians of the Andean highlands lived in a nation separate from that of the Spanish-speaking creole population in Peru's coastal cities. On the coast, large sugar and cotton plantations employed thousands of workers. A microcosm of Peru's different cultural groups and labour systems, these workers included sharecroppers of African descent, indentured Chinese labourers, and temporary indigenous workers from the Andean highlands.

In the highlands, agricultural and livestock estates or haciendas produced a variety of crops for local consumption and coastal markets, as well as alpaca and sheep wool for the booming export market. Production on these haciendas depended on a variety of coerced, servile and unsalaried labour arrangements. The workers were Quechua- and Aymara-speaking Indians who either lived on the haciendas or in neighbouring independent indigenous communities. In their communities, the Indians also produced crops and wool for the local and international markets.

On the eastern slopes of the Andes and in the Amazon rainforest, natives from the Ashaninka, Aguaruna, Shipibo, and other language groups, hunted, fished and practised subsistence agriculture. Along the river banks, newly-arrived *mestizo* colonists farmed, panned for gold, and tapped rubber.

By the early 1900s, foreign capital, particularly US and British, had begun to invest in Peruvian highland mining and wool, as well as in the coastal oil fields and sugar and cotton industries. Although these enclave enterprises increased demand for wage labour, they also relied on coerced and unsalaried labour, including payment in kind and debt peonage. In the early 20th century, US, European and Peruvian capital was drawn to Peru's Amazon region by the international

Officials from government agency for Indian affairs, Cusco, c.1920.

demand for rubber. The extreme forms of coerced labour and enslavement of Amazonian Indians generated by the 'rubber boom' brought with them a wave of violence against the indigenous lowland populations.

The elites who benefited from this expansion formed an oligarchy made up of coastal planters and financiers, highland *hacendados* and merchants, and foreign investors. With vested interests in keeping the *mestizo* and Indian majorities on the margins of political life, the oligarchy ran political debate and elections through small parties that one Peruvian historian has described as resembling 'gentlemen's clubs' more than modern political parties. Closely bound by family links and business interests, the oligarchy understood politics as the domain of an enlightened few. For the remainder of the 20th century, Peruvian politics unfolded as a struggle between those who sought to defend the traditional exclusionary politics of the oligarchic elite and those who challenged them from below.

Many of the political organisations through which the oligarchy's hold on power were challenged emerged during the 1919-1930 'Patria Nueva' ('New Nation') government of President Augusto B. Leguía. Selected in the 1919 elections as the oligarchy's inside candidate, Leguía undertook to modernise Peru's slumbering state and economy. During his eleven years in office, Leguía oversaw the expansion of state control over different areas of Peruvian society by creating departments of statistics, agriculture, mines and Indian Affairs. The expanding bureaucracy spawned a middle class of functionaries and professionals whose livelihood depended on the state. By incorporating these middle sectors into the state administration, Leguía's *'Patria Nueva'* eroded the oligarchic elite's monopoly on public affairs, while leaving their economic power intact.

Leguía's expanded state apparatus primarily served the interests of US capital. Since the turn of the century, US investment had been growing steadily. Companies such as Standard Oil, W.R. Grace and National City Bank added Peru to their roster of foreign interests. Other companies, such as the Cerro de Pasco Mining Corporation and the Northern Peru Mining and Smelting Company were created to take advantage of the Peruvian state's courtship of foreign capital. At the time of Leguía's rise to power in 1919, foreign capital controlled 77 per cent of the Peruvian textile industry, 81 per cent of sugar production and over 90 per cent of mining. US companies also controlled banking, insurance, oil, urban development, road construction and transport. 'During my administration', Leguía proudly proclaimed, 'foreign capital will be given facilities and opportunities for the development of Peruvian resources which have never heretofore been accorded and which may never be accorded again.'

The organisations which were the forerunners of today's political opposition parties and labour and peasant organisations also had their roots in the *'Patria Nueva'*. Unions and labour federations grew in strength to defend the interests of the expanding working-class population. The first workers' organisations had been created at the turn of the century. By the time Leguía took office, these organisations, which had been heavily influenced by anarcho-syndicalism, had strongholds among Lima's textile workers, bakers, and artisans. Between 1913 and 1918, they led the struggle for an eight-hour work day and headed Peru's first general strike.

During Leguía's government, rural farmworkers' and peasant politics also matured rapidly. The large foreign-owned mining centres in Peru's central highlands, which expanded under Leguía, attracted large numbers of peasants in search of wage labour. New working-class populations also spread into the northern oil fields, the coastal sugar and cotton plantations, and the factories of Lima. In the first decade of the century, indigenous peasants in the Puno provinces of Azángaro and Huancané rebelled against the illegal expansion of haciendas into community lands. In other parts of the southern highlands, Indian communities fought against abusive merchants,

Reception for President Leguía, Central Highlands, c.1925.

unfavourable wool prices, and the encroachment of haciendas. Indian workers on haciendas also demanded an end to personal services and unsalaried work in the haciendas' feudal labour relations. In the central highlands, peasant struggled with haciendas in legal disputes over property boundaries. In the north, peasants fought against bandits and abusive landlords. In July 1920, 400 delegates from across the country met in Peru's first congress of indigenous and peasant communities. Regional and local federations such as the General Federation of Yanaconas (sharecroppers) and Rural Workers, active in the central coastal cotton plantations, were the forerunners of the national CCP, formed in 1947 and today the most important peasant organisation in Peru.

Intellectuals influenced by the international socialist movement, the 1910 Mexican Revolution and the Latin American student movement joined the workers in expressing opposition to Leguía. Of particular importance were the critical writings and political organising of José Carlos Mariátegui and Víctor Raúl Haya de la Torre. The work of these two young intellectuals had an enduring influence on the ideological formation of the opposition movements which eventually undermined Peru's oligarchic state. Haya's and Mariátegui's ideas and organisations gave added strength to the workers' movement in its confrontation with the international economic crisis of 1929. APRA founded by Haya de la Torre in 1924 became the largest and most enduring political party in Peru. Mariátegui's writings and his shortlived Socialist Party (which became the PCP after his death in 1930) laid the groundwork for Peru's 20th-century socialist and popular movement.

Mariátegui and Haya de la Torre

Born in the provincial city of Moquegua, José Carlos Mariátegui was a self-educated journalist who laid the foundations of Peruvian socialism. Upon his return to Peru from Europe, where he had spent four years studying with socialist intellectuals in France and Italy, Mariátegui began working with other Peruvian intellectuals to educate the working class. He also founded *Labor*, a working-class and union newspaper which played an important role in promoting the creation of the CTGP in 1930. Although the CGTP managed to survive only a short time it was later resurrected in the 1960s as a rallying point for Peru's dynamic workers' movement.

Together with other intellectuals, workers and peasant organisers, Mariátegui created the Socialist Party of Peru in October 1928. Although the Socialist Party was affiliated to the Moscow-centred Third International, Mariátegui's ideas regarding the unique nature of Peruvian capitalism and the role of indigenous communities and traditional Andean culture in the construction of Peruvian socialism led to bitter debates with the Comintern, where universal formulas of capitalist development and working-class politics prevailed.

Mariátegui's most important legacy to Peruvian left-wing politics was his interest in expanding working-class concerns to include both intellectuals and the Andean peasantry. With this goal, Mariátegui founded *Amauta*, a literary and critical journal which carried articles analysing Peruvian society and history, as well as fiction, poetry and criticism. In addition to providing a forum for discussion of the latest European philosophy, art and political theory, *Amauta* was also one of the first publications to focus on the problems of Peru's Indian majority. In a collection of essays from *Amauta*, published in 1928 as the *Seven Essays on Peruvian Reality*, Mariátegui emphasised the political importance of the Andean Indian community, or *ayllu*, for any future socialist project for Peru. His interpretation of the communal character of indigenous Andean society, together with this critique of Peru's highly centralised political and economic structures, provided two of the central issues for the Peruvian New Left in the 1960s and 1970s.

Víctor Raúl Haya de la Torre represented another side of Peruvian intellectual life. Born to a middle-class family in the northern coastal city of Trujillo, Haya attended private schools and studied at the University of San Marcos in Lima. In 1924, while in exile in Mexico City, Haya founded APRA. The blueprint for his new party was laid out in Haya's most influential work, *Anti-Imperialism and APRA*, where he argued that capitalist economic development and nation building in Latin America would only be possible through the creation of an 'anti-imperialist state' based on corporatist principles. Through these 'functional democracies' Haya proposed to create the impossible: a pan-Latin American 'Indo-America' based on state capitalism, yet free of imperialist domination. Built around the corporatist principles developed in *Anti-Imperialism*, the APRA became Peru's strongest party and, for years, the most serious threat to the oligarchy's waning hold on power.

Since its foundation in 1924, APRA has played an important role in Peruvian politics. It is today the largest and best-organised political organisation in Peru. It is impossible to understand the enduring influence and importance of APRA without also understanding the unique nature of its organisation.

APRA's powerful *esprit de corps* has been remarkably resistant to its leaders' dramatic ideological shifts. More than any other political party, APRA was able to use its authoritarian and paternalistic structure to infuse its members with a powerful mystique of sacrifice. Within the party, Haya de la Torre, who was addressed as the 'Maximal Chief' or 'Great Teacher', exercised total authority. *Apristas* believed themselves to be creating a 'civil army' composed of new and more moral Peruvians. Through their discipline they hoped to end the 'decrepit institutions, hatreds and low passions' which they believed had made Peru a decadent nation. In his book *Fire in the Andes*, the US journalist Carleton Beals described *Apristas* as 'imbued with an almost mystical fervor; they are the material from which martyrs are made. Haya', continues Beals, 'is almost like a God for them. The APRA *locales* are completely covered with portraits of Haya in Mussolini-like poses. Their discipline is almost puritan.'

By the mid 1950s APRA had become more than just a political party. Particularly in the northern departments surrounding Haya's native city of Trujillo, APRA grew in strength by astutely blending politics with social and family life. With its newly acquired legality, APRA opened *casas del pueblo* (community centres) in every working-class neighbourhood. Students were offered remedial courses, youth camps and a wide variety of recreational activities. Good grades and participation in the party's youth organisations were rewarded in an annual ceremony in which Haya himself met the children and students.

¡SOLO EL APRISM
SALVARA AL PERU

VOTE POR
HAYA DE LA TORRE

'Only *Aprismo* will save Peru!' Election poster for Víctor Raúl Haya de la Torre.

Neighbourhood party activities, news and political gossip were channelled through *Aprista* barbers. Cheap food was available in APRA's 'peoples' cafeterias'. Free medical and legal services were offered through party professionals. Gracing the walls of every barber, restaurant, school and office was the paternal image of the party's spiritual leader, Haya de la Torre, flanked by the party flag.

Populism and APRA

Disturbed by rising working-class and peasant activism and by the new nationalist and anti-oligarchic parties, a coalition of military officers and regional politicians led by Luís M. Sánchez Cerro unseated Leguía in August 1930. Lèguía left behind him a new, more powerful state apparatus and a changed political landscape, in which the initiative had shifted from the oligarchic 'gentlemen's clubs' to the working classes and their organisations.

From his first day in office, it was clear that Sánchez Cerro's presidency was based on populism — the response of civilian and military leaders anxious to appease the poor, yet reluctant to initiate any real structural change. The enormous spontaneous public reception for the Arequipa-born president's triumphant arrival in Lima was unprecedented in the history of Peruvian politics. Hailed as Peru's 'Second Liberator', Sánchez Cerro was driven through the capital's streets carrying a bouquet of flowers given to him by a poor market vendor, and resting his other hand on his revolver. A worker interviewed decades later by historian Steve Stein, described his emotional conversion to *Sánchezcerrismo*: 'I immediately became a *Sánchezcerrista*. Everybody was a *Sánchezcerrista*. Blacks, whites, *cholos*. The people cried, they applauded, they embraced him. I have never seen anything like it. He was a hero, and we did not even know him.'

In his short first term in office, Sánchez Cerro defined a populist style which became a recurrent theme in 20th-century Peru. He appeased the oligarchy through favourable taxes, subsidies and credit guarantees, and placated the peasantry by declaring an end to Leguía's hated forced labour conscription for road building. He legalised civil marriage and divorce, personally distributed free food, and prohibited evictions. His political party, the Revolutionary Union, organised clubs in working-class Lima neighbourhoods. As would also be true of the 'populisms' that followed Sánchez Cerro, these theatrical gestures were double-edged. As he once wrote to a fellow officer long before his rise to power, 'when you see me lashing the indolent and lazy rabble with a piece of bread in one hand and a whip in the other, say that it is Sánchez Cerro who is trying to put the masses on the right track.'

The true master of populism, however, was Haya de la Torre. During the 1930s, he built APRA as a strong mass party capable of weathering his own dramatic ideological shifts. More than just a political party, APRA was a way of life which called for uncritical devotion to Haya de la Torre and commitment to the party's slogan 'Only APRA Will Save Peru'. Its membership was basically urban, with a particular strength in the northern coastal cities and plantations. APRA also became skilled in organising public protests against increasing unemployment and the rising cost of living.

One of the most important events in APRA's early history was the 1932 Trujillo insurrection. In response to Sánchez Cerro's moves to imprison and deport *Aprista* leaders, sectors of the party began to advocate armed insurrection. Acting independently from the national party leadership, APRA leaders in Trujillo, together with militants on the nearby sugar-cane plantations and others in the city, took up arms in July 1932. Their insurrection, however, failed to spread to other regions and was crushed by the armed forces. Hundreds of *Apristas* were executed, and many military personnel died in the confrontations. These deaths gave birth to a bitter enmity between APRA and the armed forces whose aftershocks affected Peruvian politics for many decades. Within APRA itself, the 'massacre of Trujillo' sustained an ideology of sacrifice and martyrdom binding *Apristas* together through the ups and downs of Peruvian political life.

Dictators and Elections

The twenty-year period following the Trujillo insurrection began and ended with harsh military dictatorship installed with the oligarchy's support. Yet despite its best efforts, the oligarchy's hold on power was severely challenged by both APRA and the popular movement.

Following Sánchez Cerro's assassination by an *Aprista* militant, the oligarchy moved in 1933 to put an end to the unruly popular movement by calling in General Oscar Benavides, a self-confessed admirer of Franco and Mussolini. Through a combination of corporatist and fascist measures similar to those in force in Europe, Benavides kept the popular movement at bay for the six years of his government.

Benavides' repressive measures could not protect the oligarchy from its own internal differences, and during his regime, it divided into two political blocs. One was made up of a residual oligarchic elite of exporters and landowners; the other brought together industrialists with the middle class and professionals. Under the leadership of the banker and entrepreneur Manuel Prado, this bloc sought to promote capitalism through industrial development, modernised farming, and some selected concessions to the working class. Both APRA and the PCP supported Prado's modernising programme in the 1939 presidential elections, from which Prado emerged the winner.

During the democratic opening provided by Prado's administration, APRA and the PCP adjusted their political strategies to accommodate their new alliance. Haya de la Torre left behind his militant anti-imperialism in favour of a new doctrine of 'democratic inter-americanism without empire'. Declaring Roosevelt's 'Good Neighbour' policy a positive development in relations between Latin America and the US, Haya supported Prado's close relationship with the US and the Allied war effort. Declaring Prado's administration a government of the 'national bourgeoisie', the pro-Soviet PCP also adopted a more conciliatory stance by calling an end to strikes which might jeopardise production in support of the Allied war effort. Prado's government, in return, eased repression against leaders of the still illegal APRA and PCP. Taking advantage of the more relaxed atmosphere, APRA and PCP union leaders formed the Labour Confederation of Peru (CTP) in 1944. The CTP filled the void left by the demise of the CGTP in 1930 and eventually fell under APRA's control, rapidly becoming the most important labour organisation in Peru.

Despite their conciliatory positions, both APRA and the PCP were banned from running candidates in the 1945 elections in which José Luís Bustamante was elected president. Backed by a broad-based and mixed political alliance including APRA and the PCP, Bustamante ran on a reformist platform which proposed income redistribution, respect for democratic rights, decentralisation, and industrial development.

Despite its wide appeal, Bustamante's government failed to achieve political and social stability. The rising cost of living (which grew by an average of 30 per cent a year between 1945 and 1949) led to urgent demands for wage increases. This in turn exacerbated conflicts between the APRA and PCP party leaders, who supported Bustamante, and their followers in the unions and popular organisations. In 1946, dissident *Apristas* and Communists joined forces with students to form the Trotskyist-influenced Revolutionary Workers' Party (POR), which rapidly gained momentum within the disgruntled union rank and file and eventually broke the PCP's monopoly over the Peruvian Left. In late 1947, POR activists together with APRA rank-and-file textile workers led a wildcat strike in Lima which attracted the support of other unions. In spite of the opposition of both PCP and APRA leaders, a majority of Lima's industrial unions called a general strike that was later called off by the CTP's leadership.

Popular anger was also directed against the right-wing parties, which for some time had been boycotting the opening of Congress. While the APRA leadership vacillated, the party's rank and file was pressing for a more effective response, and in October 1948 an *Aprista* 'revolutionary command' mounted a popular insurrection, supported by sailors from the navy base in Lima's port of Callao. Meanwhile, behind the back of the insurgents, Haya conspired with military officers to launch a coup. Haya's attitude, seen by the insurgents as a betrayal, further widened the rift between APRA's leadership and the party's radical sectors.

Faced with the possibility of further insurrections and political instability, the elites again turned to the generals. With a *bolsa* (purse) of money collected from interested groups, they struck an agreement with General Manuel Odría, Bustamante's own Minister of the Interior, to depose the besieged president. A close friend of some of Latin America's more unsavoury military dictators, Odría became known during his presidency as the 'Happy General' for his spectacular entertainments honouring such figures as Nicaragua's Anastasio 'Tacho' Somoza and Venezuela's General Marcos Pérez Jiménez.

Odría's term of office from 1948 to 1956 brought remarkable growth in US investment together with increased antagonism towards working-class and popular opposition. US capital interests in mining expanded from US$145 million to US$305 million between 1950 and 1955. During the same period, Peruvian capital investment in national industry grew by 76 per cent. To ensure the viability of these investments, Odría reinstated the ban on APRA and the PCP.

Two years after Odría's inauguration, an insurrection in Arequipa demanded his resignation. This was followed by a wave of strikes in which workers not only pressed for improved working conditions, but also demanded increased democratic rights. When even the conservative press came under fire for criticising Odría's handling of the unrest, the elite realised it was time to look for a replacement for the 'Happy General'. In an exclusive meeting at the colonial Church of Santo Domingo — three blocks from the national palace of government — prominent 'notables' met delegates from the outlawed APRA and members of Odría's own party, to decide how best to depose the president. There was a unanimous agreement to try elections again.

With APRA's endorsement, Manuel Prado, representing the modernising industrialist sector of the elite, carried the 1956 elections with 45 per cent of the vote. APRA's new status as a junior partner of the oligarchy fitted nicely with Haya's new vision of 'Indoamerican unity... driven by national capital and not only by popular parties'.

Peasant Movements and Reform

Following years of repression, local and regional trade unions and labour federations burgeoned in the new, more open political climate of Prado's administration. While many of the new unions remained loyal to the APRA-controlled CTP, *Aprista* leaders faced increasing pressure from the PCP and other emerging left-wing groups.

Important regional federations including those in Cusco, Arequipa and Puno split from the CTP. When strikes by sugar-cane workers, construction workers, teachers, miners and bank employees were met with violence, *Aprista* newspapers and spokesmen joined the anti-communist chorus orchestrated by Prado's government, the right-wing press and the military. As the culmination of a decade-long shift to the right, the APRA-led CTP's decision in 1962 to embrace the 'free trade unionism' promoted by the US government came as no surprise.

The peasant movement also gathered strength during Prado's administration. In the central highland departments of Junín and Pasco, peasant communities 'recovered' land from the large cattle and sheep-raising ranches owned by US companies and Lima-based corporations. As the movement gained confidence, communities in Pasco formed an independent federation. Pressed by the wool hacienda owners to take action, in 1961 the Prado administration sent in police to evict the peasants from the occupied lands. Although many communities lost their newly recovered lands, others were able to resist eviction. As a result of a massacre during one such eviction, miners and railway workers declared a strike in support of the peasants.

The other main centres of peasant struggle during this period were the valleys of La Convención y Lares in the eastern part of the department of Cusco. Sharecroppers and tenant farmers had begun to set up unions in 1952 with the help of legal advisers from the Communist-oriented Workers' Federations of Cusco (FTC). In 1958 the unions joined to form the Provincial Peasant Federation of La Convención (FPCC). In 1960, the FPCC called a strike demanding an end to sharecropping and unsalaried labour. Following a second strike in 1962, when the peasants seized hacienda lands, they formed self-defence committees against vigilantes and the police. In response, the government sent troops to encircle the valley and capture the peasants' leaders, in particular the young Trotskyist Hugo Blanco, who was then General Secretary of the FPCC.

The land recoveries and strikes in the central highlands and La Convención marked the beginning of a peasant movement that shook the foundations of a highland agrarian order rooted in large haciendas and landlords' power. By carrying out their own *de facto* land reform, the peasants both anticipated and forced the military's restricted 1962 land reform, the proposals that helped to bring Belaúnde to power in 1963, and the sweeping land reform which was eventually enacted in 1969.

The peasant uprisings set the agenda for the 1962 elections, dramatising the need to bridge the precarious gap between the Peruvian state and the majority of its citizens. Neither the APRA candidate Haya de la Torre, who ran with the support of three right-wing parties, nor the former dictator Odría, offered a solution. The third candidate, Fernando Belaúnde Terry, campaigned on a reformist platform that introduced the issue of land reform into Peruvian electoral politics.

When the elections resulted in a virtual tie between the three candidates, the armed forces stepped in to block a right wing-APRA coalition government headed by Odría, which they feared would further radicalise the peasant and popular movement. The coup introduced a new phase in the Peruvian military's political identity. For the first time, it had acted as a unified institution under the leadership of the General Staff, rather than as an agent of the oligarchy or a lone *caudillo*. Following years of growth and professionalisation, the armed forces had developed their own identity. With a greater social and racial mix in the officer corps, and more ideological cohesion around the anti-communism of their new national security doctrine, the armed forces were poised to take a more active role in Peruvian political life.

The military launched its new political career by clamping down on labour and the Left; in January 1963, troops arrested nearly 800 union and left-wing activists from around the country. Three months later, the junta declared Peru's first agrarian reform. Designed to quell discontent and growing left-wing influence in highland areas, the reform measures provided for only a limited redistribution of land in certain areas of the central highlands and La Convención. With no ambitions to hold on to government for any length of time, the military honoured its promise to hold elections in July 1963.

Popular Action (AP) candidate Fernando Belaúnde emerged victorious from the elections, having promised national development through road construction, rural projects, education, jungle colonisation and support for national industry. Two of his most appealing campaign pledges were agrarian reform and a solution to the long-standing problem of the US International Petroleum Company's unpaid taxes. The much-anticipated agrarian reform ran into serious difficulties on several fronts. In Congress, the scope of the reform bill was severely curtailed by APRA representatives who opposed any legislation affecting the large coastal sugar and cotton plantations. Nor did they wish to see the land reform applied to any properties that were 'efficiently managed'.

The more serious obstacle to Belaúnde's attempted reform came from the peasants themselves. Following the wave of land invasions in the late 1950s and early 1960s, peasants in Junín, Pasco and Cusco continued to carry out their own *de facto* reform without waiting for Belaúnde's legislation. Unlike the earlier land recoveries, this time both hacienda workers and peasant communities took part, supported by broad regional coalitions of students, workers and intellectuals. These coalitions effectively broke APRA's monopoly on the popular movement. In Cusco, left-wing forces and peasants formed the Departmental Peasant Federation of Cusco (FDCC). In the central highlands, peasants, students and union leaders created the Workers' and Peasants' Front (FOCEP).

Having lost the initiative on his agrarian reform proposals, Belaúnde turned to his development, road building and colonisation projects. Under the burden of these ambitious programmes, foreign debt increased significantly, forcing a devaluation of the Peruvian currency in September 1967. Despite price rises of up to 50 per cent, the government allowed only 10 to 15 per cent wage increases. Belaúnde's tough response to ensuing strikes by bank employees, teachers and metal workers quickly eroded his popularity among unions and sectors of the middle class.

Belaúnde's final promise to collect unpaid taxes from the International Petroleum Company (IPC) proved equally illusory. A subsidiary of the Standard Oil company, the IPC had been allowed to exploit Peruvian oil reserves for several decades without paying a penny of the US$144 million it owed the Peruvian government in taxes. Unable to force the company to pay, Belaúnde instead settled in mid-1968 for a deal in which the government would receive compensation in the form of old IPC equipment and exhausted oil wells. Belaúnde's deal provoked a widespread nationalist reaction; perceived as a sell-out to foreign capital, the IPC fiasco dealt a final blow to Belaúnde's troubled administration.

Overturning Tradition

On 3 October 1968, led by General Juan Velasco Alvarado and other reformist officers, the military proclaimed the creation of the Revolutionary Government of the Armed Forces. The reformist officers were angered by Belaúnde's handling of the IPC. They also feared that his new cabinet, which was made up of *Apristas* and right-wing members of his own party, would heighten social tensions and radicalise the popular movement. The reformist military had a particular interpretation of the national security doctrine in which all Latin American militaries were trained. Rather than combatting communism through force alone, it believed that it could best be contained through social and economic reforms.

Central among the new regime's goals was the modernisation and centralisation of the state through three interrelated processes: land reform, industrial development, and the creation of a state capitalist sector. Land reform would create the internal market necessary for national industrial development. Through selective nationalisations, the state would control strategic sectors of the economy by setting up state-managed enterprises. New legislation encouraged the growth of national industry and foreign investment. Through the creation of corporatist mass organisations, the state would keep control of the labour and popular movement.

The success of these plans depended on the military's vision of itself as an institution acting in the national interest and above class interests. Breaking with its past role as agent of particular class or regional elite groups, Velasco's military assumed the part of nation-builders who could resolve the class conflict, territorial fragmentation and foreign pressures which had burdened previous attempts to develop the Peruvian economy. This utopian programme envisaged a new 'socialism of full participation' which was 'neither communist nor capitalist'.

General Velasco's Third Way

While the Peruvian radical Left decried the capitalist and imperialist character of the military government, the Peruvian Right and US government reacted with alarm to what they saw as the creeping socialism and Soviet weaponry of Velasco. Their fears were in large part unfounded. Although Velasco's reform destroyed the last vestiges of an oligarchic state based on visions of foreign enclave capital and agro-export planters, it was a far cry from socialism. The military's development was premised on replacing the oligarchic state's agro-export model with a new industrial plan of state-supervised linkages between foreign, state and private capital.

A few weeks after the coup, General Velasco announced the occupation and expropriation of the petroleum deposits and installations belonging to the IPC. The company, which received no compensation for its former holdings, was then expelled from the country. The former IPC installations became the core of PetroPeru, the state oil company which came to monopolise all refining and domestic distribution. Other foreign oil companies were allowed to maintain operations in the country under strict conditions. The largest of these, Belco, was placed under contractual obligation to sell part of its production at below export price to PetroPeru. In return, the military gave Belco other incentives to increase investment.

Although economic plans were initially hampered by the strong US reaction to the IPC expropriation, the military nationalised the

US-owned Cerro de Pasco Mining Corporation in 1974. As with the IPC, nationalisation of Cerro de Pasco, which had operated in Peru since 1904, had been a long-standing nationalist goal. The military did not want, however, to nationalise all mining. Rather, as in the case of petroleum, they left the larger and more profitable companies alone in order to guarantee the sector's vitality through large inputs of foreign capital. ASARCO's Southern Peru Copper Corporation (SPCC) which already mined the biggest copper deposits in Peru, signed new contracts in 1969 to expand operations into the even more important deposits of Cuajone and Cerro Verde. By selective nationalisation of refining, processing and commercial operations in strategic sectors of the economy, the military hoped to end the enclave character of traditional foreign-controlled extractive industries. By encouraging foreign companies to invest in partnership with the new state sector, the military planned to integrate Peru's national economy through state control of foreign capital. The military government used similar mechanisms to control capital flow and banking. Under the oligarchic state, foreign capital had acquired an important presence in Peruvian banking. By the time the military took power, only one bank remained in the control of national capital. Velasco reversed this situation by 'Peruvianising' the banking system. This law limited foreign participation in Peruvian banks to a maximum of 25 per cent of the shares and prohibited foreign banks from handling public savings, while allowing them to operate in the country exclusively on their own capital. The Central Reserve Bank, which had been controlled by private banking interests, was transformed into the state-controlled National Bank. The creation of a National Bank was a key element in the centralisation and modernisation of the new national state planned by the military reformers.

Perhaps the most important component of the military project for national integration was the agrarian reform. After taking power, the military government almost immediately expropriated the coastal plantations and mills belonging to Peru's sugar and cotton barons. By transforming these properties into state-controlled peasant cooperatives, the military effectively eliminated the traditional oligarchy's stranglehold on the powerful agro-export sector. Coastal sugar plantations, ranches and other agricultural holdings belonging to foreign companies such as W.R. Grace, Gildemeister, and the Cerro de Pasco were also expropriated.

In a second stage, the military set up cooperatives on the large and more profitable livestock haciendas of the central highlands and divided estates elsewhere among their once dependent sharecroppers and peasants. In many areas of the highlands, the dispossessed *hacendados* remained in the countryside and provincial towns and continued to monopolise local political office and commerce. In other regions, they took jobs in Velasco's government bureaucracy. Although deprived of its land, this provincial elite nevertheless continued to exercise considerable power over the peasantry.

The military exploited its land reform's popularity to create its own mass organisations, the main vehicle for which was the National System of Social Mobilisation (SINAMOS), an umbrella organisation for a number of government-created trade unions, neighbourhood associations, and peasant federations. The most important of these new organisations were the National Agrarian Confederation (CNA), with provincial and departmental peasant and farmer federations in different parts of the country, the Workers' Central of the Peruvian Revolution (CTRP), a national labour federation, and the Revolutionary Labour Movement (MLR), an avowedly anti-communist organisation which mobilised shock troops for breaking strikes and demonstrations. Through these parallel organisations the military hoped to undermine the strength and legitimacy of the CGTP, CCP, and other independent labour federations such as the teachers' and miners' unions.

SINAMOS also played a role in the reorganisation of highland peasant communities. By introducing new structures of political office to replace the traditional political-religious community authorities, it brought in a fresh generation of leaders tied to the new government-sponsored agrarian leagues and the state apparatus.

Although initially successful, these organisations could not overcome widespread resentment of the authoritarianism with which SINAMOS attempted to control them. As animosity grew, many such organisations broke with SINAMOS to join forces with the other independent federations and unions which benefited from disaffection with the military reforms. The failure of SINAMOS and other state agencies to attend to provincial grievances also encouraged a movement for political and economic decentralisation. During the mid-1970s, broad-based regional movements emerged in different parts of the country. Organised into Popular Defence Fronts (FEDIPs), they brought together unions, neighbourhood and peasant organisations, student federations, professionals, small businessmen and local entrepreneurs. The FEDIPs pressed for the creation of autonomous regional governments with the power to tax local mines, oil wells, tourism and other businesses whose income was traditionally accumulated in Lima or abroad.

The revitalised urban, labour and peasant organisations which matured under the military government coalesced with Marxist and socialist parties, intellectuals, non-governmental organisations and the progressive Church to form a broad anti-military opposition. Faced with the unusual prospect of Velasco's fast-paced military reformism, the left-wing parties were forced to redefine many of their objectives. Opposed reactions to Velasco's programme sharpened the differences between the Communist Party and the parties that had emerged from the 1960s New Left. While the PCP supported Velasco as an anti-imperialist and nationalist regime, those from the newer 'radical left' parties criticised the capitalist and authoritarian nature of the military reforms. Within the labour movement and, in particular, within the CGTP, these differences exacerbated tension between the PCP-dominated bureaucracy and a rank and file with growing ties to the radical Left.

The blueprint for Velasco's industrial plans was laid out in the 1970 General Law of Industries, which placed strategic extractive industries, distribution and export-import activities under state control, and stipulated state involvement in all basic industries such as paper, tools and motors, chemicals, cement and fertiliser. As a result of these measures, the number of state enterprises more than doubled between 1968 and 1975, while firms in which the state had more than a fifty per cent stake grew from two to 95. By 1975 the percentage of GNP generated by the public sector had doubled from 16 per cent in 1968 to 32 per cent.

The larger monopolistic industries, which benefited from Velasco's new export incentives and expanded internal market, became highly visible advocates and even acted as advisers to the military government. Yet with their low profit margins and rates of reinvestment and greater dependency on the internal market, non-unionised small and medium-sized family-owned industries fared less well under the new labour code which insisted on social security payments and job security. Grouped in the National Industrial Society (SNI), these manufacturers emerged, together with the influential newspaper *El Comercio* and the conservative Peruvian Bar Association, as the Velasco regime's most vocal opponents. When, in 1973, Velasco tried to deport the president of the SNI, this right-wing opposition bloc also gained the tacit support of conservative sectors within the armed forces. The turning-point in the increasingly tense confrontation between the military reformers and the Right came in July 1974, when Velasco boldly expropriated the major national newspapers and turned their assets and control over to the popular organisations created by the government.

Tired of Velasco's authoritarianism and leftward drift, upper-class youths took to the streets in violent demonstrations against the expropriations. The Right also mounted an ideological defence of private property and democratic government and an attack on all forms of state intervention. The championing of *laissez-faire* liberalism as an antidote to 'statism' underpinned the Right's ideological renovation in the coming decades.

Mounting opposition to Velasco's reforms was fuelled by the worsening economic situation. Industrial growth fell from 13.2 per cent in 1973 to 5.2 per cent in 1975. Foreign debt rose from US$2.3 billion in 1974 to US$3.1 billion the following year. The cost of living had risen by 139 per cent since the military took power in 1968, and by 1975 real wages had fallen by over eleven per cent. Strikes in response to the industrial slowdown and failing economy increased dramatically. After an police strike was announced on 5 February 1975, there was widespread looting of shops and destruction of government offices in Lima. The military declared a state of emergency in the capital and imposed a strict curfew. Riots and protests following sharp price increases in May 1975 led to the closing of left-wing magazines and the deportation of 29 journalists, radical politicians and union leaders, as well as several *Apristas* and Popular Action party members. Three months later, moderate officers stepped in to replace Velasco with General Francisco Morales Bermúdez.

After six years of military rule, the legacy of *Velasquismo* still hung in the balance. The land reform had delivered the *coup de grace* to an already ailing oligarchy. It had also greatly empowered the peasantry and its organisations. The nationalisations highlighted the problems surrounding Peru's dependency on foreign capital, while the industrial reforms raised popular understanding of the pitfalls of capitalist development. The aspirations and mobilisation generated by the reforms went beyond the military's wildest expectations. They gave new confidence to an expanded working-class and peasant movement, whose experiences with the military's 'top-down' programme taught them the value of retaining their autonomy with respect to the state and its political interests. This vigorous popular movement became the single most important force with which the economic and political elites had to contend in their efforts to undo Velasco's reforms.

The other important legacy of the Velasco years was the sizeable state-controlled sector which would become the target of IMF-imposed austerity programmes in the 1980s and the neo-liberal reforms of the 1990s. Much of the political energy of the post-Velasco governments of Fernando Belaúnde, Alan García and Alberto Fujimori became directed towards undoing the state and economy built by Velasco.

Dismantling *Velasquismo*

The reversal of Velasco's 'revolution' began with the military government's 'second phase'. During the turbulent final year of

Velasco's rule, military opposition had been divided between a conservative faction, led by naval officers, and a moderate group, known as the 'institutionalists'. Although the institutionalists defended the military's 'revolution', they were opposed to what they saw as the excesses of Velasco's left-wing reforms. The new president, General Francisco Morales Bermúdez, who had served as Velasco's Economy Minister, had close ties to both the institutionalists and the outgoing *Velasquistas*.

It did not take long for the new president to begin his turn to the right. After a short initial period in which he allowed deported opposition leaders to return and maintained Velasco's reforms, in April 1976 in a televised speech to the nation, Morales Bermúdez outlined the *'grandes decisiones'* through which the military was now proposing to reroute the 'revolution'. Denouncing Velasco's socialist leanings as the product of 'outside infiltration', he announced important revisions to the Plan Inca which had been the blueprint for the first phase of military government. Business and industry responded with caution, requesting specific measures such as a central role for private enterprise in the military's economic planning and the elimination of Velasco's industrial reforms and job security laws.

Under pressure to refinance the foreign debt, the military government sought to regain the confidence of the IMF by introducing a package of price increases and wage stabilisation measures in June 1976. These measures led immediately to a series of uprisings and riots in Lima and other cities. The military reacted by declaring a state of emergency and curfew in Lima, and by closing all opposition newspapers. In August, the regime banned all strikes, authorising employers to dismiss any workers who took part in them. Unable to halt the momentum of unrest, in February 1977 the military announced a new plan of government known as the Plan Tupac Amaru, which outlined vague provisions for a political solution through a gradual transfer of power to civilians. Mention was made of a plan for municipal elections and a Constituent Assembly in 1980 to rewrite the constitution.

The military's hesitant moves towards a democratic transition were speeded up by unrelenting pressure from both the popular movement and the Right for further concessions. On 10 June, Walter Piazza, a well-known businessman and Morales' new Economy Minister, announced a new Emergency Programme designed to reduce price subsidies and control wages, as well as to cut arms spending and ministerial budgets. The IMF responded favourably, opening the way for negotiation of a US$250 million loan from private banks.

Piazza's measures were less popular with organised workers who formed the United Committee for Struggle (CUL), bringing together all the federations and national unions, except those controlled by APRA. The Committee called for a national 24-hour strike on 19 July in opposition to the Emergency Programme and also demanded wage increases to match price rises, price freezes on basic consumer goods, respect for labour contracts and job stability, the return of deported politicians and labour leaders, freedom for political prisoners, and full restoration of democratic rights. In the first national strike since 1919, workers, students and shanty-town dwellers took over the streets of all Peru's major urban centres in a massive show of support for the Committee's anti-IMF and pro-democracy platform.

The government answered with a blend of repression and concessions. Over 5,000 workers, among them senior union leaders, were fired. On the other hand, the government lifted the curfew, dismissed Piazza as Economy Minister and agreed to wage rises and subsidies for basic consumer goods. It also announced elections for a 1978 Constituent Assembly and general elections to be held in 1980. The proposed elections and Constituent Assembly were supported by all political forces in the country, with the exception of AP and a few of the Maoist parties, including Sendero Luminoso and *Patria Roja*.

APRA was among the most enthusiastic advocates of the Constituent Assembly. Throughout both phases of the military government, APRA had abandoned its traditional enmity towards the armed forces in favour of a cautious policy of non-confrontation. Claiming paternity for Velasco's original reforms, Haya opted to remain on the sidelines, consolidating APRA's institutional strength without confronting either the government or the Left. His chief goal was the encouragement of a select group of young *Aprista* militants for the as-yet undefined moment when APRA would once again assume a more active political role. Among this group was the future president, Alan García.

The military was similarly circumspect with APRA, excluding its leaders and organisations from the repression and vigilance with which it sought to control the Left. The fact that many *Apristas* and ex-*Apristas* held important positions in the first phase of the military government softened the long-standing hatred between APRA and the military by underscoring the similarities between Velasco's programme and Haya's original proposals for a corporatist, anti-imperialist state.

The enmity was finally bridged in 1977, when President Morales Bermúdez initiated the first direct talks between APRA and the armed forces, reaching agreement on the impending transition to democracy. APRA demanded restoration of full democratic rights and a guarantee of free elections, in return promising to use its appreciable electoral base to safeguard some of the military's reforms in the new constitution. 'The relation between the *Aprista* party and the army is like a lovers' quarrel', reflected Haya de la Torre. 'We have always wanted to approach each other, but the great achievement of the reaction, the oligarchy and the communists was to keep us apart.' For its part, the military felt reassured by APRA's proven record of anti-communism. 'The other parties had no plan of government', explained Morales Bermúdez's Prime Minister, General Pedro Richter Prada. 'We knew that APRA's non-Marxist democratic left politics were what most suited the country and the Armed Forces.'

APRA was able to honour its side of the deal in the Constituent Assembly of 1978, when it won 37 out of 100 seats. The left-wing parties (UDP, FOCEP, PCP-Unidad, and PSR) and the Popular Christian Party (PPC) ran a close second with 28 and 25 seats respectively. The pro-oligarchic parties received only four delegates. The strong showing of APRA and the Left reflected the changed political landscape following a decade of military rule. New election laws had extended the vote to illiterates and lowered the voting age to 18. As a result, sixty per cent of the electorate was voting for the first time. APRA's strong corporate party traditions attracted the vote of this new electorate, as did the Left's hard won reputation for defending the democratic rights of unions, peasants and shanty-town dwellers under the military government.

The Left was less successful in the Constituent Assembly. Divided into four groups, the left-wing representatives were split over ideological issues. For the radicals, the Constituent Assembly was merely a step towards the final goal of a socialist revolution. For the others, the constitution represented a means to guarantee the preservation of the anti-imperialist and nationalist gains achieved under Velasco's military government.

The writing of the constitution was dominated by APRA and the specialists in constitutional law who made up the minority right-wing bench. The final document reflected a compromise between APRA's social-democratic principles and the PPC's conservatism. The 1979 constitution institutionalised a parliamentary democracy with a strong executive branch, whose authority over economic decision-making proved favourable to the PPC's free-market principles. On the other hand, it also included important guarantees on workers' rights, social security, health, land reform, education and housing. Ironically in hindsight, it even included the right to insurrection.

Following the Constituent Assembly, Peru's diverse political forces geared up for the 1980 general elections. The military returned to the barracks to resolve the internal conflicts that had arisen during its twelve years in government.

Enter the Technocrats

AP candidate Fernando Belaúnde won the 1980 presidential elections by a landslide. Campaigning on a utopian programme of 'austerity without recession' and with promises to create a million new jobs, the former president made use of his populist appeal to capture 45 per cent of the vote. APRA's candidate, Armando Villanueva, ran second with 27 per cent. The Left, which split at the last moment into five different slates, took only 14 per cent.

While President Belaúnde busied himself with his long dreamed-of colonisation, irrigation and road construction projects, he turned the job of managing the economy over to US-educated Peruvian technocrats with experience working for international banks, multinational companies and the multilateral lending organisations. His first Economy Minister, Manuel Ulloa, was a wealthy businessman who favoured eliminating the state's considerable role in the economy, reducing tariffs and restoring free-market principles to attract foreign capital and boost exports of raw materials.

Ulloa and his economic team, known as 'The Dynamo', swiftly dismantled the national industrial economy set up by the military and began to restore a liberal export-led model. They began the reversal of Velasco's agrarian reform by liberalising the land market, allowing cooperatives to divide up their land and banks to hold land as collateral against mortgages and loans. They reduced the high import tariffs imposed by Velasco from 60 per cent to 32 per cent. The Dynamo also opened such strategic state-dominated economic sectors as fishing, cement and steel to competition from foreign and private capital. Their attempts to ground the economy in exports, however, did not take into account steadily declining prices for minerals and other raw materials in a recessionary world market. By 1982, raw material prices had reached their lowest point since the 1930s.

Adding to Belaúnde's economic woes was the immense cost of his own development and construction projects. Promises of new roads and development which had brought him success on the campaign trail proved harder to realise. In response to declining agricultural production in the Andean highlands, for example, Belaúnde simply turned his back on the Andes and instead proposed to expand the agricultural frontier through massive and largely unrealistic colonisation projects in Peru's jungle provinces. The increased expenditure needed for these projects also clashed with the Dynamo's calls for reduced government spending. To finance his projects, Belaúnde turned to the international banks, pushing Peru's foreign debt from US$9.6 billion in 1980 to US$11.4 billion in 1982.

Faced with imminent economic collapse, Manuel Ulloa resigned in December 1982. The new minister, Carlos Rodríguez Pastor, was vice-president of the US-based Wells Fargo bank, one of Peru's largest foreign creditors, and brought in a new team of technocrats to replace Ulloa's Dynamo. Christened 'The Stagecoach' by the press after the 'wild west' Wells Fargo stagecoaches, the new team adopted an even more radical approach. They raised interest rates, cut all remaining price and food subsidies and curtailed all state expenditure, including Belaúnde's cherished development projects.

Designed to facilitate debt service to Wells Fargo and other foreign banks, Rodríguez Pastor's policies dealt a severe blow to the already ailing national industry. In 1983, the year immediately following the austerity measures, gross domestic product dropped by 12 per cent; cumulative growth in gross domestic product for the five years of Belaúnde's administration averaged only 0.3 per cent a year. By 1984, national industry was operating at forty per cent of capacity. The textile industry and automobile assembly plants were particularly hard hit by import liberalisation. By 1984, many had been forced to close, leaving thousands of workers unemployed. Nor was the Stagecoach successful in controlling inflation. By 1985, the year Belaúnde left office, inflation had risen to 158.3 per cent annually, as compared to 60.8 per cent in the year he took office. Over this period, real wages had lost forty per cent of their value.

As the effects of the reforms became apparent, unions called general strikes to try to lead the widespread but unorganised opposition to Belaúnde. Compared with the massive and effective national strikes against the military government, the six general strikes called to oppose Belaúnde's administration met with only limited success. The once strong unions had been badly weakened by unemployment and the downward trend of real wages. The growth of the informal economy also undermined union strategies. Rather than protesting against the newly imposed wage ceilings, production cutbacks and plant closures, workers concentrated on negotiating severance payments with which to launch their own businesses in the booming informal sector.

In the countryside, peasants fought Belaúnde's attempts to roll back the agrarian reform and to weaken the juridical and land-holding status of their communities. In 1983, independent peasant communities represented by the CCP and farmers and cooperatives organised in the CNA joined efforts in the United Agrarian Council (CUNA). Peasant self-defence committees modelled on the *rondas*, or patrols, formed by peasant communities in northern Peru in the late 1970s, sprang up in different parts of the country to deter livestock theft, crime and the political violence unleashed by the dirty war between

Sendero Luminoso and the armed forces. In some regions, peasant organisations led FEDIPs in their struggle for regional autonomy. In the cities, neighbourhood and women's committees formed soup kitchens, communal canteens, and a variety of self-help organisations.

This expanding popular movement also forced the Left to forge new strategies and identities. Abandoning temporarily the divisions which had led to the 1980 electoral fiasco, the left-wing parties regrouped that year to form the United Left (IU). Conceived as a 'revolutionary mass front', the IU's objectives were 'to provide a political response to the demands for the democratic process that come from the people, [and] to become the leading force of the different classes and sectors that make up the national popular bloc.' The IU's political work paid off with thirty per cent of the vote in the municipal elections of 1983, including the election of IU mayors in Lima, Cusco, Puno and other cities, as well as in numerous provinces throughout Peru. Shortly after the elections, alliances again shifted within the IU. Three parties — the VR, the MIR and the PCR — formed the PUM in 1984. Dissatisfied with what it considered to be an over-emphasis on electoral politics, the Popular Democratic Unity (UDP) left the IU to form the UDP-*Pueblo en Marcha*. With the country's increasing militarisation and Sendero's escalating offensive against popular organisations, the Left was increasingly hard-pressed to fulfil its ambition of building a mass-based democratic movement.

When Belaúnde left office in July 1985, he left behind him a country racked by economic instability, political violence, and a military apparatus significantly strengthened by the counter-insurgency campaigns. Abandoning his original goal of national industrial development, Belaúnde had effectively handed the Peruvian economy over to the banks and multilateral lending organisations. Caught between the recessionary spiral of unemployment and industrial stagnation brought on by Belaúnde's economic policies and the proliferating violence fuelled by his dirty war, the Peruvian people had clearly come second to the international banks and the military.

A Different Future?

While Belaúnde was presiding over Peru's economic decline, APRA was busy laying its plans for 'a different future'. In the 14th Party Congress in October 1982, a young militant named Alan García Pérez was elected General Secretary. Hand-picked in 1977 as Secretary of Organisation by Haya (who had died in 1979), García was part of a rising new generation of leaders who had been carefully groomed for political power. At once more worldly in its outlook and less vehement

APRA presidential candidate Alan García at Cusco rally, 1985.   (Julio Etchart)

in its anti-communism, this young, foreign-educated generation
sought to develop APRA as a democratic left-of-centre alternative to
the Marxist Left. As a deputy to Congress, García stood out with his
eloquent speeches against the IMF and Belaúnde's policies and in
support of the Sandinista government in Nicaragua. He also took part
in workers' demonstrations and publicly supported the demands of
the CGTP and the teachers' union, SUTEP. At the same time, he
cultivated personal relations with important businessmen and
technocrats, many of whom would later be invited to participate in
formulating APRA's governmental plan, a blueprint for which had
been drawn up in García's own book, *A Different Future*.

Perfecting his populist style, García waged his campaign for the
1985 presidential elections under the slogan 'Alan: a president for all
Peruvians'. He promised his supporters a 'social democracy' in which
all citizens would have guaranteed rights to health, welfare and justice,
and toured the country giving flamboyant nationalist speeches and
offering beleaguered Peruvians the alluring prospect of an enthusiastic
37-year-old president who would restore prosperity and unity to Peru.
Inevitably, García was hard-pressed to live up to his campaign
promises.

Nevertheless, during his first 18 months in office, García achieved
the impossible through his 'Emergency Programme', which included

measures to lower business taxes, facilitate credit, raise wages and protect national manufacturers. By the end of 1986, the economy was out of its recessionary cycle. Annual growth in GDP had risen from 2.5 per cent in the last year of Belaúnde's government to 8.5 per cent. Employment in the Lima metropolitan area was also up by 3.5 per cent and private investment had grown by 23.5 per cent. Inflation went down from 158 per cent in 1985 to 63 per cent in 1986. By October 1986, the index of real wages had risen to 140 from its initial base of 100 when García took office. The spurt of economic growth and the popularity of his 'ten per cent solution' for Peru's large external debt initially bolstered García's proposal for a *concertación*, or agreement, between different economic and social actors.

The 'Ten Per Cent Solution'

Alan García's campaign promise to limit debt payment to ten per cent of export earnings formed the centrepiece of a potentially viable programme to promote economic recovery. In sharp contrast to the previous administration's policies favouring foreign capital, García's programme proposed to give priority to national capital. By restraining debt payments, García hoped to increase the availability of hard currency both to national industry and to his own government-sponsored social programmes.

Despite the confidence and enthusiasm of the recent campaign, García and his economic team proved incapable of bringing their ethereal 'ten per cent solution' down to earth. The time limits of the ten per cent solution were never made clear, nor the types of contractual relations such a solution would imply for Peru's various creditors. Nor did it supply clear answers to the creditors' concerns about who would be paid and when. Substituting bravura for diplomatic savvy and financial practicalities, García's team managed to alienate each of Peru's multilateral and private creditors. The private banks responded by cutting off commercial credit, while the World Bank and the Inter-American Development Bank both suspended previously approved loans for over US$900 million. The IMF ruled Peru out for any future credit.

García's failure to deal responsibly with the diplomatic and financial intricacies of debt negotiation had serious repercussions for his entire administration which overlooked the fact that debt payment is only one element in a comprehensive economic programme. No attention was paid to the crucial issue of how to formulate a debt payment strategy which would form part of a long-term plan for resolving the underlying structural problems of the Peruvian economy.

Lacking a complete economic strategy, García's advisers approached policy-making on an *ad hoc* basis. Although they paid lip service to the goals of rebuilding national industry and building a self-sustaining economy, they offered no concrete proposals to increase Peru's international reserves. Their failure to link a debt repayment plan with complementary strategies for either increasing exports, reducing imports, or attracting new capital, led to a rapid depletion of Peru's already meagre international reserves. Of the US$1.4 billion of international reserves which García inherited upon taking office in 1985, only US$866 million remained by 1986. By 1987, this had dwindled to only US$60 million. By 1988, international reserves were US$275 million in the red.

García's erratic economic policies and *caudillo* style eventually undermined his relationship with both industrialists and labour. The initial increase in real wages began to drop off by the end of 1986. By March 1987, the wage index had fallen from its peak of 140 to 124. Two months later, independent unions and labour federations headed by the CGTP called a national strike to demand wage increases to match the rising cost of living, respect for job stability laws, broadening collective negotiation to include workers in small enterprises, and worker participation in economic policy-making. Having trusted García for over a year, they now insisted that the president honour his calls for a dialogue with labour.

García's *concertación* with business and industrial leaders also showed increasing strain. Following a period in which the index for corporate profits had risen from 100 in 1985 and 110 in 1986 to 129 in 1987, García hardened his position towards the private sector. In April 1987, he announced the creation of investment bonds for compulsory sale to private firms. The proposal was unanimously rejected by both small businesses and the monopoly sector controlled by the twelve largest financial and industrial conglomerates. Known during García's term in office as the 'Twelve Apostles' because of their close association with the president, these conglomerates had been important supporters, and beneficiaries, of García's administration. Vindicated by the Supreme Court in their argument that the move constituted an illegal 'confiscation of profits', the industrialists and Twelve Apostles emerged victorious from the bond sales dispute only to confront García's next unpredictable move.

President García once again surprised Peruvians in his 28 July address by announcing the nationalisation of all banks, investment banks and insurance companies. He alleged that the financial institutions had made improper use of credit and unfairly favoured large industry. The announcement galvanised Peruvian political debate, with sections of the Left and labour supporting the nationalisations with varying reservations, and the Right reacting with vehement disapproval, decrying García's decree as an authoritarian blow against freedom, democracy and private property. For the Twelve Apostles, who controlled most of the financial and banking interests affected by the law, García's measure was tantamount to betrayal by the same president with whom they had supported *concertación*. Prominent *Apristas* also opposed the measure as inconsistent with Haya's original charter for APRA. Caught in endless squabbles over the interpretation and legality of nationalisation, García's original proposal was eventually reduced to near insignificance in the watered-down version which was passed months later by the Peruvian Senate. Even this modified bill was later repealed by the Supreme Court in January 1991.

Faced with increasing hostility at home and the near impossibility of raising domestic investment after the nationalisation move, García shifted gear with respect to his debt payment policies. Dropping his formerly intransigent stance against negotiation, he quietly opened talks in August 1987 with representatives of both the IMF and the World Bank. As a gesture of good faith, the government began service payments to the World Bank and later García invited delegations from the IMF and World Bank to prepare reports on the Peruvian economy. The World Bank's final report recommended implementing an 'economic restructuring programme' to include reduction of consumer subsidies, increased interest rates, a unified exchange rate, improved relation with creditors and payment of US$175 million in arrears to the World Bank.

At the same time, García also resumed discussions with creditors in the private banking sector, reaching favourable agreements with several banks. In February 1988, just as the economy hit rock bottom with accumulated inflation of over 1,700 per cent, a fall of nearly ten per cent in GDP and a precipitous drop in real wages (by now back at their 1985 level), García changed direction yet again by closing down all negotiations with both the private banks and multilateral institutions. To keep the economy working, García sold and mortgaged a large portion of Peru's remaining gold reserves. He also proposed a programme of 'selective growth' through which the government would provide favourable exchange rates and credit to those sectors of the economy which either produced basic consumer goods and exports or provided employment.

This change in economic policy was as ephemeral as those before it. In response to power struggles within APRA, García resorted to orthodox shock treatment in September 1988. The Peruvian currency was sharply devalued; consumer prices doubled or in some cases tripled overnight and wage increases were kept proportionately lower than the rising cost of living. The measures were greeted with outrage and widespread rioting and looting in Lima and other cities.

As García approached his final year in office, Peru's future seemed precarious. The president's vacillating economic policy, ineffectual dirty war strategy and arrogance had raised the hackles of the political Right, the business sector, the military and the international lending organisation and creditor banks, as well as the Left and the popular organisations. Having further weakened the Peruvian economy, García had virtually destroyed the possibility of any future compromises from the banks and multilaterals who were unimpressed by his maverick policy-making. With his abdication of responsibility for the deteriorating human rights situation and growing paramilitary threat, García had similarly paved the way for increasing military autonomy in the war against Sendero and other perceived 'subversives'. After such high hopes, the García years ended in disappointment and disillusion.

5

The Neo-Liberal Revolution

In the early 17th century, Isabel Flores Oliva had a vision of a great earthquake. The enormous tidal wave which followed it washed entire ships into Lima's central plaza. The city was swallowed by the earth and Lima's sinful population was flushed out to sea. Following Isabel's beatification as Santa Rosa of Lima in 1668, her fearful prophecy acquired a mythic life of its own in a city regularly afflicted with earthquakes and tremors. Still today, as each tremor subsides, Santa Rosa's apocalyptic vision is confirmed in the minds of Lima's seven million people.

In the 1990 electoral campaign, the image of a tidal wave once again captured the Peruvian popular imagination. In late March, as the nine candidates for Peru's presidential elections were winding up their campaigns, political analysts, pollsters and journalists began to describe Alberto Fujimori's spectacular rise in popularity as a *tsunami*. This Japanese term for a tidal wave caused by an earthquake or volcano proved an apt metaphor for the sweeping impact of Fujimori's candidacy. By building his image as a political independent, Fujimori courted the electorate's mounting frustration with traditional party politics and the inefficient state apparatus. His distinctive ethnic background as the son of Japanese immigrants and his backing by evangelical protestants heightened even further his claims to be a political outsider. In what has become an identifiable trend worldwide, Fujimori's campaign — like those of the Bolivian businessman Max Fernández, the US billionaire Ross Perot, and the Philippine candidate Miriam Santiago — stressed an anti-political message. In this new brand of international post-Cold War populism, politics and politicians are held up as the obstacle to more 'efficient' government.

Few foresaw the far-reaching effects of Fujimori's *tsunami*. Not only did his remarkable popularity shake the ground beneath Lima's political elites. Almost immediately after his elections, Fujimori also began to make use of his 'political independence' to forge ties with the military and the multinational lending technocracy, and to vilify both the judiciary and the legislature as corrupt institutions standing in the way of a 'direct democracy' linking the executive and the people. In a spectacular reversal of his electoral promises, Fujimori adopted the severe neo-liberal economic policies of his former electoral opponent, Mario Vargas Llosa, and assumed an increasingly authoritarian stance. His attacks on Congress, unions, the judiciary, political parties and other aspects of the traditional political establishment escalated during his first year in office, culminating in a military-backed *autogolpe*, or self-inflicted coup, on 5 April 1992. Though the coup came as a surprise to many, signs of Fujimori's authoritarian aspirations and pending alliance with the military began to appear immediately after the 1990 elections.

Setting the Stage

The 1990 presidential election was a record-breaking event in several respects. For the first time in Peruvian history, three consecutive general elections had taken place without military interference. A record number of voters also participated. Nearly ten million Peruvians turned out at the polls, representing almost fifty per cent of the total population. There was also a record tally of candidates; nine ran for president, 960 candidates, divided into 16 slates, ran for sixty seats in the senate. The number of candidates competing for the 181 seats in the chamber of deputies was even greater. In Lima alone, 1,160 candidates in 29 slates ran for the forty seats. The unwieldy 42-centimetre ballot paper devised to accommodate the unusual number of candidates was nearly twice the size of the 1985 paper.

The ballot's monumental scale matched the seriousness of the moment. The enthusiastic welcome which Peruvian voters had given the young Alan García in 1985 had long since been forgotten in the shambles left by his five-year term. Corruption and inefficiency had become hallmarks of García's final years. Voters were angered by García's personalist politics and the patronage system through which his government ran public services and relief programmes.

The debacle of García's government was more immediately felt by most Peruvians, however, through the effects of his economic and social policies. As voters prepared to go to the polls in April, the record-breaking inflation of recent years continued to climb, reaching 211.8 per cent during the four months preceding the elections and 38.9 per cent in April alone. In the five years since García had taken office, total accumulated inflation was over 700,000 per cent. The near total breakdown in public services made coping with the economic situation even more difficult. The government was unable to deliver even the minimal services of water and electricity. The worst drought in over thirty years devastated more than 100,000 hectares of crops in the Andean highlands, creating a double crisis for the already failing state service sector. Unable to make ends meet in their drought-stricken communities, a new wave of migrants poured into Lima and other coastal cities. Drinking water supplies for Lima were exhausted, leading to severe shortages.

People expressed their dissatisfaction by taking to the streets. In contrast to the hopeful early years when García himself was able to call mass rallies of support, his final six months in office were marked by daily demonstrations and stoppages. The regional government for the southern departments of Puno, Moquegua and Tacna called a strike to demand emergency measures and aid to counter the effects of the drought. Farmers in the central coastal valleys of Chancay, Huaura and Barranca blocked highways in protest at the suspension of a credit programme for small producers. Lima shanty-town dwellers organised huge marches demanding improved water services, equal water rationing for rich and poor neighbourhoods, increased state allocations for municipal governments, and automatic indexing of salaries to keep pace with inflation. Popular discontent and efforts to resolve the problem of housing for the growing migrant population met only with government violence. In late April, the national anti-riot police evicted 5,000 families from vacant lands they had occupied at El Naranjal, on the outskirts of Lima, tearing down and burning the small reed and cardboard shacks.

National labour federations were also demanding inflation-linked wage increases. Strikes by teachers and health workers brought home to Peruvians the chronic underfunding of basic services. The six-month strike by health workers particularly publicised the government's neglect of Peru's disintegrating health system. Affecting primarily the poor, the collapse in public health services worsened the increasingly precarious conditions of life in Lima. Water rationing and frequent power cuts contributed to the general atmosphere of anxiety and uncertainty created by the economic crisis and political violence. Everybody was hit by the recurrent electrical blackouts. Whether caused by Sendero bombings or by Lima's antiquated and largely inoperative electric power system, the blackouts added to a general mood of distrust for a government that could no longer guarantee even minimal public services.

Public fear was heightened still further by Sendero's armed campaign for a boycott of the November 1989 municipal and regional elections and the April 1990 general elections. As November approached, Sendero escalated attacks against elected mayors, popular leaders and candidates, particularly those from the United Left. In the central highlands alone, more than forty mayors were murdered, bringing to 63 the total number of mayors killed by the PCP-SL since 1987. By early 1990, Sendero had begun to target members, candidates and offices of the Democratic Front (FREDEMO), a new and growing right-wing electoral alliance supporting the candidacy of Mario Vargas Llosa.

The centrepiece of the PCP-SL's electoral boycott, however, were the so-called 'armed strikes'. Within Sendero's strategy, these are meant to provoke militarisation by creating a general atmosphere of terror and paralysis. The armed strikes are usually announced by the party several weeks in advance. Sendero then follows its strike call by intimidating merchants, taxi-drivers and bus companies and destroying several vehicles. It also circulates hit-lists of alleged 'collaborators' and commits murders as warnings against ignoring the armed strike. Car bombs, blackouts and announcements made at gunpoint on radio stations punctuate the days just before the chosen date. By the time the day itself arrives, Sendero is virtually assured of a 'successful' strike by the terrified transport workers and bus owners whose refusal to work paralyses the city. In the days preceding the armed strike of 27 March 1990, the PCP-SL threatened 200 small transport businesses and cooperatives, killed 16 people, and set off a car bomb in central Lima killing three passers-by and wounding thirty.

Military and paramilitary violence added to the fear and uncertainty. Like Sendero, extreme right-wing organisations wished to intimidate left-wing and grassroots activists. In Ayacucho a previously unknown paramilitary group, the Antiterrorist Movement of National Liberation, threatened IU leaders and candidates, while unknown individuals firebombed the offices of Ayacucho's pro-IU departmental peasant federation.

There was no let-up in the relentless pace of this dirty war during the electoral campaigns. Human rights abuses and disappearances remained daily fare in Peruvian newspapers and television. The IU's presidential candidate, Henry Pease, was himself shot and wounded by the police in a march in Lima two months before the elections. Clearly, if elections were to proceed, both candidates and voters would have to overcome some extraordinary circumstances. Together, they would also have to devise some exceptional solutions.

No Blank Cheques

As Peruvians prepared to go to the polls for the sixth time in the ten years since the military stepped down in 1980 they did so with increased awareness of the limitations of an electoral process based on demagoguery and party politics. Both Belaúnde and García had failed to live up to the expectations of those who brought them into office. Both administrations had promised that thousands of Peruvians would have an opportunity to participate in state-sponsored development and assistance programmes. Tight control of these programmes by the respective governing party's machinery, however, stifled any potential for linking state institutions and decision-making with existing grassroots organisations. For people matured through the political experiences of the military government of 1968-80, the inability of governing parties and state institutions to respond to democratic aspirations was all too clear. The result was a search for a new political identity independent of the established parties which had so often let the majority of Peruvians down.

Among the casualties of this growing disenchantment with the established political parties was the Left. In its relatively short electoral history, the Peruvian Left has ridden a veritable roller-coaster of public support. From its surprising gains in the Constituent Assembly elections in 1978, when it took 28 per cent of the vote, the Left has alternately gained and lost strength. In the general elections of 1980 and 1985, it won 15 and 24 per cent respectively; in the municipal elections of 1980, 1983 and 1986, it won 24, 29 and 32 per cent. As the Left approached the 1989 elections, it did so confident in the knowledge of its history of electoral support.

Forgetting, however, that the low points in its electoral history had coincided with periods of division, the Left once again split before the elections. Months before the 1989 municipal elections, some of the smaller parties within the IU, created in 1980 by a wide range of left-wing parties, broke away from the larger group. The splinter group was later joined by Alfonso Barrantes, the popular former mayor of Lima who had himself left the IU some months before. Together they formed the Socialist Left (IS). Made up of small groups, independent moderates and loyal *Barrantistas*, the IS proposed to modernise the economy and the state through 'a national agreement between the state, business and labour', 'competitive insertion in the international market', and 'keeping popular expectations in check'. The larger left-wing parties, such as PUM, *Patria Roja*, the Communist Party and the Christian Movement of Socialist Affirmation (MAS), remained within the United Left.

More important than the division between the IS and IU were the undemocratic practices characterising the Left as a whole. Since the mid-1970s, the Left had grown steadily in numbers and strength. The IU's first national congress in January 1989 was unprecedented in both the number of participants and the procedure of selecting delegates through local democratic elections. The event took place in Lima with more than 3,500 participants, including over 2,000 delegates elected nationwide through secret ballots and other national and local party leaders. This first experience of mass participation in a political congress generated high expectations for the possibilities of a truly united Left.

The IU national leadership, however, proved incapable of responding to this popular enthusiasm. Following the congress, the National Steering Committee met to plan for the coming municipal and general elections. As decided by the congress, electoral slates for the municipal elections were chosen through primary elections in which all IU militants voted. Yet when it came to deciding on the all-important presidential slate, sectarianism prevailed. Rejecting the two slates which had finished first and second in the primaries, Communist Party leaders entered into entirely independent negotiations with Alfonso Barrantes. When these failed, a final compromise slate, headed by Henry Pease, was agreed, but not before causing intense frustration among the rank and file whose hopes for a united Left had been first raised by the congress and then shattered by the leadership. The impact of the Left's disarray was soon to be felt. 'Some imagined that the leftist vote belonged to them', wrote Peruvian historian Alberto Flores Galindo. 'But the popular classes think for themselves, even though some do not believe so. They do not give blank cheques.'

APRA also approached the elections weakened by party in-fighting. Faced with the growing crisis during García's term, different factions began to criticise the party's role in García's administration. Radical sectors of the *Aprista* youth and unions proposed alliances with the Left; Alan García himself courted Barrantes and moderate left-wingers. All this met with disapproval from APRA's anti-communist leadership. There were also strained relations between APRA's national leadership and those provincial members who opposed García's personalist style and dependence on Lima's APRA functionaries. To some extent, APRA's resilient party structure could use clientelism to absorb these discrepancies among its membership. But these same practices alienated those non-*Aprista* voters who had supported García in 1985. It was clear to them that García had not honoured his electoral promises, but had rather promoted narrow party favouritism and corruption. Neither APRA nor the Left found a blank cheque awaiting them on election day.

Reviving the Right

During the 1980s, support for traditional right-wing parties had declined in inverse proportion to the rising popularity of the Left and APRA. In the 1985 election, Popular Action (AP) and the Popular Christian Party (PPC) obtained respectively only seven and eleven per cent of the vote — their worst ever results. These figures, claimed analysts, heralded the imminent disappearance of the traditional right-wing parties from the political scene.

In July 1987, however, President García gave the Right a new lease of life with his announcement of a plan to nationalise the banks. Led by novelist Mario Vargas Llosa and a group of friends and relatives, a 'meeting for freedom' was held in Lima's Plaza San Martín. For the first time in decades, *Limeños* were treated to the sight of elegantly dressed women and youths from the wealthy neighbourhoods of Miraflores and San Isidro taking part in a boisterous political demonstration. The traditional site for left-wing demonstrations, the Plaza San Martín was lined with Mercedes and BMWs belonging to people who seldom ventured into the Plaza or mingled with its resident population of street vendors, shoeshine boys, theatrical troupes, and working-class passers-by. Over the following months, this scene was repeated in Arequipa, Trujillo, Piura and other cities. These protests against García's ill-fated nationalisation policy resuscitated the Right from its post-Belaúnde decline and launched Vargas Llosa on his new career as one of Latin America's leading advocates of 'neo-liberal revolution'.

Literary Politics

Best known for his literary work, Mario Vargas Llosa has for decades occupied the singular position of Peru's transnational intellectual. The formal modernist language and aesthetic motifs of his early works carved an immediate place for Vargas Llosa in the international critical acclaim surrounding Latin America's literary 'boom' of the 1960s. From the vantage point of his home in Knightsbridge, London, Vargas Llosa began to acquire both the international fame and critical distance from Peru which informs all his later work. As the optimistic mood of the 1960s and its literary booms faded into the Thatcher-Reagan era of the 1980s, Vargas Llosa honed this critical distance to match with the political crusades of the 'neo-liberal revolution'. Leaving behind his earlier authorial perspective of the insider whose modernist language allows him to survey and explain the complexity of Peruvian culture and society, in later works such as *The War of the End of the World*, *The Real Life of Alejandro Mayta* and *The Storyteller*, Vargas Llosa

Mario Vargas Llosa campaigns in a Lima shanty town, May 1990. (Julio Etchart)

adopts an allegorical and moralising stance towards Peruvian society and history, attacking what he sees as 'fanaticisms' of the Left and Right.

Confusing the allegorical spirit of his novels with the realities of Peru, Vargas Llosa's speeches during the 1990 campaign painted a world divided between the dichotomies of communism and democracy, clientelistic tradition and capitalist modernity. 'We Peruvians', he proclaimed, will 'not let Alan García's APRA party become the Trojan Horse of communism.'

Since APRA's history of anti-communism and pro-capitalist reformism did not easily lend itself to such metaphors, Vargas Llosa looked elsewhere for the imagery with which to flesh out his version of a totalitarian menace. He found it in what he calls 'the vertical and totalitarian structure of the Inca Empire'. Disregarding volumes of archaeological and ethno-historical research on the extraordinary autonomy of local political and economic life in the Inca state, Vargas Llosa draws a portrait of savage totalitarianism with intended parallels for García's regime. 'The Inca', he writes, 'was the vortex towards which all the wills converged searching for inspiration and vitality, the axis around which the entire society was organised and upon which depended the life and death of every person... The individual had no importance and virtually no existence in that pyramidal and theocratic society whose achievements had always been collective.'

For Vargas Llosa, residues of this imagined past survive in the inscrutable practices and culture of the highland Andean peasants. In his first foray into Peruvian politics, Vargas Llosa was appointed by President Belaúnde to head a commission to investigate the killings of eight journalists in the Ayacucho peasant community of Uchuraccay in January 1983. Although initial evidence seemed to indicate that the peasants had killed the journalists, whom they mistook for *Senderistas*, other evidence pointed to possible army involvement in the incident. Overlooking the long history of peasant-state relations and military involvement in Ayacucho's dirty war, Vargas Llosa speculates in his final report that the terrified Indians not only acted out of ignorance of Peruvian laws, but were actually living in a time warp. For the novelist-politician, the Indians of Uchuraccay stood as poignant symbols of Peru's collective dilemma in converting 'backward' political traditions into a 'modern' democratic system. Unable to imagine a democracy which might incorporate the traditions of Peru's dark-skinned majority, Vargas Llosa laments that 'modernisation is possible only with the sacrifice of the Indian cultures'.

The novelist's allegorical language of race and modernity provided an emotional rallying point to replace the exhausted politics of Peru's dispirited Right. Unsuccessful in their age-old aim to exclude the majority, the land-owning and economic elites saw APRA, the Left and Sendero as the terrifying realisation of their worst racial fears. These political movements, together with the independent mass mobilisations and the increasingly visible dark-skinned migrant population of Lima, seemed to give substance to their colonial nightmare of Indian hordes waiting to descend on Lima. The brilliance of Vargas Llosa's political ascendancy lay in intellectualising and articulating the racialised class fears of Lima's elite.

Portrayed in the US press as a literary innocent abroad in the chaos of politics, Vargas Llosa was hardly the 'fish out of water' which he later claimed to be. As he told journalists in Lima in August 1989, 'I believe I have been doing politics for some time. My idea was that the way I would do politics would be writing, giving opinions, and only eventually participating in a more practical manner, although always on an intellectual terrain.' The decisive event which moved Vargas Llosa into 'more practical' politics was García's nationalisation speech. Returning from holiday at the beach, he wrote an editorial for Lima's *El Comercio*, entitled 'Towards a Totalitarian Peru', and a few days later, 'Opposing the Totalitarian Threat', a manifesto endorsed by hundreds of prominent right-wing politicians, intellectuals and businessmen. In both pieces, Vargas Llosa painted an alarmist portrait of the rabble-rousing APRA so long feared by Lima's elite and converted ominously into a totalitarian single-party state. 'The concentration of political and economic power in the party in power', he wrote in the manifesto, 'might well mean the end of freedom of expression and, eventually, of democracy.'

His views elicited a response that Vargas Llosa himself had not foreseen. Persuaded by friends and relatives to lead the 21 August 'meeting for freedom', he experienced the enthusiasm which his intervention aroused among Lima's 'forgotten' upper classes. The demonstration, the novelist later reflected, 'showed me that in spite of the profound inroads which decadence had made, the Peruvian people had some reserves which could be called upon to achieve a great transformation of the country.'

Two weeks later, Vargas Llosa met several prominent members of the Lima elite to found a 'new freedom movement' (*Libertad*) to give shape to the emotions raised by the anti-nationalisation rally. United by the bonds of kinship and class, this small group of professionals met — in the best traditions of Peru's 19th-century 'gentlemen's club' politics — to outline a project for bringing modernity to Peru. Their goal was to create a movement capable of replacing Peru's decrepit right-wing parties. 'Our programme', Vargas Llosa later wrote, would have 'nothing to do with the populism of Popular Action or the conservatism of the Christian Popular Party but would [instead] be associated with a radical liberalism never before put forward in Peru.' By avoiding the elitist stigma of the old Right, they hoped to win the support of an expanding informal sector for the liberal reforms which they believed would make Peru 'a prosperous modern country'.

In courting the informal sector, the *Libertad* movement combined Vargas Llosa's modernising rhetoric with the romantic fable of 'popular capitalism' promoted by Peru's leading neo-liberal intellectual, Hernando de Soto. Showing a remarkable readiness to work with all Peruvian presidents and presidential candidates, de Soto has promoted an ideological model of grassroots capitalism as the panacea for Peru's problems. For de Soto, the impoverished and desperate street vendors and artisans who line Lima's streets 'represent the new order which emerges spontaneously when men abandon the village — the tribal organisation — and go to the cities.' In his 1986 book, *The Other Path*, for which Vargas Llosa wrote the foreword, de Soto presents a scantily documented sociological portrait of Lima's faceless informal vendors and micro-entrepreneurs. On the basis of selected economic statistics and controversial analysis, *The Other Path* concludes that the entrepreneurial energies of Peru's poor have been frustrated by the ill-guided policies of an over-sized state. Peru's poor are poor, he concludes, because they have been constrained by bureaucratic paperwork, price controls, wage stabilisation and consumer subsidies.

'The informal sector': street tinsmith, Lima.
(Daniel Pajuelo/El Agustino/TAFOS/PANOS)

By rewriting both Peruvian history and the history of capitalism, Vargas Llosa and de Soto forged the sustaining myth for *Libertad's* neo-liberal political programme. Like the Thatcher and Reagan governments of the 1980s, the Peruvian neo-liberals called for restructuring the national economy to give free rein to market forces. They proposed shrinking the state sector in favour of private capital, opposed all wage controls and price subsidies, and advocated good debtor relations with the banks and multilateral lending organisations. Even before the rise of Vargas Llosa's neo-liberal crusade, these ideas had been promoted in Peru through the work of the Liberty and Democracy Institute (ILD). Founded by de Soto in 1980 and lavishly funded by US foundations, the ILD has developed proposals for streamlining state bureaucracy and facilitating paperwork and property registration. Although presented as a means to 'rationalise' the state, the ILD projects propose in reality to strengthen the power of non-elected cabinet members and technocrats at the expense of elected municipal and regional governments. Integral to these projects is the neo-liberal belief that the *informales* represent a spontaneous grassroots capitalism whose entrepreneurial energies are stifled by the state. In promoting the heroic image of the individualist entrepreneur or self-made capitalist, the ILD overlooks the popular organisations, unions and municipal governments which represent the interests of the *informales*. The 'revolution of the poor', Vargas Llosa explains in his foreword to *The Other Path*, 'is not Marxist but liberal in the classic sense of the word.'

The enthusiasm awoken by Vargas Llosa's *Libertad* movement revived the Right's hopes of capturing the presidency. Popular Action and the Popular Christian Party joined *Libertad* to create the Democratic Front, or FREDEMO, an electoral alliance with parliamentary and municipal slates and Mario Vargas Llosa as its presidential candidate. FREDEMO also provided a rallying-point for a previously apathetic upper class, which organised marches and demonstrations in support of Vargas Llosa's 'neo-liberal revolution'. Wealthy youths and women went to the poor neighbourhoods, where their maids and servants lived, to do social and charity work. With contributions from business, FREDEMO members created Solidarity Action. Headed by Vargas Llosa's wife, this programme promoted small construction projects, health care, soup kitchens and other public works.

Vargas Llosa's campaign allowed the Right to contest the political terrain which the Left had traditionally monopolised. FREDEMO's aid programmes provided a fragile electoral base in poor neighbourhoods, while the ILD and *Libertad* offered the intellectual authority to construct an ideological front. Along with their numerous publications, both the ILD and *Libertad* organised seminars and public meetings in which intellectuals discussed neo-liberal ideas. The culmination of this ideological campaign came in March 1989 with the 'Revolution in Freedom' seminar. Designed to promote Peruvian neo-liberalism as part of a wide-ranging global movement, the seminar brought together the luminaries of international neo-conservatism and discussed the economic 'shock' measures and privatisation policies necessary to transform Peru into a 'modern' economy. The seminar's lack of reference to the tremendous human cost of previous economic experiments in countries such as Chile, Brazil, Argentina, Bolivia and Poland, sealed the partnership between the new Peruvian Right and international neo-liberalism.

Challenging the Right

While FREDEMO turned for support to Europe and the US, other candidates looked towards Peru for alternatives to the traditional party structures. Chief among these was Alberto Fujimori whose *Cambio 90* (Change 1990) movement mobilised the emerging non-*criollo* elite. Formed as a non-partisan electoral movement, *Cambio 90* was a mix of micro-entrepreneurs, small businesspeople, lawyers, teachers, technicians and professionals such as agronomists and engineers.

Another important group in *Cambio 90* were protestant and evangelical leaders. As a political newcomer, Alberto Fujimori — who was himself an agronomist and former rector of the National Agrarian University — bound together these heterogeneous groups and interests around his populist appeal and personality rather than around a coherent political programme. Emphasising hard work, austerity, technical innovation and social responsibility, Fujimori's message differed from both the harsh economic platform of FREDEMO and the party-centred traditions of APRA and the Left. 'The path to true development for Peru must be exempt from partisan and ideological bombast', Fujimori told his followers, 'and instead promote technology.'

The *Cambio 90* congressional slate was made up of candidates with little or no previous political record and no ties to established political parties. As self-made professionals and entrepreneurs, their appeal to the voters lay in a straightforward message of progress through honest work and technology. A less explicit, but equally important aspect of the *Cambio 90* slate, however, was its ethnic and class origins. Most candidates were from provincial backgrounds. In striking contrast to the aristocratic FREDEMO slate, they were darker-skinned and mostly fell within the ambiguous Peruvian racial and ethnic category of *cholo*. Some, like Fujimori himself, were from Peru's Japanese community. Because of their traditional occupations as street-corner grocers and merchants, the Japanese Peruvians, or 'Niseis', were associated with hard work, small enterprise, and honesty.

These images paid off well for Fujimori. Despite predictions of a landslide victory for Vargas Llosa, the *Cambio 90* dark horse won a surprising 26.9 per cent of the vote in the April elections. Vargas Llosa obtained 35.1 per cent — far less than the 50 per cent required to take the presidency in the first round. Supported by the strength of political traditions and party structure, the APRA candidate, Luis Alva Castro, won an unexpected 14.8 per cent, despite the stigma of García's disastrous administration. In the worst performance in the Peruvian Left's electoral history, the divided slates of Pease (IU) and Barrantes (IS) obtained a meagre 6.8 and 4.3 per cent respectively. Although the Left did better in regional elections, its poor showing in the parliamentary and municipal elections seemed to confirm the voters' disapproval of its division and *caudillismo*.

The results gave a snapshot of the issues which would shape the second-round contest between Fujimori and Vargas Llosa. Despite their differences, APRA, Fujimori and the Left were united in rejecting the shock measures advocated by Vargas Llosa. The 52.8 per cent of the vote which went to their candidates expressed public support for an anti-shock platform. Shaken by the apparent decline in its hero's fortunes, the Right ignored this message and instead derided the popular vote by proclaiming that it was Peru, and not Vargas Llosa, which was the real loser in the election. The former mayor of Lima and leader of the PPC, Luís Bedoya Reyes, lamented that 'the Peruvian people are still too immature to decide on the basis of political proposals rather than [the personal qualities of] the candidates.'

Voters were also alienated by the extravagant costs of FREDEMO's political campaign. Vargas Llosa had spent over US$12 million on television commercials; the total bill for his first-round campaign came to over US$40 million. FREDEMO's parliamentary candidates also had large sums to spend. One senatorial candidate, for example, paid over US$400,000 for television advertisements. Public distaste for FREDEMO's lavish spending and US-style media campaigning in a country racked with poverty and unemployment was widespread. The Peruvian Council of Bishops issued a pronouncement condemning the expenditure as immoral and undemocratic. The stage was set for the second round.

Chinitos, Cholitos y Blanquitos

The second-round run-off between Fujimori and Vargas Llosa was scheduled for 9 June. In preceding weeks, Peruvian voters watched the two candidates tailor their images and platforms to correct the weaknesses of their first-round campaigns.

Recognising the dubious appeal of economic shock measures to an already impoverished electorate, Vargas Llosa, acting on the advice of Mark Malloch Brown, his new British campaign consultant, adopted a populist approach. He made daily visits to Lima's *pueblos jóvenes*, where he inaugurated soccer and basketball fields, drinking-water facilities and medical dispensaries. In implicit recognition of his programmes's unpopularity, he promised to create a privately funded Social Assistance Programme (PAS) to temper the harshness of economic 'shock treatment'. In a much-repeated TV commercial, Vargas Llosa promised 20,000 social programmes and public works in *pueblos jóvenes* with the US$1.5 billion he claimed to have secured from South Korea, Japan, Canada and the US.

Vargas Llosa's sudden concern for the poor, however, did not convince everybody. FREDEMO's campaign 'is nourished by patronage [*asistencialismo*] which tries to buy the people's conscience', commented a street vendors' leader in Lima. Public scepticism peaked when it was revealed that at least one of Vargas Llosa's costly TV commercials had been filmed, not in a *pueblo joven*, but rather in a 'shanty town' which had been set up in his own garden. The roles of

FREDEMO-supporting shanty-town residents had been played by the maids and chauffeurs of his relatives and friends.

Combining his populist appeal with the technological promises of *Cambio 90*'s original campaign, Fujimori made his second round campaign appearances wearing jeans and driving his tractor or 'Fujimobile'. Greeted as *'el Chino'* (the Chinaman) by enthusiastic crowds, Fujimori's problem was in many ways the opposite of his opponent's; while Vargas Llosa needed to soften his economic programme, Fujimori needed a programme to go with his already popular image. With this aim in mind, Fujimori called in a team of seven well-known specialists and academics known for their opposition to Vargas Llosa's proposed privatisation plans, as well as to the shock treatments and austerity programmes favoured by the IMF and FREDEMO. Christened 'The Seven Samurais' in the press, these independent advisers put together an economic programme based on non-recessionary anti-inflation measures, state control of strategic resources, maintenance and improvement of social services, job stability, renegotiation of Peru's substantial foreign debt with the IMF, and incentives for the informal sector, micro-entrepreneurs and small industry. In opposition to Vargas Llosa's promise to fight terrorism through harsher judicial processes and increased militarisation, Fujimori pledged not to 'respond to violence with violence', but rather to fight Sendero by 'eliminating the poverty which breeds and sustains terrorism.' Finally, he proposed to confront narcotics production through local development projects and crop substitution to offer coca farmers alternative crops.

The Holy War

Religion played an unexpectedly important role in the second round of the 1990 presidential elections. The fear generated in the upper classes by the spectre of a 'Japanese president' was worsened by the influence in *Cambio 90* of evangelical and protestant leaders. In the preceding decade, evangelical protestantism had made great inroads in Peru, particularly among the poor migrant and rural populations. The role of evangelical and protestant leaders in *Cambio 90* was an unwelcome reminder of the advances which Peru's poor majority had made in politics; it also reflected the challenge to the once monolithic power of the Catholic Church.

Described in the Lima press as the 'Holy War', the conservative Catholic campaign to discredit Fujimori began in the final days of the first round campaign, when the Archbishop of Lima dusted off a long-forgotten statue of the Virgin Mary. In her first public appearance since 1740, the Virgin Dolorosa de la Merced (who in colonial times had protected Lima from tidal waves, pirates and mob lootings) was taken in procession through the streets of the capital. Her once miraculous powers, however, could not 'protect' Lima from the *tsunami* of Fujimori. Two days after the first round elections, the Archbishop made a secret early morning visit to Vargas Llosa's house. Revelation of his visit were followed by anonymous TV commercials proclaiming 'Peru: A Catholic Country', fliers insulting the Virgin Mary, and an unprecedented defence of Peru's Catholic traditions by the avowedly agnostic FREDEMO candidate. On several occasions, both Vargas Llosa and the Archbishop publicly questioned the legitimacy, and even the 'Christianity' of the protestant sects whom they described as 'minority' and 'fanatical'. Extraordinary processions of miraculous Christ figures and Virgin Marys were organised in different cities across Peru. Most notable were the *ad hoc* processions of Arequipa's renowned Virgin of Chapi, and Lima's national patron image, the Christ of the Miracles. In an even more unusual and symbolic gesture, the Christ of the Miracles was accompanied in his procession by the oldest Marian image in Peru, the Virgin of the Evangelisation.

This manipulation of religious symbols and images for political purposes was opposed by Peru's progressive bishops and a large number of Catholics. Three thousand prominent Catholics sent the Pope a letter protesting at the Peruvian Church's attempt to 'induce Peruvian clergy and believers [to vote] against a particular candidate'.

As election day drew near, rumours began to circulate in the prosperous Lima neighbourhoods of Miraflores and San Isidro of a surefire way of stopping Fujimori. Anonymous phone calls advised residents to cut up a photograph of the *Cambio 90* candidate into small pieces, place the pieces in a glass of water and put it in the freezer. Seemingly incapable of finding a more coherent response to Fujimori's rising popularity in the opinion polls, the supporters of Vargas Llosa's crusade for modernity turned to magic to 'freeze' Fujimori's advance. Since *Cambio 90*'s surprising performance in the first round, upper-class Peruvians had succumbed to their centuries-long fear of the dark-skinned majority rejecting the very idea of a 'Japanese' president. The day after the first-round elections, young FREDEMO supporters demonstrating in front of Vargas Llosa's house, expressed their dislike of Fujimori in racial terms. In the following weeks, racially motivated incidents against Peruvians of Japanese and Chinese descent increased dramatically, particularly in Lima's upper-class neighbourhoods. Stirred by memories of anti-Japanese mobs during World War II, the Peruvian-Japanese Association issued a communiqué expressing concern over the new wave of racism.

Magic and racial intimidation were not enough to stop the *tsunami*. Fujimori won the presidency in the June run-off poll with 57 per cent of the vote. The former front-runner from FREDEMO won only 33.5 per cent and a majority in just one of Peru's 25 departments. (Void and blank votes accounted for the remaining 9.5 per cent.) With the backing of APRA and the Left, Fujimori won clear majorities in the traditionally left-voting southern departments and in APRA's 'solid north'. The closest race was in Lima, where Vargas Llosa won 42.9 per cent and Fujimori 51.9 per cent. The spread increased dramatically, however, in Peru's highland provinces. While in the coastal departments Vargas Llosa took 31.4 per cent, in the poorest and predominantly peasant highland provinces of Cusco, Huancavelica, Ayacucho, Apurímac and Puno he won a mere 14 per cent. There, as in Lima, Peru's poor turned to Fujimori in the belief that his government would fend off the shock measures and privatisation policies openly championed by FREDEMO and Vargas Llosa.

Changing Sides

Vargas Llosa greeted the news of his defeat with the simple words recorded later by his son: 'I feel sorry for Peru'. For the disillusioned novelist, the result was just one more sign of Peru's collective political and cultural immaturity. Unable to accept the voters' rejection of his proposals for austerity, Vargas Llosa would later claim that 'Peruvians did not vote for ideas', but rather 'out of some mysterious impulse'.

Reflecting on his brief political career, Vargas Llosa assured his followers in conceding defeat that 'the seeds that we have sown together during these two and a half years will continue to germinate and finally produce those fruits that we desire for Peru: the fruits of modernity, justice, prosperity, peace and liberty.'

The fruits of Vargas Llosa's ideas were soon to appear, however, in unexpected quarters. Within a week of the elections, Fujimori called for 'national unity' and announced his intention to form a multi-party cabinet representing all political forces and socio-economic groups. The proposal was cautiously supported by labour and peasant organisations. Having created widespread expectations of a broad-based government, Fujimori then announced that he would travel as president-elect to Japan and the US to initiate discussions with Washington and the IMF. Leaving behind the economic team which had advised his campaign, Fujimori unexpectedly took along as advisers Hernando de Soto and Abel Salinas. Having had his proposals for neo-liberal reform rejected at the polls, de Soto, who was well-connected in Washington, had swiftly moved from the defeated

FREDEMO to *Cambio 90*. As Alan García's former Economy Minister, Salinas, best known for the hyperinflation of 1988, was even less popular with the voters. This unlikely triumvirate would be joined in the US by Carlos Rodríguez Pastor, former Economy Minister in Belaúnde's second term and at the time vice-president of one of Peru's principal creditors, the Wells Fargo Bank.

Fujimori's trip to the US and Japan marked the beginning of a dramatic conversion to the very economic policies against which he had campaigned. One by one, with mounting evidence of Fujimori's U turn, his economic advisers began to resign. The day before he left the country, he suggested that 'drastic measures' might be required to control inflation and that US military aid might prove helpful in fighting drug trafficking. The president-elect's unexpected drift towards the language of neo-liberalism was welcomed by *Libertad* as a salutary convergence between *Cambio 90* and FREDEMO's original economic platform. Alluding to the defeated novelist's prophetic final speech, the right-wing *Expreso* newspaper assured its readers that 'the seed sown by Vargas Llosa has begun to sprout'.

Fujimori returned from abroad a changed, albeit empty-handed, man. Denied the aid he had hoped to obtain from Japan and the US, and convinced of the necessity of toeing the IMF line, he reaffirmed the need for 'drastic economic readjustment' and acknowledged that it would be difficult to honour his election promises. In what resembled FREDEMO's plan for a drastic 12-month anti-inflationary shock period, the president-elect announced measures to reduce inflation to ten per cent in the first 15 to 18 months of his government. He also traded his populist campaign style for a new image. Closing the central Lima headquarters where he had personally received delegations and requests from Lima's poor, Fujimori went to live in the *Círculo Militar*, a high-security recreational complex reserved for military officers. Closeted there, Fujimori consulted with a new team of advisers made up of prominent former ministers and technocrats known for their connections to international banking and multilateral lending agencies.

On 18 July, ten days before his inauguration, Fujimori emerged from a three-hour meeting with his advisers to announce the formation of his first ministerial cabinet. Heading it was the Economy Minister, Juan Carlos Hurtado Miller, Belaúnde's former Minister of Agriculture, and a prominent member of the Popular Action party. Honouring his pledge to form a multi-party cabinet, Fujimori also named Carlos Amat y León and Fernando Sánchez Albavera from the Socialist Left as Ministers of Agriculture and Mining and Energy, and Gloria Helfner, from the Movement of Socialist Affirmation as Minister of Education. The remaining cabinet posts were filled by *Cambio 90* members, Fujimori's personal associates, and technocrats with no party affiliation but with clear neo-liberal sympathies. The most controversial appointment was that of Augusto Antoniolli as Minister of Justice. An unlikely candidate for the highest office in the judiciary, Antoniolli had acquired an unsavoury reputation as an analyst of left-wing and union activities for the Peruvian intelligence service.

Antoniolli's appointment was attributed in the Peruvian press to the influence of Vladimiro Montesinos. Montesinos, a lawyer, had defended Fujimori against accusations of fraudulent real estate dealings during the presidential campaign. The paperwork for the case was mysteriously lost in the Ministry of Justice and the charges eventually dropped. Nicknamed 'the Peruvian Rasputin', Montesinos is a former army officer and intelligence operative, who was imprisoned in 1976 as a 'national security risk' because of his close personal ties to Washington and the CIA. Having gained a law degree through correspondence courses while in prison, Montesinos later won notoriety as the defence attorney for the police officers accused of involvement in the 1985 Villa Coca drug-trafficking case. Montesinos next worked his way into Fujimori's government, where as deputy director of the National Intelligence Service (SIN), he purged the police officers who had been involved in the investigation of the Villa Coca case. Montesinos became a key figure in Fujimori's deepening involvement with the military.

By the time of Fujimori's inauguration on 28 July 1990, public enthusiasm for the upstart president of *Cambio 90* had largely vanished. Trade unions, peasant organisations and the Left anticipated Fujimori's first acts in office with proclamations condemning the forthcoming shock measures. When he finally announced his first economic package, on 9 August, Peruvians were braced for the reverberations of the 'Fujishock'.

The Fujishock

The measures of August 1990 proved an ominous start for Hurtado Miller and the first Fujimori cabinet. Implemented as the cornerstone of the 'macro-economic stabilisation' programme required by the IMF, they were the precondition for Peru's 'reinsertion' into the international financial community following Alan García's strained relations with the multilateral lending organisations. The next step in the IMF strategy was 'structural adjustment' through liberalisation of the economy, privatisation of state-held enterprises, and reduction of tariff barriers. Peru would also be required to pay US$2.1 billion in arrears to the World Bank and IMF.

Alberto Fujimori, May 1990. (Julio Etchart)

The social cost of the anti-inflationary measures and debt servicing soon eroded Fujimori's credibility. By February 1991, only 31 per cent of Peruvians approved of his administration. Despite Hurtado Miller's repeated promises to stop inflation completely, his programme had instead failed either to reduce it significantly or to reactivate the economy. Inflation in January 1991 reached 24 per cent. By February, real wages were worth only a third of what they had been when Fujimori took office. Exports had stagnated and the industrial recession continued unabated. A majority of Peruvians were living in absolute poverty, and only eight per cent of the adult population was fully employed. Ninety-five per cent of Peruvian workers earned less than the minimum legal wage, lacked social security and worked less than four hours a day. Faced with the failure of his stabilisation programme, Hurtado Miller resigned as Economy Minister in February 1991.

The new Economy Minister, Carlos Boloña, both stepped up the pace of the adjustment process and forestalled public disappointment by promising to slow down inflation rather than stop it altogether. At the time of his cabinet appointment, Boloña, an Oxford graduate, was Director of Economics at Hernando de Soto's ILD. More importantly, he was also well connected with the same multilateral lending institutions that had had difficulties with Hurtado Miller. In Belaúnde's cabinet, he had developed a close working relationship with Carlos Rodríguez Pastor, the then Economy Minister and now Fujimori's link with the international financial community. With the liberalisation of the economy as his main goal, Boloña now set out a programme to transform Peru's productive structure, consolidate 'economic stabilisation' and boost production. These objectives were to be reached by reducing tariffs, slashing ministerial budgets and privatising state-owned enterprises. Most importantly, Boloña proposed to open such strategic areas of the economy as mining, agriculture, and banking and securities to foreign capital. With respect to the debt, he endorsed Hurtado Miller's policy of honouring interest and arrears payments to the multilaterals, regardless of the social cost. Like other neo-liberal technocrats, Boloña approached the task of economic 'readjustment' as a purely technical problem, far removed from the unpalatable realities of hunger, unemployment and malnutrition.

Boloña's plan had a temporary effect on inflation, which fell from 17.8 per cent in February to 5.8 per cent in April, climbing again to 9.3 per cent in June. His image was enhanced by accumulated inflation for the six-month period between January and June 1991 of only 62 per cent. (Total accumulated inflation for the ten months since the Fujishock was 1,381 per cent.) Boloña also succeeded in making strides towards 'reinsertion'. The Inter-American Development Bank approved credit for road construction, Japan pledged an additional US$400 million for debt relief, and the US promised US$60 million in aid as part of a proposed anti-narcotics agreement.

The 'social indicators', however, fared less well. One month after Boloña's anti-inflationary success in April, thirty per cent of the students registered for the 1991 school year (which began in April) had dropped out. According to a spokesperson for the teachers' union, SUTEP, this decline in attendance — which SUTEP correctly forecast would increase to over fifty per cent by the end of the year — was due to malnourishment and to children leaving school to supplement dwindling family incomes. More than 10,000 schoolteachers had left teaching due to salary constraints imposed by Boloña's ministerial budget cuts. A similar situation prevailed in Peru's public sector, where over 50,000 employees in ministries and para-statals handed in 'voluntary resignations'. Following a three-month strike of public health workers, 3,500 out of 5,000 trained public-sector nurses left their jobs to accept work offers in Spain, Italy and Brazil.

Industrialists and businessmen were initially critical of Boloña's handling of the economy. The National Society of Industries (SNI) predicted that the recession would force the dismissal of over 100,000 workers. It also feared the effects of increasing imports of basic consumer and manufactured goods, following Boloña's drastically reduced tariffs. Salvador Majluf, a prominent businessman and president of the SNI, correctly warned that such policies would generate recession and widespread unemployment.

The centrepiece of Boloña's new economic programme, however, were his proposals for structural adjustment through privatisation and liberalisation. On 13 March, Fujimori's Labour Ministry issued a decree enabling employers to fire striking workers. Other decrees eliminated job security and curtailed collective bargaining. In late March, Fujimori announced Executive Decree 009-91, later christened the 'counter-agrarian reform', which liberalised Peru's land market by allowing peasant community members and cooperatives to sell or rent their landholdings to third parties. Denounced by the CCP as a 'neo-liberal offensive... against the victories of poor peasants, tenant farmers and rural cooperatives', the Decree effectively paved the way for new large landholdings and the re-emergence of a private agro-export sector. This was followed in April by a new banking law, deregulating interest rates, opening banking to foreign investment, and eliminating subsidised development banks such as the Agrarian Bank and Industrial Bank with ties to specific sectors of the economy.

In June, Mining Minister Sánchez Albavera announced the sale of state-owned mining companies, allowing private investors to become majority shareholders. He also declared that Petroperu's monopoly on refining and distribution of petroleum products would be removed. A few weeks later, the government announced the privatisation of the state-owned airline, the national railway system and the ports.

The effects of privatisation were immediate. Speculation inspired by the new banking law drove prime interest rates up to 22 per cent per month. The scrapping of the national development banks caused widespread bankruptcies in small and medium-sized businesses. The disappearance of agrarian credit programmes sponsored by the national Agrarian Bank severely cut food production for the internal market. In the Huallaga Valley, land planted with credit assistance plummeted from 106,000 hectares in 1989 to 6,000 hectares in 1991. With no alternative sources of credit, farmers in that area have been forced to turn from rice and corn to growing coca for the narcotics market (see chapter 6).

The beneficiaries of Boloña's economic programmes were primarily foreign, and particularly US businesses which have benefited from expanding investment opportunities and low tariffs. A second sector to profit from the new reforms were Peru's monopolistic 'power groups', whose diversified financial and investment portfolios and links with foreign finance have given them advantages in the liberalised economy. Finally, the IMF, World Bank and other international agencies welcomed Peru's US$50 million in monthly payments, as did the transnational technocracy of advisers and 'specialists' who patch together deals between such lending institutions and the debtor countries. This technocracy was well represented among the advisers such as de Soto, Rodríguez Pastor and Boloña himself who negotiated Peru's 'reinsertion' into the international financial community. Signed in January 1991, the Reference Programme defining the terms of Peru's 'reinsertion' included none of the socio-economic relief loans and assistance which are customarily offered by the multilaterals as an antidote to the human cost of economic 'shock treatment'. Nor does the Programme stipulate when, if ever, renewed loans shall be forthcoming in return for debt servicing and economic restructuring.

The consequences of Boloña's and Fujimori's programme led inevitably to a wave of strikes and demonstrations beginning in January 1991 and keeping pace with the government's neo-liberal reform programme. In response to cuts in the Social Emergency Programme, women from Lima's 9,000 local *Vaso de Leche* committees demanded increased funding and direct, autonomous management for the municipal *Vaso de Leche* organisation. When the women marched to Congress on 15 January, they were dispersed with tear gas and water cannons. Two weeks later, they rallied again to take over Lima's city hall, forcing the government to sign an agreement to consider their proposals.

Fujimori also faced opposition to his Lima-centred policies, in particular a freeze on transfers of public enterprises to regional governments and delays in creating regional development banks. In the southern highlands, the new economic reforms cut off credit to peasants and small producers who had already been hard hit by droughts. In the north-east jungle region of Loreto, the government had ignored both environmental and regional interests by granting oil exploration rights in the National Pacaya-Samiria Reserve to the Texas Crude Exploration Company. Moved by long-standing antipathy towards Lima's centralisation of power, as well as by environmental and economic concerns, broad-based social and political movements organised a series of regional strikes and demonstrations. In Loreto, a defence front made up of environmentalists, indigenous organisations and a spectrum of political parties, led demonstrations and a regional strike. Other regional strikes were mounted in Cusco, Arequipa, Huancayo, and the southern José Carlos Mariátegui Region (comprising the departments of Puno, Tacna and Maquegua). In all cases, the strikers linked local demands with a broader political challenge to Fujimori's neo-liberal programme. The strikes highlighted the extent to which Fujimori had reneged on his electoral promise to promote decentralisation and autonomous regional development.

The Interunion Confederation of State Workers (CITE) and workers in public enterprises also protested against Fujimori's plans to cut payrolls and privatise state-controlled enterprises in energy, oil and mining. Mounting discontent climaxed in early June with a national call for a *Jornada Cívica* (Civic Day of Struggle) in support of prolonged strikes by health workers and teachers, and in opposition to the controversial anti-narcotics agreement between Peru and the US (see chapter 6).

The marches and strikes met with violence from the security forces and won only symbolic concessions. Several people were killed and hundreds imprisoned during the unrest, while some peasant leaders and teachers' union representatives were 'disappeared' by the army. When the government did agree to talks with the protest movements, it made vague promises which it later refused to honour. Faced with the new anti-strike legislation, increased repression and frustration at the government's unwillingness to consider even minimal demands, the popular movement began to lose momentum. When a national strike was called by labour confederations in July 1991, it failed to take hold.

The popular movement's waning energies were a victory not only for Fujimori's government but also for Sendero Luminoso, which had infiltrated marches and demonstrations in an attempt to provoke confrontation with the police and the military. Sendero sympathisers accused political and grassroots leaders of 'restraining the energies of the masses' and called for their overthrow. Several such leaders were killed by *Senderistas*.

In the aftermath of an exhausting and unproductive six-month process of anti-government activity, the popular movement was left in disarray. As it surveyed the new political landscape of Fujimori's regime, it found itself faced with three alternatives: an authoritarian and unresponsive government unable or unwilling to provide the most basic services; a traditional left-wing and union leadership, discredited by the failures of recent struggles and by its inability to offer a convincing alternative programme; and a violently authoritarian, but well-organised and effective Sendero Luminoso. As people took stock of their new situation, some began to reconsider Sendero's argument that fighting for specific goals was in itself pointless unless geared also towards the ultimate goal of seizing political power. A majority, however, simply returned to the individual struggles of a daily life which has become even more demanding under the new economic regime. In the lull left by this last wave of popular mobilisation, Sendero's objective of polarising social forces has come another step closer.

Between Friedman and the Führer

Emboldened by the opposition's temporary retreat, in November 1991 Fujimori presented Congress with a package of 126 decrees for the reorganisation of the state and economy. The package, providing for total privatisation of the economy and further escalation of the war against Sendero, became known in Peru as the *decretos-bomba* ('decrees-bomb') for its explosively controversial nature. As political and constitutional analysts observed, the decrees would lift remaining controls on foreign investment, grant almost unlimited powers to the military and intelligence services, and greatly enhance the power of the executive branch. The radical nature of the proposed reforms led the conservative magazine, *Caretas*, to describe Fujimori as caught 'between [Milton] Friedman and the Führer.'

Fujimori's autocratic tendencies were already the subject of speculation; his quick temper and arrogance had earned him the popular sobriquet of 'the Emperor'. Since taking office, his relations with Congress had been extremely tense and often confrontational. Having built his electoral campaign around the image of a political independent, Fujimori had used his inaugural address to rail against Peru's 'professional politicians' and 'corrupt institutions'. On other occasions, he called Peruvian judges 'jackals'. When Congress baulked at his proposed anti-narcotics policies, he accused it of bowing to the 'drug-traffickers' lobby'.

Despite Fujimori's hostility, Congress had in fact cooperated with him on many occasions. The Right saw him as a means to carry out a neo-liberal economic programme. APRA kept its distance from the president, but cooperated with *Cambio 90* representatives in Congress to smooth over the allegations of corruption and mismanagement levelled against Alan García and his former functionaries. The Left was split in its attitude towards the new government. While the IS and parts of the IU had accepted cabinet positions in order to support what they initially viewed as a 'weak government', others including PUM and Patria Roja had maintained a critical distance from the beginning. In exchange for *Cambio 90*'s support in the November 1990 vote absolving García of responsibility for the 1986 prison massacre, APRA had backed *Cambio 90* delegates for the positions of speaker in both chambers. One month later, APRA and FREDEMO representatives joined *Cambio 90* in approving the promotions of General José Valdivia Dueñas — responsible for the killings of more than thirty peasants in Cayara in 1988 — and General Jorge Rabanal Portilla — who led the military forces which stormed the prisons in June 1986.

In late May 1991, in a further gesture of cooperation, Congress granted Fujimori the extraordinary legislative powers which he later used to promulgate the controversial *decretos-bomba*. The special powers, which were opposed by left-wing representatives to Congress, stipulated three areas in which the president could act: national pacification, employment law, and promotion of private investment. Fujimori made use of the special powers to propose a new social order, described by Economy Minister Boloña as 'economic growth with law and order'. Inspired by the models of the south-east Asian 'tigers' of Thailand, Malaysia, Singapore, South Korea and Taiwan, more than seventy decrees relating to economic reform eliminated all barriers to foreign investment, dismantled the entire state sector and privatised public and social services including education, social security, health care, water and electricity. All restrictions on exports of capital and profits by foreign companies and multinationals were removed, as were such basic labour rights as the eight-hour working day and job security.

Along with the so-called 'savage capitalism' of the south-east Asian tigers, the decree package also adopted many of their authoritarian structures. Snubbing Peru's fledgling regional governments, the decrees called for the centralisation of the newly-formed regional development banks into a single, Lima-based development bank. All international development aid and NGOs were placed under direct government control. Fujimori also proposed to expand greatly the powers of military commanders in the emergency zones and the system of national intelligence. The armed forces were given the authority to establish educational and development programmes in the emergency zones. Citizens would be obliged, on pain of imprisonment, to provide information and support to any military personnel engaged in counter-insurgency operations. Journalists would be liable to terms of five to ten years in prison for publishing information on activities described as 'secret' by the military or intelligence service. In addition, Peruvian citizens would be subject to charges of treason if they published information in the foreign press critical of the Peruvian military's counter-insurgency campaign.

At the centre of Fujimori's proposals was a decree creating a military-dominated 'Unified Pacification Command' (CUP), to be headed by the president, who would have powers to appoint the commanders-in-chief of the three branches of the armed forces and other top-ranking security personnel. By granting Fujimori the authority to make top military appointments, the decrees proposed to override the traditional system of promotions by rank and seniority and to eliminate Congress' role in approving military promotions. Drastically extending the executive's powers, this provision would have created an alarming concentration of power among those closest to the president and his inner circle of military and civilian advisers.

The *decretos-bomba* took Congress by surprise. Issued just two days before Fujimori's special legislative powers were due to expire, and a month before the annual congressional recess, the decrees were designed to provoke further friction in the already divided legislature. The right-wing *Libertad*, PPC and AP supported them; APRA expressed concern over their constitutionality; The Left rejected them on the grounds that they worsened the militarisation and polarisation of Peruvian society. Unable to overcome its differences in the short period left by Fujimori, Congress called an extraordinary legislative session in January 1992 to debate the decrees. The session approved a majority of the economic decrees with only minor revisions, but the decrees regarding state centralisation and the military's increased role were either amended or rejected.

Unwilling to accept even minor modifications, Fujimori reacted angrily and over the next few months launched a series of confrontations, refusing to sign a compromise budget negotiated between Congress and his own Economy Minister, and repeatedly vetoing congressional nominations to the supreme court. APRA, and especially Alan García, were particular targets and scapegoats, since García and other *Aprista* senators and deputies had played highly visible roles in the congressional debates over the budget and implementation of economic reforms.

Fujimori was also antagonistic towards the legislature because of recent congressional investigations into the military's human rights record and charges of corruption against his own administration. In separate investigations, Congress and independent human rights organisations had identified the recently-promoted General Valdivia as responsible for the 1988 Cayara massacre. Valdivia's case was further complicated for Fujimori by investigations into the Justice Ministry's unsuccessful attempts to prosecute the general. Responsibility for the mysterious disappearance of the relevant paperwork was credited to none other than Vladimiro Montesinos, who had also 'disappeared' the evidence for an earlier investigation into Fujimori's real estate dealings.

An inquiry with even more direct repercussions for Fujimori was the congressional investigation into a scandal involving the president's family. Less than two weeks before the coup, Fujimori's wife, Susana, had alleged that the president's brother, sister and sister-in-law had stolen and resold clothes donated by the Japanese government for distribution to the poor. This accusation followed new revelations regarding the nature and extent of the president's brother's role in the government, where he enjoyed unprecedented power in controlling access to the president, channelling foreign aid donations and approving contracts for lucrative public works projects.

A final blow for the administration came in late March, when Fujimori's already notorious personal adviser, Vladimiro Montesinos was accused of using his contacts to place Fujimori loyalists in important positions in the armed forces, intelligence service and Justice Ministry as a prelude to the planned CUP. Nor was Fujimori's association with the intelligence community restricted to Montesinos. As Fujimori's popularity had risen during the first round of the 1990 presidential campaign, President García, who saw him as the best means to divert votes from Vargas Llosa, had arranged for the National Intelligence Service to provide opinion polls and political advice to *Cambio 90*'s 'politically independent' candidate.

A Coup Foretold

On the evening of 5 April 1992, the owners of Peru's main television networks were telephoned and told that President Fujimori wished to talk to them. Arriving at the presidential palace in Lima's Plaza de Armas, the men were surprised to find that the president was not at home. To talk to him, they were told, they would have to go to the Ministry of Defence, known in Lima as the *Pentagonito* ('little Pentagon'). There, they met Fujimori, his Foreign Minister Augusto Blacker Miller, and the commanders-in-chief of the army, navy and air force, who asked them to broadcast an important pre-recorded 'message to the nation'.

In the message, President Fujimori announced the establishment of an 'emergency government of national reconstruction'. Blaming 'chaos and corruption' and 'lack of identification with great national interests', he said that he was dissolving Congress and reorganising the judicial branch and general accounting office. The parliament's 'ineffectiveness and the judiciary's corruption' had been compounded, the president explained, 'by the obstructionist attitude and covert plans of certain party leaders' against his government's economic measures. Parliament, moreover, had 'displayed weakness and inconsistency' in its efforts against drug-trafficking and terrorism. Fujimori also stated that he was disbanding Peru's twelve regional governments and suspending all articles of the constitution that were not 'compatible with the government's goals'. He concluded his message by announcing that he had ordered the armed forces and national police to enforce the measures.

The joint chiefs of staff wasted no time in showing their support. Tanks encircled the Congress building and the Justice Ministry, and troops and police arrested several congressional leaders and placed others under house arrest. When police arrived at Alan García's home, the former president had already escaped. Military forces occupied newspaper and magazine offices. The media were permitted only to publish the official text of Fujimori's speech and the joint chiefs' communiqué. Journalists were instructed to avoid using the word *golpe* or coup, in their headlines. Security forces also visited radio stations which had begun to broadcast interviews and talk shows opposed to the president's *autogolpe*.

Both the substance and tenor of Fujimori's 5 April message, as well as the cast of characters involved, make it clear that the *autogolpe* was not a last-minute decision. All the basic elements of Fujimori's 'government of national reconstruction' had been spelled out in the *decretos-bomba* the previous November. In a *New York Times* interview a week after the coup, a retired US officer with close ties to the Peruvian military confirmed that the coup 'had been discussed for at least six months.' The original plan was devised within Fujimori's inner circle of military and civilian associates and advisers. Principal among these was the ubiquitous Vladimiro Montesinos, who mediated between the presidential palace and Fujimori's allies in the upper echelons of the armed forces. Other important figures in planning and execution of the coup were General Luís Salazar Monroe, his brother General Julio Salazar Monroe, Chief of the National Intelligence Service, General José Valdivia Dueñas, Chief of the General Staff, and General Nicolás de Bari Hermoza, chairman of the Joint Chiefs of Staff. Those sectors of the military, in particular within the navy and air force, who were reluctant to support the coup eventually agreed to cooperate either as a matter of obedience to Fujimori, in his capacity as commander-in-chief of the armed forces, or out of fear of Montesinos' considerable power and influence.

In the days following the presidential message, Peruvians considered the implications of Fujimori's dismantling of the country's democratic institutions. Unions, regional governments, intellectuals, NGOs and church organisations all issued strong statements of opposition. In an unprecedented display of unity, all Peru's ideologically diverse political parties, including some members of *Cambio 90*, denounced the *autogolpe*. Fujimori's own Prime Minister, Alfonso de los Heros, resigned, along with high-ranking officials in the judiciary and other branches of the national government. Locked out of their offices in the Congress building, senators and deputies met in emergency sessions to condemn the president's unconstitutional move. Declaring Fujimori's presidency illegitimate, parliamentarians used their constitutional mandate to elect Vice-President Máximo San Román as president.

While the vast majority of political leaders opposed the coup, influential sectors of Peru's business and industrial community began to rally behind the new 'government of national reconstruction'. Both the National Confederation of Business Institutions of Peru (CONFIEP) and the Exporters' Association (ADEX) came out in support of Fujimori. Jorge Camet, the acting president of CONFIEP and long time associate of Fujimori, was later named Minister of Industry and Commerce. Fujimori also received the tacit support of the large television networks. In the first days after the coup, television cameras followed him on his well-publicised walks through Lima's downtown area to film him being congratulated by enthusiastic crowds. In the following weeks, news programmes devoted extensive coverage to his new populist image, showing almost daily visits to schools, orphanages, hospitals, universities and *pueblos jóvenes*, where he gave away computers, clothes, medicine, and, in one dramatic appearance, amnesty to a prisoner in a juvenile detention centre. Along with the distribution of goods, Fujimori would make quick speeches asking the recipients of his gifts whether they approved of his attempts to fight corruption, inefficiency, terrorism and drug-trafficking. The people invariably answered 'yes'.

Populist rhetoric also lay behind the public opinion polls that followed the coup. When asked whether they supported Fujimori's extraordinary measures, over seventy per cent of interviewees responded positively. Ninety-five per cent agreed that there was a need to reorganise the judiciary, and over eighty per cent agreed with the decision to dissolve Congress. Over the next few weeks, Peruvians were subjected to an avalanche of opinion polls, most purporting to demonstrate massive public backing for Fujimori's coup. Most were simple 'yes or no' polls, suggesting widespread support. More sophisticated polls, however, revealed other attitudes. One poll in May showed that only 47.2 per cent of those asked believed that they were living in a democracy. When asked whether they would prefer to live in a democracy or dictatorship, only 10.9 per cent favoured a dictatorship, and 73.1 per cent a democracy. Only 55 per cent believed that Fujimori would honour his promise to restore democracy within a year, whereas nearly 30 per cent did not believe the president would keep his word.

What the polls clearly revealed was the potency of Fujimori's 'anti-political' and 'anti-establishment' stance. For people exhausted by ten years of unrelenting violence, chronic unemployment, escalating inflation and a near-total collapse of public services, democratic ideals may be secondary to more immediate problems. For a public desperate for any solution to the violence of Sendero Luminoso, Fujimori's claims that Congress and the judiciary had to be overhauled in order to fight terrorism more effectively appeared reasonable. While pointing to the drop in inflation which accompanied his neo-liberal reforms, Fujimori could explain that its benefits were not yet felt by the 12 million impoverished Peruvians because of an incompetent *'partidocracía'* ('partyocracy'). It was the corrupt and self-serving political parties, he claimed, which had fostered an inefficient government, obstructed his economic reforms and prevented Peru from becoming a modern country.

An Uncertain Future

While Fujimori and his supporters were prevented by Congress from imposing the 'counter-insurgency state' laid out in the November *decretos-bomba*, little stood in their way, following the *autogolpe*. Having eliminated the legislature and with the judiciary under the virtual control of the executive branch, Fujimori was free to stack the cards even further in favour of the military.

One source of opposition is Congress and its 'alternative' president, Máximo San Román. With the exception of some *Cambio 90* senators and deputies, Congress has repeatedly expressed its opposition to the coup and the violation of democratic and constitutional principles. Its gestures, however, have remained largely symbolic. Well before the coup, Congress — along with most other branches of central government — was discredited in the eyes of many Peruvians. With no clear majority, many debates had succumbed to overt partisan in-fighting; others were resolved through deals and trade-offs, as in any other multi-party parliamentary system in the world.

Even though Congress debated, modified and passed much new legislation, it had failed to create the channels for more direct democratic participation necessary to dispel public suspicion of corruption and inefficiency. For the majority of the electorate, Congress' activities had very little direct impact on their daily lives. Mired in poverty and faced with an uncertain future, many Peruvians came to resent the high salaries, pensions and fringe benefits that come with congressional office. Fujimori's campaign against Congress capitalised on public scepticism to alienate Congress and the political parties even further from the population.

Another potential centre of opposition is APRA. Although it officially supports the congressional front, APRA has tried to set up its own independent opposition. Alan García has resurrected the best theatrical traditions of APRA and its founder, Víctor Raúl Haya de la Torre, to rebuild the party's combative image and myth. Immediately after the coup, García went into hiding as troops surrounded his home.

APRA and García's wife called press conferences, made dramatic telephone appeals for help to a popular Mexican news programme and marched to the Justice Ministry (which Fujimori had closed) to denounce the former president's 'disappearance' or arrest. Some days later, García reappeared in a well-staged press conference where he called on Peruvians to rise up against Fujimori and vowed himself to lead the struggle. Following several threats to himself, his family and other *Aprista* leaders, García invoked the ghost of Haya — who lived for six years in asylum in the Colombian embassy — by seeking asylum in the Colombian embassy in Lima, from where he left for exile in Colombia in early June. With their eyes firmly fixed set on the 1995 presidential elections, it is unlikely that García and APRA will bring the considerable organisational strength of their party into a unified opposition.

A final source of domestic pressure is the Left and the popular movement. Weakened by the cumulative effects of the economic crisis, frustrated by the intransigence of Fujimori's government and intimidated by Sendero, the popular organisations have done little more than condemn the coup. The Left has proved equally ineffective; in a large part because long-standing ideological differences have worsened with the general political crisis. Only months before the coup, some within the IS and the IU had been calling for the army and the popular movement to join forces in fighting Sendero Luminoso. Others strongly opposed the implied subordination of popular organisations to a military with a proven record of human rights violation. Meanwhile, the Left's leadership has become increasingly divorced from the rank and file. The forced suspension of parliament has also deprived it of a forum from which to voice opposition to the government.

Perhaps the most effective pressure on Fujimori has come from outside Peru. The US and Japan, with Latin American and European countries, condemned the coup with varying degrees of severity. Some countries, such as Chile and Argentina, recalled their ambassadors; Spain suspended technical assistance and development projects, while Germany cancelled Fujimori's planned May visit to Bonn, and announced that it would review its economic cooperation with Peru. The US cut off US$275 million in pending economic and military aid, plus US$45.4 million of aid already in the pipeline. Only Japan, which has decided not to halt the US$126 million in aid it offered to Fujimori in March, has refused to cooperate in the US-led effort.

The US has also rallied the support of the powerful multilateral lending institutions. The IMF and Inter-American Development Bank (IDB) froze credit to Peru soon after the coup. A major loan from the IDB, which was to have been signed on 6 April, was postponed, and a US$100 million payment on a US$625 million trade and adjustment loan from Japan and the IDB was placed on temporary hold. Japan and the IDB also stopped a US$300 million financial sector loan, placing the total amount of international loans jeopardised by the coup at over US$400 million.

Both the US and the multilaterals face a dilemma in their relations with Fujimori's new regime. Both are pleased with its commitment to neo-liberal reforms and privatisation. Two weeks after the coup, an IMF board meeting was held to review Peru's status. The overall tone of the meeting was congratulatory, and the board was told by the IMF's managing director, Michel Camdessus, that, current circumstances notwithstanding, the political situation in Peru was not 'an issue'. The US representative praised the Peruvian government for its 'dedication' to the IMF's economic plan.

President Bush also views the combination of free-market policies and democratisation in Latin America as an important test of his 'New World Order'. As a symptom of the incompatibility between neo-liberal programmes and democratic process in the Third World, Fujimori's coup has been unwelcome, especially in the US election year. In a continent where the military has traditionally played an important political role, Fujimori's civilian-military coup sets a disturbing example. Echoing Fujimori's language, shortly after the coup the Bolivian president, Jaime Paz Zamora, called for a 'more efficient Congress'. The coup also has meaning for Latin American officers unhappy with the chaotic political and social situations created by neo-liberal reforms. In Venezuela, there had already been one coup attempt against President Carlos Andrés Pérez. In Brazil, the military has voiced its fears of a possible left-wing electoral victory as a consequence of the extreme social polarisation and economic disarray following President Fernando Collor de Mello's free-market reforms. These and other political actors in Latin America are waiting to see the outcome of Fujimori's experiment in authoritarianism with a civilian face.

Another factor complicating the US reaction is the 'war on drugs', in which the Peruvian government is an indispensable ally. Having signed a comprehensive anti-narcotics agreement with the Fujimori administration in May 1991 and successfully sidestepped the human rights objections raised by the US Congress (see chapter 6), the State Department was poised to take action against Peruvian military officers with connections to drug-traffickers. Hours before the coup, Assistant Secretary of State Bernard Aronson, who had been asked beforehand by the Fujimori administration to delay his scheduled trip, arrived in Lima for a meeting to discuss anti-narcotics strategy. The Peruvian press reported that Aronson had brought with him a list of names of officers involved in drug-trafficking. Surprised by the coup, Aronson was recalled to Washington the next day.

The Bush administration is caught in a series of dilemmas and has had to tread cautiously in developing a strategy to deal with Fujimori. It is dependent on the Peruvian government in its 'war on drugs', yet reluctant to endorse an overtly undemocratic regime. It is fully aware that the coup plays into the hands of Sendero Luminoso, yet unable to risk any real threat to Fujimori's already fragile economic programme.

The Organisation of American States (OAS) has been more direct in its response to the coup. In an emergency session, the OAS deplored Fujimori's move and called for an immediate restoration of democratic institutions, respect for human rights and the immediate release of the legislators, union and political leaders detained after the coup. The meeting resolved that the OAS's Inter-American Human Rights Commission should visit Peru, and that a special committee appointed by the OAS should travel to Peru to encourage dialogue between Fujimori, Congress and the political parties.

Subsequently, the OAS has persuaded Fujimori to amend his original twelve-month proposal for constitutional reform and election of a new Congress, which provided for the constitution to be rewritten by a team of chosen 'specialists in constitutional law' and approved in a plebiscite. Elections for Congress were to have been held in spring 1993 under terms defined in the new constitution. Adopting the opposition proposal for a democratically elected constituent assembly, the OAS has been able to convince Fujimori to instead call elections for a 'democratic constituent Congress' in November 1992.

The nature of the constituent Congress, however, remains unclear. One of Fujimori's first acts following the coup was to dismiss the National Electoral Board and replace it with hand-picked appointees. Nor has Fujimori yet spelt out the terms under which the elections will take place. To date, he has announced only that 'traditional politicians' and members of the deposed Congress will not be allowed to participate. Some political observers in Peru question the legitimacy of the elections. Others doubt that the elections will ever take place. Many believe that if elections do take place, they will be staged for the exclusive benefit of Peru's foreign critics. Such scepticism is not shared, however, by the US and the multilaterals, which have taken the promise of elections as a signal for resuming business as usual. By 17 June, the IMF and the IDB had already announced that they were relaxing their 'freeze' on Peru.

The final, and perhaps decisive, actor in the unfolding crisis is Sendero Luminoso. Fujimori has justified closing Congress and reorganising the judiciary as necessary to the fight against 'terrorism'.

In the months following the coup, the military and police dealt several severe blows to Sendero, with the violent attack on the Castro Castro prison and the arrest of Guzmán.

Yet Fujimori's coup provides Sendero with the ideal enemy: an illegitimate, authoritarian and repressive government. Far from deterring terrorism, Fujimori's displays of military strength challenge the PCP-SL to respond with its own show of force. From Sendero's point of view, the generalised and indiscriminate repression with which the military and police have responded to its actions is welcome in that it further polarises society between Sendero and the state.

The Peruvian armed forces have two possible responses to Sendero's strategy. At one extreme, an influential faction in the high command favours a doctrine of total war. Similar in many ways to Sendero's own military philosophy, the total war doctrine calls for mobilising the entire civilian population under military leadership. This sector of the military has influence in the new 'government of national reconstruction'. The government has already proposed organising vigilante patrols in all Lima's residential neighbourhoods and in a high-level meeting at the *Pentagonito* an intelligence officer suggested imprisoning all the relations of existing *Senderista* prisoners.

At the moment, it is unclear how far the proponents of a total war solution will be permitted to carry out their strategy. Many within the armed forces disagree with an exclusively military solution to Sendero's violence. These officers believe that a successful counter-insurgency campaign must combine military and political means within the framework of a constitutional order. Their differences with the proponents of total war have begun to create divisions within the military. Although the armed forces backed the 5 April *autogolpe* as a united institution, these incipient divisions within the ranks could deepen if the government fails to deliver its promise to eliminate terrorism by 1995.

The increasing power of Fujimori's right-hand man, Vladimiro Montesinos, has also angered many military officers. They see his manoeuvring of promotions and appointments as a threat to the institutional integrity of the armed forces. Finally, a moral movement against corruption within the high command has gained ground among junior officers. As Fujimori retreats further into the bunker of the *Pentagonito* — where he now lives — these tensions within the armed forces may prove decisive in determining the direction his government will take and the outcome of the war against Sendero Luminoso.

6

Coca Capitalism and the New World Order

The 'people's trial' took place one January evening in the central plaza of the small town of Barranca. The accused was Tito López, the biggest coca grower and cocaine base producer in the Upper Huallaga Valley, itself the largest coca-producing region in the world. The prosecutors were a group of *Senderistas*, who had waited in ambush all day for López to return to his farm. The onlookers were the peasants and villagers whom the *Senderistas* had rounded up from surrounding communities as witnesses to the trial.

The *Senderistas* played on the peasant audience's animosity towards the prosperous coca-grower. 'How much land do you own?', they asked him. 'How much do you pay your labourers? How much do you pay peasants for their coca leaf? For how much do you then sell the cocaine paste?' Having found López guilty of cheating the peasants and paying his workers a pittance, the *Senderistas* took him to one side of the plaza for execution. Kneeling in front of his executioners, López begged for mercy. Deaf to his pleas, their decision was only overturned by López's observation: 'For you guys, I'm more useful alive than dead. I can supply you with food, clothing, boots, sneakers, all the money you need, everything that I can.' The *Senderistas* accepted López's offer. He was to go immediately to buy the supplies and the money was to be delivered the following day. They would also see to it that, in the future, López would pay fair wages to his peons and market prices to the peasants who sell him coca leaf.

The booming coca economy of the Huallaga Valley has provided Sendero with one of the most successful settings for its unfolding 'people's war'. Through 'agreements' with men such as López, the party has been able not only to benefit from the huge profits of the drug trade, but also to obtain benefits for its peasant 'bases' in the coca-producing areas. The PCP-SL is not alone, however, in its interest in the Huallaga coca leaf producers and drug trade. For Peruvian bankers and importers, as well as for the government itself, the dollars generated by the coca economy are the principal source of foreign exchange. For the peasants who grow coca leaf and those who produce cocaine paste, the coca crop is an assured source of income in an otherwise failing economy. For the thousands of street vendors and money changers who make up Peru's 'informal economy' and for millions of Peruvian consumers, coca dollars are an inflation-proof currency for savings or a business. Finally, for the MRTA, whose presence in the region precedes the PCP-SL's by over a decade, the Huallaga coca-growers are an important base of support, while the drug trade provides arms and cash.

Of all the different parties to the Huallaga coca economy, however, the most powerful by far is the US government. Classified by both Presidents Reagan and Bush as a 'national security threat', cocaine production and the Latin American narcotics trade have replaced communism as the principal enemy around which to rally public support for continuing military intervention overseas, tighter law enforcement at home, and a more powerful executive branch. Unlike the distant Soviet threat upon which national security arguments rested for decades, the new enemy can be personified in the form of the Latin American migrants, dark-skinned youth, and drug users who are already in the US. As such, drugs provide a 'foreign enemy' upon whom blame can be laid for a number of domestic social ills including crime, poverty, violence and unemployment. As a Massachusetts mayor reported to the Senate Committee on Foreign Relations, 'we are not being invaded by Russians. We are not being invaded by Savings and Loans. We are daily... being invaded by foreign people... carrying foreign drugs.' The resulting witchhunt has made drugs, in the words of the historically symbolic mayor of Salem, Massachusetts, 'public enemy Number One'.

By invoking the menace of Latin 'drug lords' and 'foreign drugs', the Reagan and Bush administrations have presented themselves as defenders of western democracy and civilisation. This ideological posture can do little, however, to turn the tide of rising unemployment, industrial recession, poverty and social polarisation which has resulted from their own economic policies and which provides the environment in which the drug economy thrives. At one extreme of this economy are the US working-class Latino and black youth who have been marginalised by Reaganomics and racism. At the other, are the Andean peasants whose economies have been destroyed by US-backed IMF austerity measures and neo-liberal reforms. For both these disenfranchised populations, the drug economy offers their only source of security. While Washington's xenophobic portrait of 'Latino drug lords' provides a politically expedient scapegoat, economic analysts and Wall Street maintain a more realistic vision of the Colombian cartels and the drug economy. It is neither the violence nor underworld connections of the Latin American cartels, but rather their capitalist spirit and 'businesslike mentality' which *Fortune* magazine credits for their success 'in turning cocaine trafficking into a well-managed multinational enterprise.'

Coca Capitalism

Following wool and guano in the 19th century and rubber, copper, fishmeal and oil in the 20th century, Peru's 'coca boom' took off in the 1970s. This latest cycle in Peru's export economy actually started in 1969 when demand for cocaine first began to grow in the North American drug market. As a result of the equivalent criminal penalties imposed by the Nixon administration on marijuana, heroin and cocaine, trade in the bulky and less easily smuggled marijuana declined sharply. The competitive advantage afforded to more compact and portable narcotics, such as cocaine and heroin, actually helped to expand the niche for these drugs in the US market.

The ups and downs of the drug market also reflect shifting social needs and cultural fashions. Cocaine's fast 'high' was the perfect stimulant for people living through the highly energised and short-lived financial booms of the Reagan-Thatcher era. Demand for cocaine in the US climbed steadily with the yuppie culture and consumer binges of the late 1970s, and peaked during the 'fast-track' 1980s. In 1984, drug entrepreneurs in the US began to manufacture a less expensive and more physiologically destructive form of mass-marketed rock cocaine known as 'crack'. Crack took hold quickly, allowing more Americans to buy into what Jefferson Morley has described as the 'consumptive sensuous pleasures' of the Reagan era. Crack caused a dramatic leap in both the demand for coca leaves and the quantity of processed cocaine shipped abroad. It also opened unrivalled opportunities for entrepreneurship in the depressed inner city economies of the urban US. By the late 1980s, the cocaine trade, with its retailers, wholesalers and money launderers in the US, and its manufacturers and exporters in South America, had matured into a well-oiled industry with a clearly defined international division of labour between production, refining, distribution and financial operations.

The cocaine on US streets is the final product of a process in which raw coca leaves are chemically transformed into cocaine hydrochloride. The process begins with leaves gathered from industrial varieties of the *Erythroxylum* coca plant cultivated on the

Traditional coca-chewing, Bolivia.   (Jenny Matthews)

eastern slopes of the Peruvian and Bolivian Andes. In its raw form, the coca leaf contains a negligible amount of the cocaine alkaloid substance that, in a highly concentrated form, constitutes the basis of cocaine. Traditionally, peasants and Indians throughout the central Andes and western Amazon have chewed coca leaves as a mild form of stimulant whose effects on the user are similar to those induced by drinking a cup of coffee or tea. For Andean peasants, coca leaves are the social lubricant for all manner of activities, ranging from the short work breaks which punctuate a hard day in the fields to the more highly structured etiquette of ritualised coca chewing through which peasants maintain and renew spiritual and religious ties to the earth and sacred mountains.

Coca leaves are also widely used by Peruvians and Bolivians of all social classes for the therapeutic teas prescribed as home remedies for gastro-intestinal disorders, altitude and motion sickness, hangovers and headaches. In Peru, the coca leaves sold for teas and chewing, as well as the small amount of legally produced cocaine which is sold to the national and international pharmaceutical industry, is marketed by the state-owned National Coca Enterprise (ENACO). The coca leaves purchased and marketed by ENACO are produced on the 10,000 hectares of legally registered coca fields located in the Cusco province of La Convención y Lares, the Huallaga Valley and other much smaller coca-producing areas in the departments of Huánuco, La Libertad, Ucayali and Puno.

The precise number of hectares of coca grown in the Huallaga Valley for the illegal cocaine market is more difficult to ascertain. Estimates based on US satellite images and calculations derived from cocaine and cocaine paste seizures vary between 100,000 and 300,000 hectares. Most analysts prefer to work with a median figure of 200,000 hectares, resulting in the production of 323,000 metric tons of Peruvian coca leaf per year. This coca is cultivated and harvested by small peasant producers, as well as by commercial growers, such as Tito López, who own large and medium-sized farms. Whereas the small peasant producers depend on family labour, commercial growers employ a labour force drawn from both the local population and seasonal highland migrant workers.

For the small growers and labourers alike, the coca harvest provides more money than any other crop. In the Huallaga Valley, one acre of coca produces an income equivalent to five acres of coffee, or seven acres of corn. Daily wages in 1989 in the Huallaga coca fields averaged 20,000 Intis, as compared to 5,000 for work in crops such as coffee, rice and cacao. Moreover, while annually or twice annually harvested crops such as rice, coffee and maize require substantial inputs such as fertiliser and pesticides, as well as labour-intensive irrigation and

What crack is like

... An individualistic drug, crack is often enjoyed in silence. The silence ends when that last sliver of rock is gone and you want to go out and find another $25 rock. When you're back outside prowling the lunar landscape of post-Reagan urban America at two in the morning with your high fading and your heartbeat racing, you'll begin to learn that crack is both a mental and a material phenomenon. You want your next rock, you want to get off, get out of this world — or at least transform it for a few minutes. You can be a moral tourist in the land of crack and still get a sense of how the drug can make sick sense to demoralized people. If all you have in life is bad choices, crack may not be the most unpleasant of them.

... I put on my clothes and thought, for obscure reasons, of a yuppie acquaintance. I am sure she has never tried crack. 'I just bought a CD player,' this young woman announced proudly to her sister one day when it was still morning in America. 'Do you know of any music I should listen to?' Yuppies are just the crackheads of consumerism, I thought, their CDs just so many rocks of consumptive, sensuous pleasure. My mood was improving already. Crack was a parody of Reaganism, I concluded, a brief high with a bad aftertaste and untold bodily damage.

'What Crack is Like', Jefferson Morley, *The New Republic*, 2 October 1989

The Etiquette of Coca Chewing

For the Quechua-speaking peasants of Cusco, *hallpay* (to chew coca) provides a framework within which peaceful and constructive social interaction takes place. An invitation to chew coca is an invitation to social intercourse. Friends who meet on the road pause to chat and to chew coca; men gathering to work in a field settle down to chew coca beforehand. When serious or troubling problems are at hand, *hallpakuy*, or the shared chewing of coca leaves, expresses the participants' commitment to rational and peaceful discourse. For the solitary individual, the brief *hallpay* break provides a meditative interlude in which to gather stray thoughts and prepare mentally for the task ahead.

'The Etiquette of Coca Chewing', excerpts from Catherine Allen, *The Hold Life Has. Coca and Cultural Identity in an Andean Community*, Washington, Smithsonian Institution Press, 1988 weeding, the hardy coca plant is virtually maintenance-free and produces four harvests a year.

After harvest, the next step in the production process is the transformation of the leaves into 'basic cocaine paste' (PBC). The leaves are placed in swimming pool-sized cement or plastic-lined pits, and are soaked and pounded in a mixture of sulphuric acid, lime (or cement), kerosene and sodium carbonate. After the resulting residue is drained and formed into small balls of paste, the chemicals from the pit are released into surrounding rivers where they cause severe ecological damage. With the exception of lime, which is produced locally, the other chemical inputs are produced in Lima and brought into the Huallaga Valley by specialised merchants and truckers. Since trade in these substances is tightly controlled in the coca regions, there is a considerable price mark-up between Lima and the Huallaga maceration pits. The pits are operated by local growers and merchants with access to the capital and trucks necessary to purchase and transport the large quantities of leaves and chemicals necessary to make PBC. At least 100 kilos of leaves go into the production of just one kilo of PBC.

These leaves are purchased from local growers at prices which fluctuate between US$1.20 and US$3.00 per kilo, equivalent to roughly seven to eight times that which ENACO pays for legally-produced coca leaf. As a result of the disarray in distribution and production networks caused by the US-backed Colombian military anti-narcotics offensive in 1990, prices dropped briefly to US$0.25 per kilo, well below the US$0.80 per kilo needed for farmers to make a profit. The effects of the crackdown were shortlived, however, and prices soon shot back up to previous levels. In addition to the cost of purchasing the leaves from farmers, local coca entrepreneurs must also pay bribes to police and local authorities, a salary to the 'chemist' who directs the operation, and wages to the 'stompers' who pound the corrosive mixture with their bare feet. All workers in the PBC production pits risk arrest and, in the case of the stompers, severe chemical burns and poisoning, but the wages paid for such work far exceed the minimum wage paid for other jobs.

The finished PBC is sold to three markets. The vast majority goes to agents of the two large Colombian cartels. The better-known of these is the highly publicised Medellín cartel of Pablo Escobar, Carlos Lehder, the Ochoa brothers and others who first began their careers and fortunes in the 1960s and 1970s marijuana trade. The other less visible cartel, centred in the Colombian city of Cali, is made up of members of well-known political and industrial families, whose wealth and power predate their involvement with the cocaine industry. Through its social connections, the Cali cartel has been able to maintain

close relations with Colombia's national and regional political and
economic establishment.

Agents for the cartels purchase the PBC in Peru. Organised in
well-armed gangs, these young Colombian agents, known in Peru as
narcos or *colochos*, often use violence and intimidation to secure
supplies, and bribery to assure compliance from local authorities.
Armed confrontations have often erupted between gangs working for
competing cartels. A much smaller amount of the PBC remains in Peru,
where it is processed into cocaine for the Peruvian market and for
export. The remaining PBC is sold for direct consumption as *pasta* or
basuco, an unrefined and highly toxic form of cocaine which is smoked.
Of these three markets, it is the Colombian export market which
defines the parameters and character of Peru's coca economy. In 1989
alone, an estimated 3,230 metric tons of Peruvian PBC were exported
to Colombia. Over the past years, prices paid for Peruvian PBC have
fluctuated between US$250 and US$1,500 dollars per kilo, reaching
their lowest levels during the Colombian military offensive in 1990.
Given their position in the cocaine trade, the Colombian cartels control
prices, supply and distribution.

The PBC purchased for the cartels is sent by plane or boat to
factories, or 'laboratories', along the large tributaries of the upper
Amazon near the Colombian-Peruvian-Brazilian border. In the
laboratories, workers 'wash' the PBC into cocaine base, which is in
turn refined into crystallised cocaine hydrochloride. Each kilo of
hydrochloride requires 2.5 kilos of PBC (equal to 250 kilos of coca leaf).
Industrially manufactured chemicals, such as acetone, potassium
permanganate and sodium sulphate, are imported from the US and
Europe. Although imports of these 'precursor' and 'essential'
chemicals to Colombia and Peru are strictly controlled, the cartels
make use of a network of proxies and industrial fronts to obtain them.

The cocaine is then shipped out to warehouses and distribution
centres in Mexico, Ecuador, Brazil, Honduras, Panama and the
Caribbean. From there, the cargoes are broken down into smaller units
for delivery to the US and Europe. Small volume wholesale shipments
(under ten kilos) from these distribution centres sold for between
US$14,000 and US$17,000 per kilo in 1989, while larger volumes cost
US$9,000 to US$12,000 per kilo. These prices include a percentage
mark-up to cover expected losses through interdiction. After being cut
two or three times, the retail value of the same cocaine in the US ranged
from US$80,000 to US$100,000 per kilo. While the stages of production
and distribution remain under the control of the Colombian cartels, a
number of independent Peruvians have recently begun to manufacture
and export cocaine in response to an enlarged foreign market and to
temporary disruptions in the cartel networks following the 1990

Colombian campaign. Once in the vast US market, distribution and sales fall beyond the scope of any one national group. While the Colombian cartels continue to control a substantial part of the US wholesale business, their monopoly breaks down once the drugs leave their offshore distribution centres.

Like other consumer markets during the 1980s, the US cocaine market conformed to what Barbara Ehrenreich calls the 'deepening fault lines within American society'. While cocaine catered to the tastes of the 'designer' market, crack filled the needs of 'less discriminating' mass-market consumers. Mirroring the larger rifts within society, these two markets were divided along lines of race and class at both ends of the trade. White middle- and upper-class professionals became involved in wholesaling and retailing cocaine to the fashionable market of their peers. Only occasionally surfacing in US media reports (which prefer to devote coverage to the BMWs and cellular phones of young black inner-city drug dealers), this economic elite of the cocaine trade consists, in the words of a US Treasury Department official, of 'Members of a wealthy, highly-skilled professional class, many of whom do not have previous criminal records, some of whom are highly respected members of their community. They are attorneys, accountants, bankers and money brokers'.

Unlike the upmarket cocaine entrepreneurs, the wholesalers, distributors, pedlars and crack house managers for the urban mass market are usually black or Latino youth, excluded from participation in the mainstream economy. For youth whose only other alternative are often dead-end jobs or unemployment, the drug trade provides an entry into the hyper-consumerism championed by US culture. As California assemblywoman Maxine Waters has trenchantly pointed out, 'in an affluent society in which only dollars appear to matter, some young people will find drug-pushing a seductive (or desperate) alternative to low-paying jobs. For the truly entrepreneurial the drug trade fits neatly into the American concept of free enterprise.' In an unlikely fellowship, the inner-city drug dealer and the impoverished coca-producing peasant of the Huallaga Valley occupy the lowest echelons of both their national economies and the international cocaine industry.

Inner-city drug pedlars and Peruvian peasants are also alike in their relatively minuscule share they receive of the profits generated by the cocaine industry. According to a 1991 *New York Times* investigation, small-scale drug dealers in Harlem barely earn as much as the government-established minimum wage for New York City. The approximately 200,000 Peruvian peasants who produce coca leaf for the drug market receive only US$300 to US$450 million a year for their crops, a per capita annual average of US$1,500 to US$2,250 dollars.

Peruvian PBC exporters and processers, by comparison, receive between US$1.3 and US$2.8 billion, compared to Peru's 1989 legal export income of US$3.5 billion.

Coca dollars, which account for over seventy per cent of all the dollars that move through Peru's thriving national currency exchange market, flow easily into the legal economy through established financial circuits. A portion of the dollars which the Peruvian coca leaf and PBC producers and exporters receive from the Colombian buyers is traded for Peruvian currency at the currency exchange houses and bank branches which have been set up in the Huallaga Valley. Another portion is deposited directly in dollar accounts in Peruvian banks. This busy market in dollars is not restricted to the Huallaga Valley. Large currency exchange businesses and banks regularly send in small planes to the Huallaga to pick up dollars for shipment to Lima, where they are sold wholesale to industrialists, importers and wealthy individuals, as well as to the numerous street retailers who turn a small profit by selling on to small businesses and individuals. Given the instability of the Peruvian economy and the constant devaluations of its currency, many day-to-day transactions are conducted with dollars. For the middle classes, paying rent, buying imported luxury goods and family savings all require dollars. The Peruvian government also relies heavily on coca dollars for foreign debt payments. According to the president of Peru's Central Reserve Bank, in late 1990 the Central Reserve made daily purchases of US$2 million 'in order to accumulate reserves for debt payment'.

Like other Third World agricultural export industries, in the cocaine economy the vast majority of profits are accumulated at the consumer end of the chain. According to a study by the London-based *Latin American Newsletters* over ninety per cent of the 83 to 197 billion dollars spent on cocaine in the US remains in the US. The anti-narcotics commission of the Group of Seven has speculated that US$600 to US$800 billion have been injected into the international financial system by the narcotics industry. The US Senate Subcommittee on Narcotics places this figure at US$300 billion, of which a third is estimated to be held in US banks. Estimates of narco-dollars entering the economy are derived from statistics on the amount of cash which banks turn over to branch offices of the Federal Reserve. When cash deposits begin to exceed payouts, there is good reason to suspect an influx of narco-dollars. The currency surplus figures of Miami — the early centre for drug money laundering — rose from US$576 million in 1970 to US$1.5 billion in 1976 with the growth in the US cocaine market. Today Los Angeles has surpassed Miami in both the amount of cocaine distributed through the city and the currency surplus which provides tell-tale signs of money-laundering.

Rather than go after the cocaine capitalists in Los Angeles and Miami, Reagan and Bush have opted for the ineffective but ideologically useful measures of criminalisation at home and eradication at the supply end abroad. Through the spectres of drug-frenzied criminals and foreign 'drug lords', the Reagan and Bush administrations have used the image of a narcotics underworld divorced from 'respectable' business and finance. Such is the importance of this narcotics underworld to the ideological underpinning of Bush's New World Order that an entire subsidiary of what Edward Hermann and Gerry O'Sullivan have aptly called 'the terrorism industry' has emerged to manufacture and market the concept of 'narco-terrorism'. As defined by Rachel Ehrenfeld, the high priestess of this new industry, narco-terrorism is 'a particularly sinister manifestation of the international terrorist phenomenon [whose] effects are insidious, persistent, and more difficult to identify than the sporadic, violent outbursts of the armed assailant.' Combining the worst of both worlds, the narco-terrorist is seen to act both through violence and by attempting 'to weaken the moral fiber of the target society by encouraging widespread addiction and by nurturing the socially enervating criminal activities that flourish around the drug trade.'

Narco-terrorism provides policy-makers and ideologues with a convenient concept through which to avoid addressing the links between the narcotics industry and the financial establishment. When defined as such, the political insurgencies of far-off lands, such as Peru, appear to have necessary causal links to the moral and criminal effects of drug-use in the US. Conversely, the drug trade appears to have necessary links to political terrorism and the undermining of democracies. The 'narcotics underworld' in Latin America, writes William J. Olson, the former Assistant Secretary of Defense for Low Intensity Conflict and current Senior Deputy in charge of Plans and Policy for the State Department's Bureau of International Narcotics Matters (INM):

> challenges enfeebled governmental capabilities... eating up what human and material resources exist to cope with existing problems, a situation that then compounds the whole in a vicious downward way. The future model for political order could well be Lebanon... Nowhere is this potential more dramatically revealed than in Peru, where the combination of insurgency, drugs, local mismanagement, debt and centuries old antagonism have brought the country to the verge of collapse.

The New El Dorado

For centuries, Peruvians have looked towards the lush eastern slopes of the Andes for a solution to their problems. Spurred by legends of the mythical El Dorado, Spanish conquistadors, Peruvian colonial subjects and 19th-century European explorers have each in turn pursued the dream of a fortune in gold. When the quest for gold became supplanted by the 20th-century search for industrial progress and development, Peruvian planners, politicians and presidents continued to look towards the country's vast and largely unsettled eastern lowlands for the panacea for Peru's many ills. Encouraged by government incentives, extractive industries have exploited the rubber, lumber, placer gold, oil and tropical forest fauna found in Peru's jungle. Along with these cyclical booms has gone a steady drive to colonise the eastern agricultural frontier in the rich zone just above the tropical forest known as the *ceja de selva* or 'the jungle's eyebrow'.

The leading champion of *ceja de selva* colonisation was President Fernando Belaúnde, with his grand plan for a network of roads and colonisation projects in the eastern lowlands of the departments of San Martín, Junín and Huánuco. Central to Belaúnde's plan for opening a new agricultural frontier was the Marginal Forest Highway which would run the length of the eastern slopes of the Andes, connecting the different eastern river drainage basins and uniting the newly developed eastern slopes with the highlands and coast.

Today Belaúnde's Marginal Highway is the central artery for the transport of the coca leaves and precursor chemicals that are the lifeblood of Peru's latest economic boom. Beginning in the highland city of Huánuco, the highway runs along the Huallaga Valley through the towns of Tingo Maria, Tocache, Uchiza, Juanjui and Tarapoto, in the department of San Martín. From there it divides into two branches that extend into the departments of Loreto and Amazonas. The towns through which the highway passes on its way towards the jungle form the heartland of Peru's coca-rich Huallaga Valley. The valley is divided into two regions with distinct histories of colonisation and political organisation. These regions are known as the Upper Huallaga Valley and the Central Huallaga Valley. The Upper Huallaga Valley, which runs from Huánuco to Juanjui, was initially colonised by highland migrants in the 1940s. Belaúnde's first administration promoted further agricultural colonisation projects in conjunction with the construction of the Marginal Highway.

In the first decade of colonisation, agriculture in the Upper Huallaga was highly diversified and self-sufficient, but during the mid-1970s farmers began to move increasingly towards monocrop coca production. By 1989, half the rural population in the department of

UPPER MAYO

Mayo River

LOWER MAYO

AMAZONAS

Moyobamba

Tarapoto

Lamas

Huallaga River

SAN MARTIN

CENTRAL HUALLAGA

Saposoa

Bellavista

Juanjui

Campanilla

Barranca

LORETO

Biabo River

LA LIBERTAD

Tocache

Santa Lucia

Uchiza

UPPER HUALLAGA

Aucayacu

ANCASH

Tingo María

HUANUCO

Huallaga River

Huánuco

PASCO

HUALLAGA VALLEY,
DEPARTMENTS OF SAN MARTIN
AND HUANUCO

Huánuco was directly involved in the coca economy. The reasons were obvious: coca cultivation yielded a profit margin of 200 per cent. Stimulated by the coca boom, the small frontier settlement of Tingo Maria has grown from a population of 5,000 in 1961 to over 50,000 today. Its few paved streets are incongruously lined with branches of Peru's major banks and currency exchange houses, as well as with the electronics, automobile, and motor-boat dealers who have moved in to take advantage of the coca-dollar boom.

The smaller settlements along the Upper Huallaga have experienced similar bonanzas. Makeshift airstrips dot the countryside around the 'coca capitals' of Tocache and Uchiza, north of Tingo Maria. The massive amounts of dollars brought into these two towns by the Colombian *narcos* have in turn attracted banks, money exchange houses and commerce, as well as a host of thieves, prostitutes, gamblers and fortune-seekers. A resident of Tocache described the rapid changes to the magazine *Quehacer*, 'in the mid-1970s this whole region was invaded. New patterns of consumption were introduced and the lifestyle changed. The people with money — those who make PBC from coca leaves — hired big bands from Lima or Huánuco and spent the nights dancing and drinking.' The Upper Huallaga also experienced escalating levels of violence, brought by the presence of well-armed Colombian *narcos*, the Peruvian police and Sendero.

The Central Huallaga Valley extends north from the town of Juanjui to Tarapoto and Moyobamba on the Mayo River. Unlike the Upper Huallaga, the Central Huallaga has a long history of agricultural settlement. The majority of its population are natives of the area with deeply-rooted traditions of community organisation. Until the economic crisis of the late 1980s, the Central Huallaga was one of Peru's largest producers of rice, corn, fruit and beef. Confronted with the disappearance of credit guarantees and state-controlled marketing outlets, multi-crop farming is increasingly giving way to coca production. Whereas in 1980 only around 10,000 hectares of land were planted in coca, by 1986 195,000 hectares of coca fields were being worked in the region. Along with the coca plantations, the *narcos* have extended their operations from Tocache and Uchiza into the Central Huallaga and Lower Mayo River valleys. With the worsening economic situation and the escalating international demand for cocaine, a wave of new migrants from Peru's highland and coastal regions has begun to pour into the Central Huallaga. From a total population of 319,000 in 1980, the department of San Martín had grown to 460,000 in 1990.

The Central Huallaga Valley is also home to a thriving network of grass-roots and community organisations. An affiliate of the Peasant Federation of Peru (CCP), the Selva Maestra Agrarian Federation of

San Martín (FASMA) is made up of committees representing rice growers, corn and sorghum farmers, and peasant communities in the region. Since its foundation in the late 1970s, FASMA has grown to include numerous community assemblies and has led marches, strikes and demonstrations to demand fair prices, credit and government support for farmers, and an end to police and military repression of popular organisations. In September 1989, FASMA led a successful twenty-day department-wide strike against the ailing García government, demanding fair crop prices, low interest credit, and payment of the money owed to producers by the state agencies in charge of marketing of corn, sorghum and rice.

With the neo-liberal reforms passed by Fujimori in late 1990, the situation has worsened. Instead of providing support for corn and rice farmers in the Huallaga, Fujimori's government opted to eliminate price subsidies, abolish low-interest credit programmes for farming, and dismantle state-managed marketing networks. In response, corn cultivation in San Martín fell by fifty per cent. Rice cultivation in the department fell even more dramatically, from 50,000 hectares to only 10,000 in 1991. As costs of production rose under Fujimori's economic regime, prices paid to farmers by the state agricultural marketing agency remained below cost. To meet the demand for basic foodstuffs, Fujimori turned his back on the Huallaga and began to import corn and rice. Faced with the withdrawal of all state aid and the drying up of credit sources, large numbers of farmers turned to coca cultivation.

The other important popular organisation in the Central Huallaga is the Defence Front for the Interests of San Martín (FEDISAM), an umbrella body for the department's numerous local community organisations and unions, including FASMA. Since its creation in 1987, FEDISAM has worked to support peasant and farmer demands and the creation of municipal and provincial defence fronts. It has also led the broad-based and highly popular movement to win regional autonomy for San Martín. Following Alan García's 1987 announcement of the creation of regional governments and assemblies, the department of San Martín was joined with the coastal department of La Libertad to form the Gran Chimu Region. Building on long-standing antipathy towards the coastal elites of La Libertad and Trujillo, the people of San Martín banded together to demand the formation of their own autonomous region. FEDISAM successfully led the movement which culminated in a February 1990 plebiscite in which over 75 per cent of voters supported secession from the Gran Chimu Region.

As elsewhere, San Martín's popular organisations have been supported by various left-wing parties. PUM, Patria Roja and MIR have played important roles in the FASMA and FEDISAM, as well as in other grass-roots and neighbourhood organisations. The 1980s coca boom, however, created special problems in creating and maintaining viable grass-roots organisations while confronting the violence of corrupt police and armed *narcos*. In response, rural communities began to organise self-defence committees with the help of left-wing parties. These committees gave advance warning of the frequent police raids made on communities with the pretext of searching for coca. They also confronted the *narcos'* armed gangs to demand fair prices for coca and to prevent other abuses such as theft and rape.

The *Movimiento Revolucionario Tupac Amaru*

Another important political force in the Central Huallaga is the Revolutionary Movement — Tupac Amaru (MRTA). The MRTA was formed in 1984 as an armed organisation, conceived as part of a front in which popular organisations, unions and parties would combine political, electoral and armed actions with mass mobilisation. Because it views itself as part of the national Left and popular movement, the MRTA supports the efforts of existing labour and peasant federations, neighbourhood associations, self-defence committees, and the IU parties. 'The political and mass struggle', states a 1987 MRTA document, 'plays a fundamental role, and within it, political centralisation constitutes the central axis. In this respect, the formation of a revolutionary political movement is a task of primary importance. This task requires the development of a united front with the IU and its member parties.'

In both its political identity and strategy, the MRTA differs substantively from the PCP-SL, which considers all existing popular organisations and parties as 'revisionist' enemies. 'Our differences with the *Senderistas* have different dimensions', explained an MRTA national leader in 1986. 'With respect to tactics, we think that the enemy that has to be defeated is militarisation and the government, whereas the *Senderistas* believe that the main enemies are *Apristas*. We do not agree that it is necessary to kill common people, *Apristas*.'

In line with this political philosophy, the MRTA has aimed its armed actions at police and military installations, banks, and US interests. MRTA members have also 'expropriated' food and clothing for redistribution to poor shanty-town dwellers. While MRTA has, for the most part, avoided execution and indiscriminate use of force, it has been less scrupulous in dealing with internal differences. Several dissident members have been executed, and the MRTA has often been troubled by conflict between factions in the leadership. In a widely condemned action, in late December 1989 MRTA members executed

MRTA guerrillas with leader Víctor Polay (centre), 1987.   (Alejandro Balaguer)

Alejandro Calderón Espinoza, the *pinkatzari* or leader of the Ashaninka Federation of the Pichic River (ANAP), whom they accused of collaboration with the army in the death of a MIR guerrilla leader in 1965. In the ensuing backlash by the Ashaninka, the MRTA was expelled from the Gran Pajonal region and lost important support from certain sectors of the Ashaninka.

The MRTA has had some success in the Central Huallaga. With the incorporation of the MIR into its ranks in 1986, it gained important links with popular organisations with whom the MIR had worked for almost a decade. MRTA members frequently participate as equals in community assemblies and meetings of popular organisations. Armed MRTA platoons have protected coca producers from abusive authorities and *narcos*. The MRTA also actively supported the FASMA peasant strike of September 1989, helping blockade roads and rivers, and protect marches and demonstrations. In the 1990 plebiscite, the MRTA sided with FEDISAM in supporting the creation of an autonomous regional government.

In their first major armed action in the region, a column of 100 MRTA guerrillas tried in mid-March 1987 to occupy the 'cocaine capital' of Tocache in the Upper Huallaga Valley. On entering the town, they were ambushed by a combined force of *narcos* and Sendero Luminoso. Sendero's participation in the attack was motivated not only by its animosity towards the MRTA, whom it dismisses as 'armed revisionists'. It also reflected Sendero's close working relationship with the Colombian *narcos* in Tocache, where Sendero's headquarters were housed in the home of a famous Colombian trafficker known as '*El Vampiro*'. After a prolonged battle lasting over five hours, the MRTA column lost more than fifty combatants and was forced to retreat north to the area between Tarapoto and Moyobamba. Following the fighting, a state of emergency was once again declared in the Upper Huallaga. The ensuing police offensive temporarily pushed both the *narcos* and Sendero out of their former strongholds in Tocache and Uchiza, to an area near the town of Campanilla.

Seven months later, the MRTA renewed its initiative in the Central Huallaga. In a symbolic tribute to the 20th anniversary of Che Guevara's execution, on 8 October 1987 the MRTA took over a radio station in Lima and announced the imminent opening of a guerrilla front. In the following weeks, MRTA fighters temporarily occupied Soritor, Tabalosos, San José de Sisa, and other small towns along the Central Huallaga and lower Mayo Rivers. On 5 November they occupied the provincial capital of Juanjui, a city of over 20,000 inhabitants. These occupations consisted of locking up the local police in their barracks, convening community meetings and finally organising soccer games, parties and dances with the residents. On several occasions, such as during the spectacular takeover of Juanjui, the guerrillas invited in television crews who broadcast the events nationwide. Following the Juanjui occupation, a state of emergency was proclaimed in the department of San Martín. A military offensive followed which dealt a series of severe blows to the MRTA's military organisation from which it did not recover until mid-1990.

During the year following the spectacular and well-publicised prison tunnel escape (see chapter 1), the MRTA reorganised its forces in San Martín. In May 1991, over 500 well-armed and uniformed MRTA guerrillas simultaneously occupied the cities and towns of Tarapoto, Moyobamba, Saposoa and Rioja, where they captured nine policemen. The MRTA used these actions to call attention to government neglect of the region, the corruption of local authorities and human rights abuses. Following the occupation of Rioja, the guerrillas offered to turn their police prisoners over to the International Red Cross, an offer which President Fujimori and the military refused. Over the following months, they maintained an active military presence in the Central Huallaga, launching the campaign 'Punishment to the Assassins of the People' with an attack on the army and police barracks in San José de Sisa. This campaign was intended to publicise the deteriorating human rights situations in San Martín as a result of violence from Sendero, the Peruvian military and police forces, and the anti-narcotic police forces supported by US Special Forces military advisers and US Drug Enforcement Agency (DEA) operatives.

The Huallaga Republic

While the MRTA's stronghold has traditionally been centred in the Central Huallaga and Mayo valleys, Sendero has concentrated its actions in the Upper Huallaga, where popular organisations are weaker (or non-existent) and where the monocrop coca economy has attracted *narcos* as well as the US-backed Peruvian anti-narcotics forces. Sendero first moved into the area in the early 1980s with the wave of immigrant colonisers who settled around Aucayacu and Puerto Pizana, north of Tingo Maria. Over the following years, it worked to establish a presence in the different communities along the Upper Huallaga. In some cases, as it had done in the highlands, it executed *narcos*, authorities, and merchants who had mistreated peasants and coca farmers. After 1985, it focused its efforts on undermining the fledgling producers' committees and self-defence groups which were beginning to form in the area. It also killed MRTA militants and sympathisers in an attempt to push its rival out of the Biabo valley in the Upper Huallaga region. In some instances, as in the MRTA attack on Juanjui, Sendero allied with the *narcos* in order to keep the MRTA at bay. For their part, the *narcos* adopted a pragmatic approach towards both the PCP-SL and MRTA. In areas in which Sendero threatened to disrupt their business through enforcement of coca prices or punishment of abuses, the *narcos* allowed the MRTA to work with community self-defence groups. In other areas where the police were interfering with their activities, the *narcos* encouraged Sendero to attack the police.

Following the MRTA's defeat at Uchiza, Sendero moved to create a 'liberated zone'. Having driven the police out of the area between Tocache and Uchiza, it turned against the *narcos*, forcing them to disband their armed groups. When conflict erupted, Sendero confronted the armed gang belonging to 'Cejitas', a renowned *narco* working in the area, killing 13 of its 18 members. According to Peruvian sociologist and journalist Raúl González, the surviving five gunmen then joined forces with Sendero.

During the next two years the Upper Huallaga Valley was the scene of a pitched battle between the PCP-SL, the *narcos*, and the combined anti-narcotics forces of the Peruvian police and the DEA. Because the anti-narcotics efforts concentrated exclusively on the unpopular policy of destroying coca fields, Sendero emerged the victor. As the dominant military force in the area, it was able to consolidate its intermediary position between the *narcos* and the coca-producers to form a quasi-state organisation that became known in Peru as the 'Huallaga Republic'. Sendero enforced price controls on coca, collected taxes or 'quotas' from the Colombians who buy PBC, and, in return, forced

PBC manufacturers to sell to narcos who had paid their quotas. It continued to enforce the moral order, punishing criminals and corrupt authorities, as well as homosexuals, adulterers, prostitutes, drug-users and others who transgressed its conservative moral code. Finally, Sendero succeeded in keeping the unpopular DEA-supported anti-narcotics police at bay. Lucas Cachay, president of FEDISAM, described the situation in 1991 to Raúl González: 'What the coca-producers want is to be protected and to make more money. The *narcos* always tell them that coca prices are low because of overproduction. The peasants know this is not true, but they don't have anyone to protect them. That is what Sendero offers them. On the other hand, there is a lot of money, alcohol, loose life and violence in the region. Sendero puts an end to all that and makes everybody work. They also close the discotheques and brothels, kill the homosexuals and deport the prostitutes.'

By imposing economic and moral order, Sendero's Huallaga Republic enabled an economy which is otherwise riddled with instability and violence to function smoothly. Buyers were assured of a steady supply of coca and producers were assured of a fair market price for their crop. The PCP-SL also took over responsibility for administering justice. 'Before [the arrival of Sendero]', explains a lawyer from Tingo Maria, 'the peasants came to Tingo Maria to seek justice. Now their problems are settled by Sendero's committees. Formal justice here is inefficient, corrupt and drawn out, while Sendero's is free, fast and effective.' As the overseer of this new civil order, the PCP-SL is also assured of direct economic and political benefits. As a bank employee explained to *Quehacer*, 'since April of this year when Sendero began to govern, they have prohibited the Colombians from exchanging their dollars for Peruvian currency in the banks. [Instead] they pressure them to do their currency exchanges with outsiders who are said — although in fact everyone is suspicious — to be agents from the exchange houses in Lima'. In addition to the obvious financial benefits of controlling currency exchange operations, it has been estimated that the five per cent quotas charged to the Colombian buyers yield at least US$30 million a year for the PCP-SL.

Sendero's hold on power in the Upper Huallaga was helped by the continuing eradication campaigns of the US-created Upper Huallaga Valley Coca Reduction Programme (CORAH). CORAH was provided with logistical support and armed protection by Mobile Rural Patrol Units (UMOPAR), the Peruvian anti-narcotics police trained by US Special Forces personnel at the Mazamari camp in the department of Junín. Besides the widespread abuses committed by UMOPAR, the very idea of eradication threatened the economic livelihood of the region. Initially, CORAH workers uprooted the coca plants by hand.

The impracticality of such efforts was made evident by the fact that, in 1988 only 680 hectares of coca fields were destroyed by manual eradication, whereas an estimated 5,000 hectares of new coca plantations were planted in the area.

Faced with the failure of the manual eradication efforts, the DEA attempted to introduce aerial spraying of Spike, an ecologically destructive and highly controversial herbicide. Even after the manufacturer, Eli Lilly, refused to supply the herbicide to the US government and the director of the DEA's herbicide testing programme resigned in protest at the State Department's indifference to environmental issues, the State Department continued to insist on Spike. The US government's obstinate preference for using Spike to eradicate coca never came to fruition. It was, however, the best thing that could have happened to Sendero.

Spike provided Sendero with a useful new issue around which to rally the coca growers. *Senderistas* devoted their military and political efforts to driving out the eradication teams. Coca producers were mobilised for attacks on CORAH teams and anti-narcotics police. Sendero also shot at UMOPAR helicopters, putting several of them out of service. In August 1988 Sendero called an armed strike to protest against the US government's plans to use Spike. In response to Sendero's offensive and the local population's opposition, in February 1989 UMOPAR and the DEA temporarily halted field operations in the area. The final obstacle standing in the way of Sendero's hold on regional power was the police barracks in Uchiza. In April 1989, PCP-SL cadres led local residents in a massive attack on the police headquarters there.

Following the attack on Uchiza, a new state of emergency and military jurisdiction was imposed on the region. General Alberto Arciniega, commander of the new emergency zone that included the central and Upper Huallaga, moved the army headquarters from Tarapoto to Uchiza, and implemented a counter-insurgency strategy aimed at breaking Sendero's ties to the coca growers. 'What Sendero wants', explained General Arciniega in November 1989:

> is to win the support of a population who depend on monocrop coca agriculture and who are repressed [by the police]...The CORAH which eradicated their crops harassed them, the police harassed them because they consider coca farming to be crime. We are talking about eighty per cent of the population! What we must do, therefore, is to change this situation in order to prevent the *cocalero* peasant — the base on which Sendero thrives — from being harassed.

In the following months, Arciniega successfully carried out a military campaign against Sendero and a 'hearts and mind' strategy to win over the loyalties of the local coca-producing population. Sendero columns retreated from the area and the population shifted their pragmatic relationship with the PCP-SL to a new alliance of convenience with the military. Central to Arciniega's counter-insurgency strategy was his refusal to accept DEA and CORAH programmes against the coca-producers. 'I don't have any problem, even a moral one, with treating the *cocalero* peasant as a normal person... The police have to fight against what drives the production of cocaine — against the [chemical] inputs, against the laboratories, against the airfields — not against the population.' In addition to opposing the eradication campaigns, Arciniega repaired roads and bridges which had been destroyed by Sendero, so that peasants could ship their fruit crops, coffee and cacao to markets outside the region. He also created a civic committee and brought back the local authorities and judiciary who had left during Sendero's reign. Finally, he broke with previous military policies in the area by declaring a truce in the harassment of popular organisations such as FASMA and FEDISAM in the Central Huallaga.

Although Arciniega's counter-insurgency strategy worked in undermining Sendero's presence in the coca-producing regions, it was not exempt from human rights abuses. During Arciniega's anti-Sendero campaign, whole villages suspected of supporting the PCP-SL were bombed, according to a report by the Peruvian human rights organisation APRODEH. Six extrajudicial executions, thirty disappearances, and hundreds of cases of torture, rape and illegal detention were also reported to APRODEH by local human rights organisations in the department of San Martín.

Despite driving Sendero out of the Upper Huallaga, Arciniega was deeply resented by the Peruvian police forces. With the military takeover of the Upper Huallaga region, the anti-narcotics police lost territorial control of an area which was central to both their institutional identity and their continuing DEA funding. As a result, Arciniega's attempts to coordinate military and police actions in the area were seen as interference with police jurisdiction.

More importantly, Arciniega's refusal to endorse the coca eradication programmes also met opposition from the US embassy and State Department. In conversations with US officials and DEA personnel, Arciniega was repeatedly urged to cooperate with the eradication campaigns which lay at the heart of US anti-narcotics efforts in the region. In September 1989, US Assistant Secretary of State for International Narcotics Matters, Melvyn Levitsky, testified before a congressional hearing that General Arciniega was involved in

Sendero slogan adorns farmers' roadblock to protest against use of Spike
herbicide in anti-drugs campaign.   (Alejandro Balaguer)

narcotics trafficking. Although Levitsky offered no proof to back his
allegations, any signal of State Department dissatisfaction was
unwelcome news for Alan García who was then renegotiating Peru's
status with the IMF and World Bank. As García knew, the US
Anti-Drug Abuse Act of 1986 specifies mandatory sanctions for failure
to comply with US anti-narcotics efforts. These sanctions include
withholding foreign aid and voting against loans from the multilateral
development banks to non-compliant countries.

Three months after Levitsky's allegations, Arciniega was transferred
out of the Huallaga by the army central command. His successors
moved the military headquarters from Tocache back to Tarapoto,
where they concentrated their counter-insurgency efforts on the MRTA
and the popular organisations of the Central Huallaga. With the DEA
and its anti-narcotics forces entrenched in the US-built Santa Lucia
police base and the military busy fighting popular organisations in the
Central Huallaga, the Upper Huallaga was once again left to Sendero.

From Megatons to Kilos

On February 8 1988, retired army general Paul Gorman testified before
the Senate Subcommittee on Terrorism, Narcotics and International
Operations. 'The American people', he said, 'must understand much
better than they ever have in the past how our safety and that of our

children is threatened by Latin drug conspiracies (which are) dramatically more successful at subversion in the United States than any that are centered in Moscow.' As former head of the Panama-based US Southern Command, or SouthCom, Gorman was in a good position to appreciate the value of the so-called 'drug war'. Under the urging of Presidents Reagan and Bush, SouthCom has declared counter-narcotics the top priority for US forces in Latin America and the Caribbean. As US military strategy makes the transition 'from megatons to kilos', the Latin American 'drug menace' provides a safety net for a military establishment threatened by budget cuts in an era of waning foreign and nuclear threats to US global power. As General 'Mad Max' Thurman, Gorman's successor at SouthCom and commander of the 1989 US invasion of Panama, has put it, 'the Latin American drug war is the only war we've got.'

The association between drugs and foreigners has been a recurrent theme in American political life for much of the 20th century. It was not until the 1960s, however, that a US administration successfully took hold of the 'narcotics menace' to forge a link between foreign and domestic policy. Building on his image as anti-communist crusader and law-and-order candidate, Richard Nixon revamped the existing institutions to bring narcotics issues under direct control of the executive branch by forming the Justice Department's Drug Enforcement Agency or DEA. Since its creation, the DEA has been the single most important agency in governmental anti-drug initiatives with jurisdiction over all international and interstate drug-related criminal offences. As a *de facto* narcotics police force, the DEA manages a national narcotics intelligence system, coordinates anti-narcotics programmes overseas, and has the power to make arrests and seize property.

By the time Ronald Reagan took office, the drug law enforcement system had mushroomed into a complex network of agencies and a global army of US narcotics agents. During the Reagan administration the budget for this drug law enforcement system grew from US$705.3 million in 1981 to US$1.221 billion in 1985. In George Bush's first year in office, Congress approved five billion for drug enforcement activities. By 1990, the budget appropriations for Bush's 'War on Drugs' had reached over nine billion dollars.

Reagan and Bush justified these skyrocketing budgets by describing the drug trade — and specifically the Latin American drug trade — as a national security threat. On 8 April 1986, Reagan signed a National Security Directive declaring drugs a national security matter, thereby authorising the military to provide support for anti-drug operations overseas. Reagan's attempts to militarise the drug war, however, were opposed at the time by the Department of Defense.

Under Bush, the military has come to see the 'war on drugs' in a different light. Faced with increasing talk of a 'peace dividend', Defense Secretary Richard Cheney on 18 September 1989, ordered the Pentagon to develop a plan for border control, aerial and maritime surveillance, intelligence gathering and military training in the Latin American and Caribbean drug producing and drug transit countries. Cheney's directive was embraced by the military for ideological, as well as pragmatic, reasons. As the resulting Pentagon plan made abundantly clear, the military saw in the 'war on drugs' an opportunity to obtain state of the art radar and satellite equipment. For Colonel John Waghelstein, former commander of US military advisers in El Salvador, the 'war on drugs' could be merged with ongoing military concerns with the 'low-intensity conflict' needed to 'counter the guerrilla/narcotics [sic] terrorists in [the Western] hemisphere.' For others the 'war on drugs' offered a lifeboat in a time of fiscal austerity. 'In a time when there will be increasing demands for fiscal constraints and selective spending', wrote Major Susan Flores in a 1990 article for the *Marine Corps Gazette*, 'Congress has already demonstrated that it is willing to provide funding for counternarcotics programs. Before the Marine Corps says "no" to drugs,' she concludes, 'it should think seriously about what is to be gained.'

On 5 September 1989, President Bush gave the military the opening it needed by announcing the Andean Initiative, a five-year strategy to deal with the drug problem 'at its source'. Ignoring the well-documented failures of President Reagan's 'war on drugs', Bush's Andean Initiative maintained the questionable principle of concentrating US anti-narcotics efforts on the producing countries and included for the first time an active role for both the US and Andean militaries. On the ground, the Andean Initiative provides for military and police training, technical assistance and personnel in a 'phased approach' that includes coca eradication programmes, crop substitution, interdiction and enforcement efforts. It also expands on Reagan's strategy by including military and economic aid for those countries who cooperate with the programme. Through the incentive of military aid, Bush hopes to convince reluctant militaries in Peru, Bolivia and Colombia to play a direct role in anti-narcotics operations traditionally reserved for police forces. Through the incentive of economic aid, the Andean Initiative offers compensation to Andean governments for the destabilising economic effects of eliminating their countries' major source of foreign exchange.

Although the Andean Initiative recognises the diplomatic importance of multilateral and bilateral agreements such as those reached at the presidential summits in Cartagena in 1990 and San Antonio, Texas, in 1992, all economic and military decisions remain the unilateral prerogative of the US. In order to qualify for economic aid, recipient countries must adhere to 'sound economic policies' — a clause meant to ensure that they follow strict IMF guidelines and keep their markets open to US exports. Economic aid also depends on meeting eradication and interdiction targets set for each country in consultation with the State Department's bureau of International Narcotics Matters (INM). Although military aid is not directly tied to meeting anti-narcotics targets, the Foreign Assistance Act makes delivery of military aid conditional on annual human rights certification. According to the same law, however, this certification can be waived at the White House's discretion in matters of 'national security'. In addition, in 1991 Congress allowed for further military escalation by approving Bush's request for a waiver permitting economic aid to be used for military financing, thus effectively erasing the boundaries between economic and military aid.

US anti-narcotics operations in Peru go back at least a decade. During 1979-80, the DEA launched Operation Green Sea, a 'cooperative enforcement effort' with the Peruvian government. Green Sea provided technical support for coca eradication efforts and for the destruction of PBC-processing laboratories. It also laid the institutional groundwork for future US-Peruvian programmes with the creation of CORAH, UMOPAR, and PEAH (Special Upper Huallaga Project), a short-lived and under-financed crop substitution programme. The next major US initiative came in 1985 and 1986 with Operation Condor. This time the targets were the airfields and processing laboratories. Peruvian military aircraft were used to transport UMOPAR personnel and equipment.

Soon after Operation Condor came Operation Snowcap, the US government's largest Andean anti-drug initiative and the direct predecessor to the Andean Initiative. Snowcap, launched in April 1987, was first presented as a three-year 'comprehensive international cocaine suppression strategy' for twelve Latin American countries. It has since been extended and incorporated into the Andean Initiative. Snowcap's goal was to reduce cocaine supply in the US by fifty per cent. Its objectives were, in the words of a DEA administrator, 'to control the growing areas, locate and destroy processing facilities, identify and neutralize trafficking organisations, reduce the chemical flow, and interdict transshipment.' Snowcap operations included intelligence gathering, diplomatic initiatives, enforcement, and training for Peruvian police forces.

In Peru, Snowcap began in July 1987 and concentrated on a 'relatively small area' of the Upper Huallaga Valley. Developed by the DEA, together with the State Department's bureau of International Narcotics Matters, its activities were closely coordinated with a dozen other US agencies. The DEA provided advisers; INM provided support; the Department of Defense provided training and transport; and the Coast Guard and Border Patrol assisted with riverine interdiction and patrol. During its first two years of operations, 83 PBC labs were destroyed, 1,800 metric tons of coca leaf were confiscated or eradicated, and two metric tons of PBC were seized. In 1989, a fortified police base was constructed at Santa Lucia base in the Upper Huallaga Valley. Described by one veteran as being 'just like a firebase in Vietnam', Santa Lucia has sandbagged fortifications, guard towers and is encircled by minefields and razor wire.

Besides erecting this highly symbolic target for Sendero, Operation Snowcap has accomplished very little. During 1989, anti-narcotics operations seized less than one per cent of the total PBC produced in Peru, and made only 44 arrests. The labour-intensive process of manually uprooting the sturdy coca plants likewise proved ineffective. The introduction of motorised trimmers merely led to the discovery that cutting the plants just above the roots actually increased farmers' yields by making the bushes grow back stronger than before. Peruvian CORAH workers also had to deal with hostile farmers, and on several occasions they and their police escorts were stoned by irate peasants. Between 1983 and 1989, 27 eradication workers were killed by Sendero. Cumulative figures for eradication reflected these endemic problems. In 1989, less than one per cent of the total coca crop in the Huallaga Valley was eradicated.

In a congressional hearing in October 1989 to evaluate Operation Snowcap, a State Department official reported that total Andean coca cultivation had actually increased by ten per cent a year, doubling since the 1970s. Farmers proved much more adept at clearing new fields than CORAH and the DEA were at eradicating old ones. Members of the House Committee on Foreign Affairs who visited the Huallaga Valley in 1989, reported that 'US antinarcotics aircraft cannot even fly due to the extensive smoke produced from the slash and burn techniques used to clear new land for coca production.'

With such derisory results, Snowcap fell well short of its goal of reducing cocaine supply in the US by fifty per cent. According to the December 1989 *DEA Review*, 'cocaine availability [has] increased dramatically since 1983'. In 1989, estimated cocaine production was 695 tons, nearly double the estimated 361 tons produced in 1988. The 1989 State Department Inspector General confirmed that total annual coca production was sufficient to satisfy US demand four times over.

Both the supply-side philosophy to drug enforcement and the specific programmes and strategies used in Snowcap have been incorporated wholesale into the Andean Initiative. The difference is one of scale. Instead of pulling up mature coca plants, the DEA now focuses on destroying coca seedbeds. The Initiative's budget for 1990 was fifteen times greater than the US$7 million which the DEA spent on Snowcap in 1988. Bush's resolve to militarise the 'war on drugs' has also heightened the political stakes both in the US and in Peru.

The Andean Initiative has also inherited Snowcap's operational difficulties and turf battles between the many different US agencies involved. As a House of Representatives Staff Study Mission to Peru reported in late 1988, 'the DEA is being thrust into essentially a paramilitary role for which it is ill-equipped; INM is operating an air wing for which it has no expertise; DOD's [Department of Defense] role remains murky; and the intelligence community's record ranges from very good to non-existent. Eradication and interdiction efforts in-country are coordinated on an ad-hoc basis while AID [the Agency for International Development] remains an unwilling or largely disinterested partner.'

Other investigations have confirmed the report with a tragi-comedy of bureaucratic foul-ups, inter-agency squabbles and sheer incompetence. Many of the DEA agents sent to coordinate the Peruvian police's air assault operations frequently could not speak Spanish and had received no military training beyond a two-week course in 'jungle survival'. Long-standing rivalries between the DEA, the Department of Defense, and the State Department's INM and Narcotics Assistance Unit (NAU) have frequently led to what one congressional committee described as 'confusion and conflict at the operational level'. The DOD has refused to provide regular supply flights to DEA agents at the Santa Lucia base, and SouthCom has kept DEA agents in the Huallaga Valley waiting over a year for the communications equipment required to do their work. NAU, the anti-narcotics unit attached to the embassy in Lima, has also refused DEA agents' requests to use their helicopters, because NAU prefers to lend them directly to Peru's UMOPAR.

These seemingly petty turf battles reflect discrepant views of what is at stake in the 'war on drugs'. While DEA agents and officials take seriously their mission of 'fighting drugs', SouthCom, Pentagon and State Department priorities lie elsewhere. Conceived and marketed as an anti-narcotics operation, the Andean Initiative has brought the 'war on drugs' into countries where armed insurgencies and popular organisations provide attractive targets for a US military establishment which is redefining its post-Cold War identity in terms of a focus on 'low intensity conflict' (LIC). As defined in President Reagan's 1987 outline for a new US national security strategy, LIC covers those situations which threaten US national interests, values and free institutions. Such situations exist 'at levels below conventional war but above the routine, peaceful competition among states. They often involve a protracted struggle of competing principles and ideologies [and they can be] waged by a combination of means, including the use of political and economic, informational, and military instruments.' As LIC expert and current INM plans and policy director, William J. Olson explains, LIC reflects an effort to replace the outdated counter-insurgency models which failed in Vietnam, with new conceptual models and strategies for fighting 'terrorism, insurgency and subversion'.

The Andean 'war on drugs' provides the resources and physical theatres of operations necessary for the high-technology intelligence gathering and surveillance systems and the new tactical strike units and special forces that are integral to the LIC concept. A key component in the Andean Initiative is the development of blanket radar and satellite coverage for South America. State-of-the-art radar and electronic surveillance stations have been built in Peru, Colombia and Bolivia. The Pentagon plan for the Andean Initiative also allots forty per cent of total AWACS (Airborne Warning and Control System) flying time to the region. Navy Hawkeye E-2C radar planes, Coast Guard Aerostats, Army UH-60 helicopters, and F4 Phantom and F-14 Tomcat fighter planes are also included in the air surveillance and interdiction package. Allowance has been made for the eventual inclusion of aircraft carriers, destroyers and other naval support units. With the US$15 million allocated for improving SouthCom's command, control and intelligence centre, a 'prototype Command and Management System' has been installed in Panama to provide field agents with satellite hook-ups to a central computer intelligence network that includes the Defense Intelligence Agency and the secretive National Security Agency. According to the Pentagon plan, all intelligence information analysis will be centralised at SouthCom in Panama, making use of an underground counter-narcotics command post manned by thirty military personnel. The CIA counter-narcotics unit created by President Reagan has also used NASA and Pentagon satellites to take aerial photographs of all major coca and marijuana fields in South America.

The Andean Initiative also includes provision for on-site ground units. Exact figures for the number of military personnel working in Peru at any one time are impossible to come by. Military 'tactical analysis teams' based at the US embassy in Lima coordinate activities with the DEA and decide what intelligence information will be made available to the Peruvian government. Starting in 1990, an estimated 200 US Special Forces have been deployed as 'mobile training teams' to the Andean countries. Some of these Special Forces conduct 'anti-narcotics' and counter-insurgency training for Peruvian *sinchis* (anti-subversive troops) at the Mazamari base in the eastern lowlands of Junín. Department of Defense 'rules of engagement' prohibit US military personnel from assuming 'any operational role' in counter-narcotics activities. According to these rules, US personnel may defend themselves if attacked using 'the minimum amount of force, proportional to the threat'. Despite Defense Secretary Dick Cheney's assertions that US troops only provide training and support, US Special Forces routinely lead Peruvian military patrols outside the Mazamari base. Moreover, according to a July 1990 *Los Angeles Times* report, in Panama 'Special Operations forces rehearse anti-drug missions at a US military jungle training school [where] a cocaine laboratory has been added to the collection of mock targets.'

In addition to active duty Special Forces, retired Special Forces personnel have also been hired as mercenary labour by the INM. The INM, which operates a fleet of over fifty planes and helicopters in the Huallaga region, was forced to turn to contracted expertise because, as INM chief Melvyn Levitsky told the *Philadelphia Inquirer*, 'I cannot find many Foreign Service [State Department] officers who know anything about aircraft.' The pilots hired by the INM are former Special Forces, or Green Berets, contracted through the privately owned Arizona-based National Air Transport, Inc. Most have combat experience in Vietnam and many worked as well for the illegal 1984-5 contra resupply mission orchestrated by Lt Col Oliver North and retired air force Major General Richard Secord.

One 'contragate' insider now in the Huallaga is Richard J. Meadows, described in the *Philadelphia Inquirer* as 'one of America's most influential clandestine operatives'. Before retiring from the army, Meadows led many Special Forces missions in Vietnam, and took part in the failed 1980 US hostage rescue mission in Iran. Meadows, who is also 'said to have advised key figures in the contra supply effort', arrived in the Huallaga in 1983. By 1990, he was working as chief of security on a large private plantation conveniently adjacent to the Santa Lucia base. According to the *Philadelphia Inquirer*, Meadows was, at the time, adviser to the US Special Operations Command and the National Security Council's deputy for counter-narcotics, counter-terrorism and low intensity conflict. In the Huallaga, Meadows has also worked to recruit 'soldiers of fortune' — generally retired Special Forces operatives — to serve as gunners and pilots for the INM's helicopters.

The Fujimori Doctrine

On 14 May 1991, President Fujimori informed the Peruvian Congress of the contents of the US-Peruvian anti-narcotics agreement which had been signed only an hour before. 'In this enterprise', he declared, 'Peru is the partner of the United States of America. Peru will not be converted into anybody's satellite and there will be no subordination.' 'Drug trafficking', he pointed out:

> is not just any criminal activity. It is a cancer which advances relentlessly. It degrades our country's image [abroad], violates our sovereignty and upsets the economic stabilisation process, besides being now in a phase of coexistence (*convivencia*) with subversion.

As well as fighting both 'illicit drug trafficking and psychotropic substances' (meaning coca leaf which was incorrectly classified as a 'dangerous psychotropic substance' in a 1947 UN resolution), Fujimori claimed that the agreement '[would] serve as an effective instrument for structural reforms, anti-subversive policies, and in [Peru's] reinsertion into the international financial community.'

The agreement, Fujimori explained, required economic, legal and administrative reforms leading to 'true structural adjustment'. As part of this adjustment, it would 'promote and implement alternative development' in coca-producing areas. Alluding to widespread concerns regarding militarisation and human rights offences, Fujimori optimistically told his audience that the agreement 'clearly subordinates military forces to civilian power'. In a final attempt to convince critics that the US had broken with its long history of failed promises and disregard for Latin American economic development, Fujimori claimed that the agreement 'recognised the possibility of a reduction or "swap" of Peru's debt to the United States.'

After a long period of tense negotiations, the details of the agreement came as no surprise to the senators and representatives gathered to hear Fujimori's speech. Various versions of its ever-changing text had been published in Lima newspapers, and its contents had been the subject of intense public debate for some time. What did surprise Fujimori's audience that day was the fact that the agreement had been signed without first having been presented for parliamentary debate. Anticipating the parliament's objections to his violation of democratic procedures, Fujimori presented his own curious reinterpretation of democracy: 'One cannot consult the citizens about something that does not yet exist. Before being signed, there is no agreement and, as a consequence, there is nothing that can be the object of public debate.'

Parliamentary and public opinion was outraged at Fujimori's offhand treatment of the democratic process. Ignoring established government channels, Fujimori had instead chosen in the months preceding the agreement's signing to contract Hernando de Soto's ILD (see chapter 5) to develop an alternative anti-narcotics policy — later to be christened the 'Fujimori Doctrine' — and to negotiate the terms of the agreement with Washington. De Soto saw in the anti-narcotics agreement an opportunity to bring to fruition his own ideas about the ways in which the lack of individual property titles and bureaucratic obstacles had supposedly blocked Peruvians' capitalist spirit. In the text of the agreement, these ideas drawn from de Soto's *The Other Path* are interwoven with more comprehensive clauses outlining a neo-liberal restructuring project for Peru. The clauses coincide with recommendations made in a 1991 policy report on US policy towards Peru by the Heritage Foundation, a conservative US think-tank which both finances and provides ideological guidance for the ILD. The Heritage Foundation report concluded that the US should seek to implement a free trade treaty 'to develop free market enterprise' in Peru and to deregulate agricultural markets in the coca-producing zones. It also recommended that the Peruvian government appoint a 'drug czar' to oversee all anti-narcotics operations.

The Fujimori Doctrine was developed in the six-months after Fujimori rejected the initial draft of a bilateral agreement in September 1990 when he had taken the Bush administration by surprise by turning down an offer of US$34.9 million in military aid. Ostensibly because of inadequate accompanying development aid, his decision was also motivated by public opinion. In Peru, the US 'Donation Agreement' had insulted nationalist sensibilities across the political spectrum due to wording which portrayed Peru as the 'recipient' and the US as the 'donor'. Peruvians across the political spectrum also objected to clauses in which exclusive jurisdiction over conflicts arising from the use of the aid would be granted to US courts. The agreement also contravened previous accords reached at the Cartagena summit, where President Bush and the presidents of Peru, Bolivia and Colombia had agreed that anti-narcotics initiatives would focus equally on supply and demand, and that any future bilateral agreements would include provisions for alternative economic development. The most serious obstacle to the agreement, however, was posed by the Peruvian military. In a report for the Washington Office on Latin America, Coletta Youngers underscores the importance of military objections to the agreement: 'Within the Peruvian military, there is significant debate over whether or not to accept US aid; some want to accept it because they feel the military needs the resources, while others fear the leverage such assistance could give the United States and potential US meddling in the Peruvian military's affairs.'

In rejecting the aid, Fujimori hoped to buy time to appease the numerous and highly vocal critics of the agreement. However, by late October, Fujimori was already making overtures to the US. In a speech on 26 October, he outlined a programme to deregulate agricultural markets, grant land titles to coca farmers, and support eradication and interdiction efforts. Working with State Department representative Ann Wroblesky, who had been hired as his adviser on narcotics affairs, Fujimori next criminalised both cocaine and coca leaf production, in a show of support for the US anti-drug crusade. In November he announced a decree reorganising ENACO, the only legal outlet for coca leaf production and one of Peru's only profitable state enterprises.

The following month, another presidential decree created the Autonomous Alternative Development Authority (AADA), 'a public institution with economic, technical and administrative autonomy' with ministerial rank and answering directly to the executive. Fujimori named Miguel González del Rio, a close associate of de Soto at the ILD, as its director. AADA was to have complete authority over decisions regarding the development and economic restructuring of the coca production zones and was charged with establishing free-market mechanisms and free enterprise zones to 'promote economic activities distinct from coca leaf cultivation.'

AADA's first blueprint for the Huallaga Valley proposed relocating the population along the Marginal Highway and creating a free enterprise zone for commercial farming and agribusiness. Crops designated for cultivation in the planned smaller commercial farms included flowers, fruit and vegetables destined for the export market. Other larger farms and plantations would produce palm oil, drawing on the labour force concentrated in AADA's newly created settlements.

With the creation of AADA, Fujimori was ready to make his final move. In January 1991, Hernando de Soto officially unveiled the Fujimori Doctrine in Washington. As an outline plan of cooperation to fight drug trafficking, it specified that a bilateral agreement would have to include debt relief, crop substitution programmes, and access for alternative crops to international and US markets. In an effort to assure the US of the viability of AADA's 'free enterprise' programmes, it also spelt out the Peruvian government's commitment to grant legal property titles and to remove 'bureaucratic obstacles to agricultural production'. As the congressional deadline for budget allocations drew closer, Bernard Aronson, Assistant Secretary of State for Interamerican Affairs, announced the US government's acceptance of the Fujimori Doctrine. Ignoring overwhelming evidence of Peru's failure to meet US anti-narcotics targets, Bush quickly certified Peru for economic and military aid.

Criticism of Fujimori's quick deal with Washington and AADA's 'free market' plans came from all quarters of Peruvian society. The CCP and other peasant federations expressed strong opposition to the Doctrine's equation of cocaine with coca leaves and its proposal to eliminate coca cultivation completely. The Doctrine, the CCP objected, dismissed completely the importance of coca to peasant culture in the

Peruvian highlands and jungle, and provided no margin for the development of alternative legal uses of coca. Human rights organisations, NGOs and the Church, in turn, deplored its emphasis on military solutions. In a rare consensus, intellectuals and politicians from both Left and Right joined voices with some sectors of the military to protest against the Doctrine's violation of Peruvian national sovereignty and the sweeping powers given to the US government. Many of these same critics also pointed out the unconstitutional character of AADA as an entity created by presidential decree and having no public accountability. Finally, both Sendero and the MRTA found in the Fujimori Doctrine the ultimate confirmation of the need for further armed struggle against 'yankee imperialism'.

Five days after Bush's certification of Peru, the CCP delivered a manifesto to Fujimori rejecting AADA and calling for a programme to develop alternative uses of coca. The peasants demanded that their organisations be included in all discussions preceding the signing of the bilateral agreement. They also informed the President that these demands would be included in the platform of the national peasant strike called for 21-23 March. In late March, the First Andean Meeting of Coca Producers was held in La Paz, Bolivia. More than 500 delegates including peasants, intellectuals and agronomists from Peru attended, expressing unanimous rejection of attempts to criminalise coca and coca-producers. A week later, the prestigious Andean Commission of Jurists held an international conference on drug-trafficking in Latin America, in which experts, academics, politicians, and representatives of international organisations from the US, Latin America and Europe criticised Bush's plans to further militarise anti-narcotics efforts, as well as the equation between coca leaf production and cocaine trafficking.

As momentum built against Fujimori's and de Soto's plans, the US and Peruvian administrations were pressed to find a quick resolution. In April the US embassy in Lima staged a teleconference between Melvyn Levitsky of the INM and Peruvian journalists. 'The most important issue in our relations with Peru', Levitsky announced:

> is drugs. That is the 'number one' problem and all other issues depend on its solution. If there were more collaboration between the Peruvian military and police in the struggle against drugs, economic aid would increase... Accusations regarding the supposed militarisation [of our anti-narcotics efforts] are part of a disinformation campaign mounted by the drug-traffickers in order to ensure that our programmes are not effective against their illicit activities.

Levitsky also made explicit the benefits of complying with the US plan: 'We would be able to provide not only economic assistance, but also very important support for Peru's international economic status, in such a way that Peru could also work with multilateral organisations such as the IMF, World Bank and Inter-American Development Bank, as well as with the European Economic Community.' A week later the agreement was signed behind closed doors.

The final obstacle in the Bush administration's path was that of certifying Peru's human rights record. According to the International Narcotics Control Act of 1990 (ironically known in Washington circles as 'INCA'), countries receiving military aid must have acceptable human rights records. Realising that Congress might well baulk at the idea of certifying one of the worst human rights offenders in the world, the Bush administration waited until late July and submitted its certification application just three days before Congress's annual August recess. Since the INCA specifies that once an application has been presented, Congress has only 15 days to decide on whether to grant or withhold aid, this meant that the congressional committees had only three days to reach a decision. Angered by Bush's methods and incredulous at the State Department's written certification request asserting that, 'no major human rights organisation has reported a consistent pattern of gross abuses of human rights', Congress blocked the military aid.

As Congress reconvened in September 1991 Bush invited Fujimori to Washington for photo opportunities, speeches and lunches with strategically placed senators and congresspeople. In a meeting with the *Washington Post*, Fujimori charmed reporters and congressional aides with his assurances that the programme would avoid confrontations between the military and coca-producers, and that US advisers would not become involved in military actions. Soothing Congress's fears of an electoral backlash against further US involvement in Peru, Fujimori insisted that 'we don't want a little Vietnam in the Huallaga'. The following day, President Bush complimented the Peruvian president: 'Rights abuses have fallen sharply since you took office. You are a man of vision and courage.' 'We have a policy', Fujimori replied, 'for the protection of human rights which will complement our fight against drug trafficking and terrorists.'

When Congress reconsidered Peru's case the following month, it approved US$25 million of the US$34.9 million requested by Bush for military aid. This aid was to be released in instalments conditional on Peru's performance in meeting anti-narcotics targets and on improvements in human rights. Following Fujimori's April 1992 coup, the prospects for compliance with either condition appears even more remote. On the day of the coup, Assistant Secretary of State Bernard Aronson arrived in Lima with a list of Peruvian military personnel which the State Department believed to have close ties with drug trafficking. Far from purging such officers, Fujimori's new government gave them an even more prominent role. According to an 18 April article in *The Miami Herald*, Montesinos was able after the coup to strengthen the position of military officers with known ties to the drug trade. In reorganising the judiciary, Fujimori and Montesinos also favoured judges known for their leniency towards drug traffickers. The State Department's inability to enforce a purge of military officers and judges connected with the narcotics trade was compounded by evidence that the CIA which has for years cultivated Montesinos as an intelligence 'asset' in Peru, provided financial support and vehicles for Montesinos and his acolytes in the National Intelligence Service. Given Fujimori's proven sympathies towards both Montesinos' intrigues and the hardliners in counter-insurgency, the US government will be hard-pressed to justify a continuation of its present anti-narcotics policies in Peru.

Sources and Further Reading

1. War Against Democracy
For human rights statistics, see Amnesty International and Americas Watch's annual reports, as well as the comprehensive chronology of the war, *Violencia política en el Perú*, 1980-1988 (Lima, DESCO, 1989). For an account of the internal refugee problem, see Robin Kirk, *The Decade of Chaqwa: Peru's Internal Refugees* (Washington DC, US Committee for Refugees, 1991).

Statistical information on Peru can be found in Richard Webb and Graciela Fernández Baca (eds), *Perú en números* (Lima, Cuanto SA, annual); the World Bank's annual World Development Report; and the Inter-American Development Bank's yearly Economic and Social Progress in Latin America.

For accounts of the daily life and survival strategies of Peru's poor, see Jurge Golte and Norma Adams, *Los Caballos de Troya de los invasores* (Lima, IEP, 1987); and Cecilia Blondet, *Las Mujeres y el poder: una historia de Villa El Salvador* (Lima, IEP, 1991). See *Sólo organizados podemos vencer* (Lima, SER, 1989) for peasant accounts of community life and organisation.

The major Peruvian periodicals from which material in all six chapters of this book has been drawn are the magazines *Quehacer, Caretas, Sí* and *Actualidad Económica*, and the daily newspapers *El Comercio, la República* and *Expreso*. A weekly summary of the Peruvian press can be found in *Resumen Semanal* (Lima, DESCO).

2. The Shining Path
For Sendero's political strategy and the philosophy and thought of its leader, Abimael Guzmán, see Luís Arce Borja (ed), *Guerra popular en el Perú: el pensamiento Gonzalo* (Brussels, 1989) and the interview with Guzmán published in *El Diario* (Lima, 24 July 1988).

The origins and early history of the PCP-SL are discussed in Carlos Iván Degregori, *Ayacucho 1969-1979: el surgimiento de Sendero Luminoso* (Lima, IEP, 1990); Lewis Taylor, 'Maoism in the Andes: Sendero Luminoso and the Contemporary Guerrilla Movement in Peru' (University of Liverpool, 1983); and Gustavo Gorriti, *Sendero Luminoso: historia de la guerra milenaria en el Perú* (Lima, Apoyo, 1990).

3. Time of Fear
For the PCP-SL's military programme, see especially *Desarrollemos la guerra de guerrillas* (Lima, Bandera Roja, 1982) and 'Bases de discusión' in Luís Arce Borja, *op.cit.*

Analyses of Sendero's war in different regions of Peru can be found in Carlos Iván Degregori, 'Jóvenes y campesinos ante la violencia política: Ayacucho 1980-83' in H. Urbano (ed), *Poder y violencia en los Andes* (Cusco, Bartolomé de las Casas, 1991); Ponciano del Pino, 'Los Campesinos en la guerra' (Iquitos, SEPIA, April 1991); José Coronel A. and Jorge C. Loayza C., 'Violencia política: formas de respuesta comunera en Ayacucho' (Iquitos, SEPIA, April 1991); Billie Jean Isbell, 'Shining Path and Peasant Responses in Rural Ayacucho' in D.S. Palmer (ed), *The Shining Path of Peru: A Study of Sendero Luminoso* (London,

Hurst, 1992); Ronald Berg, 'Sendero Luminoso and the Peasantry of Andahuaylas', *Journal of Inter-American Affairs* (28, Winter 1986-7); José Luís Rénique, 'La Batalla por Puno: violencia y democracia en la sierra sur', *Debate Agrario* (10, 1991); Michael Smith, 'Sendero Luminoso's Urban Strategy: Ate-Vitarte as a Case Study' in D.S. Palmer, *op.cit.*; Nelson Manrique, 'La Década de la violencia', *Márgenes* (5/6, 1989); and the articles on Sendero by Raúl González published in *Quehacer* between 1983 and 1990. For accounts in English, see NACLA *Report on the Americas* (XXIV, 4, January 1991) with articles by Nelson Manrique and Carlos Iván Degregori.

4. A Nation for the Few

For histories of the modern Peruvian state and economy, see Julio Cotler, *Clases, estado y nación en el Perú* (Lima, IEP, 1978); Alberto Flores-Galindo and Manuel Burga, *Apogeo y crisis de la república aristocrática* (Lima, Editorial Rikchay Peru, 1987); Aníbal Quijano, *Imperialismo, clases y estado en el Perú, 1890-1930* (Lima, Mosca Azul, 1978); David Slater, *Territory and State Power in Latin America: The Peruvian Case* (London, Macmillan, 1989); and Rosemary Thorp and Geoff Bertram, *Peru 1890-1977: Growth and Policy in an Open Economy* (London, Macmillan, 1978).

The work and influence of Mariátegui and Haya de la Torre are analysed in Aníbal Quijano, *Introducción a Mariátegui* (Mexico, Era, 1981); Alberto Flores-Galindo, *La Agonía de Mariátegui* (Lima, DESCO, 1980); Steve Stein, *Populism in Peru* (Madison, University of Wisconsin Press, 1980); Imelda Vega Centeno, *Aprismo popular: mito, cultura y historia* (Lima, Tarea, 1985); Heraclio Bonilla and Paul Drake (eds), *El APRA: de la ideología a la praxis* (Lima, Nuevo Mundo, 1989); and Frederick Pike, *Politics of the Miracle in Peru: Haya de la Torre and the Spiritualist Tradition* (Lincoln, Neb, University of Nebraska Press, 1986).

For histories of the Peruvian Left and labour and peasant movements, see Ricardo Letts, *la Izquierda peruana* (Lima, Mosca Azul, 1981); Roger Mercado, *Los Partidos políticos en el Perú* (Lima, Fondo de Cultura, 1985); Denis Sulmont, *Historia del movimiento obrero peruano* (Lima, Tarea, 1977); Rodrigo Montoya, *Lucha por la tierra, reformas agrarias y capitalismo en el Perú del siglo XX* (Lima, Mosca Azul, 1989); Diego García Sayán, *Tomas de tierras en el Perú* (Lima, DESCO, 1982); Hugo Blanco, *Land or Death: The Peasant Struggle in Peru* (New York, Pathfinder, 1972); and Gavin Smith, *Livelihood and Resistance: Peasants and the Politics of Land in Peru* (Berkeley, University of California Press, 1989).

Alan García's government is analysed in Cynthia Sanborn, 'El Apra en un contexto de cambio' in Bonilla and Drake, *op.cit.*; Francisco Durán, *La Década frustrada: los industriales y el poder* (Lima, DESCO, 1982); Carlos Monge, 'La Práctica política aprista como respuesta a la crisis de los 80' in Bonilla and Drake, *op.cit.*; John Crabtree, *Peru Under García: An Opportunity Lost* (London, Macmillan/Pittsburgh, University of Pittsburgh Press, 1992).

5. The Neo-Liberal Revolution

For a critical analysis of the Peruvian debt crisis, see Oscar Ugarteche, *Inserción y deuda: Peru 1985-90* (Lima, FONDAD-DESCO-CEPES, 1991).

The history of neo-liberalism in Peru and the Andean region is discussed in Catherine M. Conaghan, James M. Malloy and Luis A. Abugattas, 'Business and the "Boys": The Politics of Neoliberalism in the Central Andes', *Latin American Research Review*, XXV, 2, 1990.

For a critical analysis of Hernando de Soto's *The Other Path*, see Alberto Flores Galindo, 'Los Caballos de los conquistadores otra vez' in *Tiempo de plagas* (Lima, Caballo Rojo, 1988).

For Mario Vargas Llosa's 1990 election campaign and politics, see 'Vargas Llosa for President', *Granta*, 36, Summer 1991; Mario Vargas Llosa, 'Inquest in the Andes', *New York Times Magazine*, 31 July 1983; 'In Defense of the Black Market', *New York Times Magazine*, 22 February 1987; 'Questions of Conquest', *Harper's*, December 1990.

Carlos Iván Degregori, 'El Aprendiz de brujo y el curandero chino' in *Demonios y redentores en el nuevo Perú* (Lima, IEP, 1991) provides a critical assessment of the 1990 elections.

6. Coca Capitalism and the New World Order

For overviews of the Andean drug economy and anti-narcotics policy, see Eduardo Crawley, *Tráfico de drogas en América Latina* (London, Latin American Newsletters, 1990); Diego García Sayán (ed), *Coca, cocaína y narcotráfico: laberinto en los Andes* (Lima, Comisión Andina de Juristas, 1989); and 'Assessing America's War on Drugs', special issue of *Journal of Interamerican Studies and World Affairs*, XXX, 2-3, Summer-Fall 1988.

Accounts of US anti-narcotics policies are to be found in Edward Jay Epstein, *Agency of Fear: Opiates and Political Power in America* (London, Verso, 1990); Jefferson Morley, 'Contradictions of Cocaine Capitalism', *The Nation*, 2 October 1989; and Steven Wisotsky, *Beyond the War on Drugs: Overcoming a Failed Public Policy* (Buffalo NY, Prometheus Books, 1990).

For critical analyses of US drug policy in the Andes, see Peter Andreas, 'Drug War Zone', *The Nation*, 11 December 1989; Michael Klare, 'Fighting Drugs with the Military', *The Nation*, 1 January 1990; Peter Andreas and Coletta Youngers, 'US Drug Policy and the Andean Cocaine Industry', *World Policy Journal*, Summer 1989; and Coletta Youngers, 'The War in the Andes: The Military Role in US International Drug Policy' (Washington, Washington Office on Latin America, 1990).

See Deborah Poole and Gerardo Rénique, 'The New Chroniclers of Peru: US Scholars and their "Shining Path" of Peasant Rebellion', *Bulletin of Latin American Research*, X, 2, 1991, for analysis of the narco-terrorism industry.

The traditional uses of coca leaf in the Andes are described in Deborah Pacini and Christine Franquemont (eds), *Coca and Cocaine: Effects on People and Policy in Latin America* (Cambridge, Mass, Cultural Survival, 1985); and Catherine Allen, *The Hold Life Has: Coca and Cultural Identity in an Andean Community* (Washington DC, Smithsonian Institute Press, 1988).

Acronyms

AADA	*Autoridad Autónoma de Desarollo Alternativo*
	Autonomous Alternative Development Authority
ADEX	*Asociación de Exportadores*
	Exporters' Association
AID	Agency for International Development (US)
ANFASEP	*Asociación de Familiares de Secuestrados y Detenidos-*
	Desaparecidos en las Zonas Declaradas en Estado de Emergencia
	del Perú
	National Association of Families of the Disappeared
AP	*Acción Popular*
	Popular Action
APRA	*Alianza Popular Revolucionaria Americana*
	American Popular Revolutionary Alliance
APRODEH	*Asociación Pro-Derechos Humanos del Perú*
	Peruvian Pro-Human Rights Association
CCP	*Confederación Campesina del Perú*
	Peasant Confederation of Peru
CEAPAZ	*Centro de Estudios y Acción para la Paz*
	Episcopal Commission of Action for Peace
CGTP	*Confederación General de Trabajadores del Perú*
	General Confederation of Workers of Peru
CITE	*Confederación Intersectorial de Trabajadores Estatales*
	Interunion Confederation of State Workers
CNA	*Confederación Nacional Agraria*
	National Agrarian Confederation
CONFIEP	*Confederación Nacional de Instituciones Empresariales del Perú*
	National Confederation of Business Institutions of Peru
CORAH	*Proyecto Especial de Control y Reducción de los Cultivos de Coca*
	en el Alto Huallaga
	Upper Huallaga Valley Coca Reduction Programme
CTIM	*Centro de Trabajo Intelectual José Carlos Mariátegui*
	José Carlos Mariátegui Centre of Intellectual Work
CTP	*Confederación de Trabajadores del Perú*
	Labour Confederation of Peru
CTRP	*Central de Trabajadores de la Revolución Peruana*
	Workers' Central of the Peruvian Revolution
CUAVES	*Comunidad Urbana Autogestionaria de Villa El Salvador*
	Urban Self-Managed Community of Villa El Salvador
CUNA	*Consejo Unitario Nacional Agrario*
	United Agrarian Council
CUP	*Comando Unificado de Pacificación*
	Unified Pacification Command
DEA	Drug Enforcement Agency (US)
DIRCOTE	*Dirección contra el Terrorismo*
	Anti-terrorism Agency
EGP	*Ejército Guerrillero del Popular*
	People's Guerrilla Army

ENACO	*Empresa Nacional de Coca*
	National Coca Enterprise
FASMA	*Selva Maestra Agrarian Federation of San Martín*
	Selva Maestra Agrarian Federation of San Martín
FDCC	*Federación Departmental de Campesinos del Cusco*
	Departmental Peasant Federation of Cusco
FDCP	*Federación Departmental de Campesinos de Puno*
	Departmental Peasant Federation of Puno
FEDCCA	*Federación Departmental de Comunidades Campesinas de Ayacucho*
	Departmental Federation of Ayacucho Peasants and Communities
FEDIP	*Frente Defensa de los Intereses del Pueblo*
	Popular Defence Fronts
FEDISAM	*Frente de Defensa de los Intereses de San Martín*
	Defence Front for the Interests of San Martín
FER	*Frente Estudiantil Revolucionario*
	Revolutionary Student Front
FNTMMSP	*Federación Nacional de Trabajadores Mineros, Metalúrgicos y Siderúrgicos del Perú*
	National Federation of Miners, Metalworkers and Steelworkers
FOCEP	*Frente Obrero, Campesino, Estudiantil y Popular*
	Workers', Peasants' and Students' Front
FPCC	*Federación Provincial de Campesinos de La Convención*
	Provincial Peasant Federation of La Convención
FREDEMO	*Frente Democrático*
	Democratic Front
FTC	*Federación Trabajadores del Cusco*
	Workers' Federations of Cusco
FUCAM	*Federación Unificada de Campesinos de Melgar*
	United Peasant Federation of Melgar Province
IDL	*Instituto de Defensa Legal*
	Institute for Legal Defence
ILD	*Instituto Libertad y Democracia*
	Liberty and Democracy Institute
INCA	International Narcotics Control Act of 1990 (US)
IS	*Izquierda Socialista*
	Socialist Left
IU	*Izquierda Unida*
	United Left
LIC	low intensity conflict
MAS	*Movimiento de Afirmación Socialista*
	Movement of Socialist Affirmation
MCB	*Movimiento Clasista Barrial*
	Neighbourhood Class Movement
MCP	*Movimiento de Campesinos Pobres*
	Poor Peasants' Movement
MFP	*Movimiento Feminino Popular*
	Popular Women's Movement

MIP	*Movimiento Intelectual Popular*
	Popular Intellectual Movement
MIR	*Movimiento Izquierda Revolucionaria*
	Revolutionary Left Movement
MLR	*Movimiento Laboral Revolucionario*
	Revolutionary Labour Movement
MOTC	*Movimiento de Obreros y Trabajadores Clasistas*
	Class Workers' and Labourers' Movement
MRDP	*Movimiento Revolucionario por le Defensa del Pueblo*
	Revolutionary Movement for Defence of the People
MRTA	*Movimiento Revolucionario Tupac Amaru*
	Revolutionary Movement — Tupac Amaru
NAU	Narcotics Assistance Unit (US)
PBC	*pasta básica de cocaína*
	basic cocaine paste
PCP	*Partido Comunista del Perú*
	Peruvian Communist Party
PCP-BR	*Partido Comunista del Perú — Bandera Roja*
	Peruvian Communist Party — Red Flag
PCP-PR	*Partido Comunista del Perú — Patria Roja*
	Peruvian Communist Party — Red Fatherland
PCP-SL	*Partido Comunista del Perú — Sendero Luminoso*
	Communist Party of Peru — Sendero Luminoso
PCP-U	*Partido Comunista del Perú — Unidad*
	Peruvian Communist Party — Unity
PCR	*Partido Comunista Revolucionario*
	Revolutionary Communist Party
POR	*Partido Obrero Revolucionario*
	Revolutionary Workers' Party
PPC	*Partido Popular Cristiano*
	Popular Christian Party
PUM	*Partido Unificado Mariáteguista*
	United Mariateguista Party
SAIS	*Sociedades Agricolas de Interés Social*
	Agrarian Society of Social Interest
SIN	*Servicio de Inteligencia Nacional*
	National Intelligence Service
SINAMOS	*Sistema Nacional de Apoyo a la Movilización Social*
	National System of Social Mobilisation
SNI	*Sociedad Nacional de Industrias*
	National Industrial Society
SUTEP	*Sindicato Unico de Trabajadores de la Educación*
	Union of Peruvian Education Workers
UDP	*Unidad Democrático Popular*
	Popular Democratic Unity
UMOPAR	*Unidades Móviles de Patrullas Rurales*
	Mobile Rural Patrol Units
VR	*Vanguardia Revolucionaria*
	Revolutionary Vanguard

Index

The Latin America Bureau is a small, independent, non-profit-making research organisation established in 1977. LAB is concerned with human rights and related social, political and economic issues in Central and South America and the Caribbean. We carry out research, publish books, and establish support links with Latin American groups. We also brief the media, run a small documentation centre and produce materials for teachers.